# RICK STEVES'
# FRENCH, ITALIAN & GERMAN
## PHRASE BOOK & DICTIONARY

**2nd Edition**

**John Muir Publications**
**Santa Fe, New Mexico**

Thanks to the team of people at *Europe Through the Back Door*
who helped make this book possible: Dave Hoerlein, Mary
Carlson, Mary Romano, and . . .

French translation: Scott Bernhard, Steve Smith, and
  Paul Desloover
Italian translation: Giulia Fiorini and Alessandra Panieri
Italian proofreading: Manfredo Guerzoni
German translation: Julia Klimek
Phonetics: Risa Laib
Layout: Rich Sorensen
Maps: Dave Hoerlein

Edited by Risa Laib and Rich Sorensen

John Muir Publications, P.O. Box 613, Santa Fe, NM 87504

Second edition. Second printing March 1998
Printed in the U.S.A by Quebecor Printing

ISBN 1-56261-314-6

Cover photo by Leo de Wys, Inc./Steve Vidler

Distributed to the book trade by
Publishers Group West
Emeryville, California

*While every effort has been made to keep the content of this
book accurate, the author and publisher accept no responsibility
whatsoever for anyone ordering bad beer or getting messed up
in any other way because of the linguistic confidence this phrase
book has given them.*

**JMP travel guidebooks by Rick Steves:**

*Rick Steves' Best of Europe*
*Rick Steves' France, Belgium & the Netherlands*
   (with Steve Smith)
*Rick Steves' Italy*
*Rick Steves' Germany, Austria & Switzerland*
*Rick Steves' Great Britain & Ireland*
*Rick Steves' Scandinavia*
*Rick Steves' Spain & Portugal*
*Rick Steves' Russia & the Baltics* (with Ian Watson)
*Rick Steves' Europe Through the Back Door*
*Europe 101: History and Art for the Traveler*
   (with Gene Openshaw)
*Mona Winks: Self-Guided Tours of Europe's Top Museums*
   (with Gene Openshaw)
*Rick Steves' Phrase Books: French, Italian, German,*
   *French/Italian/German, and Spanish/Portuguese*
*Asia Through the Back Door* (with Bob Effertz)

Rick Steves' company, *Europe Through the Back Door,*
provides many services for budget European travelers,
including a free quarterly newsletter/catalog, budget
travel books and accessories, Eurailpasses (with free video
and travel advice included), free-spirited European tours,
on-line travel tips, and a Travel Resource Center in
Edmonds, WA. For a free newsletter, call or write:

**Europe Through the Back Door**
120 Fourth Avenue N, Box 2009
Edmonds, WA 98020 USA
Tel: 425/771-8303, Fax: 425/771-0833
Web: www.ricksteves.com

# Contents

**Hi, I'm Rick Steves.**

I'm the only mono-lingual speaker I know who's had the nerve to design a series of European phrase books. But that's one of the things that makes them better. You see, after twenty summers of travel through Europe, I've learned first-hand (1) what's essential for communication in Europe, and (2) what's not. I've assembled the most important words and phrases in a logical, no-frills format, and I've worked with native Europeans and seasoned travelers to give you the simplest, clearest translations possible.

This three-in-one edition is a lean and mean version of my individual French, Italian, and German phrase books. If you're lingering in a country, my individual phrase books are far better at helping you connect with the locals, but if you're on a whirlwind trip, this handy three-in-one book gives you all the essential phrases.

This book is more than just a pocket translator. The words and phrases have been carefully selected to make you a happier, more effective budget traveler. The key to getting more out of every travel dollar is to get closer to the local people, and to rely less on entertainment, restaurants, and hotels that cater only to foreign tourists. This book will not only help you order a meal at a locals-only European restaurant—it will help you talk with the family that runs the place. Long after your memories of the museums have faded, you'll still treasure the personal encounters you had with your new European friends.

A good phrase book should help you enjoy your

European experience—not just survive it—so I've added a healthy dose of humor. But please use these phrases carefully, in a self-effacing spirit. Remember that one ugly American can undo the goodwill built by dozens of culturally-sensitive ones.

To get the most out of this book, take the time to internalize and put into practice the pronunciation tips. I've spelled out the pronunciations as if you were reading English. Don't worry too much about memorizing grammatical rules, like which gender a particular noun is—forget about sex and communicate!

Along with a four-language dictionary, this book has nifty menu decoders (to help you figure out what's cooking). You'll also find tongue twisters, telephone tips, and handy tear-out "cheat sheets." Tear out the sheets and keep them handy, so you can easily memorize key phrases during otherwise idle moments. As you prepare for your trip, you may want to have a look at my annually-updated *Rick Steves' Europe* guidebook or my country guides: *Rick Steves' France, Belgium & the Netherlands; Rick Steves' Italy;* and *Rick Steves' Germany, Austria & Switzerland.*

My goal is to help you become a more confident, extroverted traveler. If this phrase book helps make that happen, or if you have suggestions for making it better, I'd love to hear from you.

Happy travels, and good luck as you hurdle the language barrier!

*Rick Steves*

4

# FRENCH

# Getting Started

### Challenging, romantic French

...is spoken throughout Europe and considered to be one of the most beautiful languages in the world. Half of Belgium speaks French, and French rivals English as the handiest second language in Spain, Portugal, and Italy. Even your U.S. passport is translated into French. You're probably already familiar with this poetic language. Consider: *bonjour, c'est la vie, bon appétit, merci, au revoir, bon voyage!*

As with any language, the key to communicating is to go for it with a mixture of bravado and humility. Try to sound like Maurice Chevalier or Inspector Clouseau.

French has some unusual twists to its pronunciation:

*Ç* sounds like S in sun.
*CH* sounds like SH in shine.
*G* usually sounds like G in get.
   But *G* followed by *E* or *I* sounds like S in treasure.
*GN* sounds like NI in onion.
*H* is always silent.
*J* sounds like S in treasure.
*R* sounds like an R being swallowed.
*I* sounds like EE in seed.
*È* and *Ê* sound like E in let.
*É* and *EZ* sound like AY in play.
*ER*, at the end of a word, sounds like AY in play.
*Ô* sounds like O in note.

French has a lot of strange-looking accents. The cedilla makes *Ç* sound like "s" (*façade*). The circumflex makes *Ê* sound like "eh" (*crêpe*), but has no effect on the sounds of *Â*, *Î*, *Ô*, or *Û*. The grave accent stifles *È* into "eh" (*crème*), but try as it may, cannot change the stubborn *À*. The acute accent opens *É* into "ay." Ponder (or forget) this at a *café*.

French is tricky because the spelling and pronunciation seem to have little to do with each other. *Qu'est-ce que c'est?* (What is that?) is pronounced: kehs kuh say.

The final letters of many French words are silent, so *Paris* sounds like pah-ree. The French tend to stress every syllable evenly: pah-ree. In contrast, Americans say **Par**-is, emphasizing the first syllable.

In French, if a word that ends in a consonant is followed by a word that starts with a vowel, the consonant is frequently linked with the vowel. *Mes amis* (my friends) is pronounced: may-zah-mee. Some words are linked with an apostrophe. *Ce est* (It is) becomes *C'est*, as in *C'est la vie* (That's life). *Le* and *la* (the masculine and feminine "the") are intimately connected to words starting with a vowel. *La orange* becomes *l'orange*. (No risk! Safe sex.)

French has a few sounds that are unusual in English: the French *u* and the nasal vowels. To say the French *u*, round your lips to say "oh," but say "ee." Vowels combined with either *n* or *m* are often nasal vowels. As you nasalize a vowel, let the sound come through your nose as well as your mouth. The vowel is the important thing. The *n* or *m*, represented in this book by <u>n</u> for nasal, is not pronounced.

There are a total of four nasal sounds, all contained in the phrase *un bon vin blanc* (a good white wine).

| Nasal vowels: | Phonetics: | To make the sound: |
|---|---|---|
| *un* | uh<u>n</u> | nasalize the U in lung. |
| *bon* | oh<u>n</u> | nasalize the O in bone. |
| *vin* | a<u>n</u> | nasalize the A in sack. |
| *blanc* | ah<u>n</u> | nasalize the A in want. |

In phonetics, *un bon vin blanc* would look like this: uh<u>n</u> boh<u>n</u> va<u>n</u> blah<u>n</u>. If you practice it, you'll learn how to say the nasal vowels . . . and order a fine wine.

Here's a guide to the rest of the phonetics we've used in the French section of this book:

| | |
|---|---|
| ah | like A in father. |
| ay | like AY in play. |
| eh | like E in let. |
| ee | like EE in seed. |
| ehr | sounds like "air." |
| ew | pucker your lips and say "ee." |
| g | like G in go. |
| ī | like I in light. |
| or | like OR in core. |
| oh | like O in note. |
| oo | like OO in too. |
| s | like S in sun. |
| uh | like U in but. |
| ur | like UR in purr. |
| zh | like S in treasure. |

# French Basics

## Greeting and meeting the French:

| | | |
|---|---|---|
| Good day. | **Bonjour.** | bohn-zhoor |
| Good morning. | **Bonjour.** | bohn-zhoor |
| Good evening. | **Bonsoir.** | bohn-swahr |
| Good night. | **Bonne nuit.** | buhn nwee |
| Hi. (informal) | **Salut.** | sah-lew |
| Welcome! | **Bienvenue!** | bee-an-vuh-new |
| Mr. | **Monsieur** | muhs-yur |
| Mrs. | **Madame** | mah-dahm |
| Miss | **Mademoiselle** | mahd-mwah-zehl |
| How are you? | **Comment allez-vous?** | koh-mahnt ah-lay-voo |
| Very well, thank you. | **Très bien, merci.** | treh bee-an mehr-see |
| And you? | **Et vous?** | ay voo |
| My name is... | **Je m'appelle...** | zhuh mah-pehl |
| What's your name? | **Quel est votre nom?** | kehl ay voh-truh nohn |
| Pleased to meet you. | **Enchanté.** | ahn-shahn-tay |
| Where are you from? | **D'où êtes-vous?** | doo eht voo |
| I am / Are you...? | **Je suis / Êtes-vous...?** | zhuh sweez / eht-vooz |
| ...on vacation | **...en vacances** | ahn vah-kahns |
| ...on business | **...en voyage d'affaires** | ahn voy-yahzh dah-fair |
| See you later. | **À bientôt.** | ah bee-an-toh |
| Goodbye. | **Au revoir.** | oh vwahr |
| Good luck! | **Bonne chance!** | buhn shahns |
| Have a good trip! | **Bon voyage!** | bohn voy-yahzh |

## Survival phrases

During the liberation of Paris in 1945, American G.I.s stormed the city using only these phrases. They're repeated on your tear-out cheat sheet near the end of this book.

## The essentials:

| | | |
|---|---|---|
| Good day. | **Bonjour.** | bohn-zhoor |
| Do you speak English? | **Parlez-vous anglais?** | par-lay-voo ahn-glay |
| Yes. / No. | **Oui. / Non.** | wee / nohn |
| I don't speak French. | **Je ne parle pas français.** | zhuh nuh parl pah frahn-say |
| I'm sorry. | **Désolé.** | day-zoh-lay |
| Please. | **S'il vous plaît.** | see voo play |
| Thank you. | **Merci.** | mehr-see |
| No problem. | **Pas de problème.** | pah duh proh-blehm |
| It's good. | **C'est bon.** | say bohn |
| You are very kind. | **Vous êtes très gentil.** | vooz eht treh zhahn-tee |
| Goodbye. | **Au revoir.** | oh vwahr |

## Where?

| | | |
|---|---|---|
| Where is...? | **Où est...?** | oo ay |
| ...a hotel | **...un hôtel** | uhn oh-tehl |
| ...a youth hostel | **...une auberge de jeunesse** | ewn oh-behrzh duh zhuh-nehs |
| ...a restaurant | **...un restaurant** | uhn rehs-toh-rahn |
| ...a supermarket | **...un supermarché** | uhn soo-pehr-mar-shay |

| ...a pharmacy | ...une pharmacie | ewn far-mah-see |
| ...a bank | ...une banque | ewn bahnk |
| ...the train station | ...la gare | lah gar |
| ...the tourist information office | ...l'office du tourisme | loh-fees dew too-reez-muh |
| Where are the toilets? | Où sont les toilettes? | oo sohn lay twah-leht |
| men / women | hommes / dames | ohm / dahm |

## How much?

| How much is it? | Combien? | kohn-bee-an |
| Write it? | Ecrivez? | ay-kree-vay |
| Cheap. | Bon marché. | bohn mar-shay |
| Cheaper. | Moins cher. | mwan shehr |
| Cheapest. | Le moins cher. | luh mwan shehr |
| Is it free? | C'est gratuit? | say grah-twee |
| Included? | Inclus? | an-klew |
| Do you have...? | Avez-vous...? | ah-vay-voo |
| I would like... | Je voudrais... | zhuh voo-dray |
| We would like... | Nous voudrions... | noo voo-dree-ohn |
| ...this. | ...ceci. | suh-see |
| ...just a little. | ...un petit peu. | uhn puh-tee puh |
| ...more. | ...encore. | ahn-kor |
| ...a ticket. | ...un billet. | uhn bee-yay |
| ...a room. | ...une chambre. | ewn shahn-bruh |
| ...the bill. | ...l'addition. | lah-dee-see-ohn |

## How many?

| one | **un** | uhn |
|-----|--------|-----|
| two | **deux** | duh |
| three | **trois** | twah |
| four | **quatre** | kah-truh |
| five | **cinq** | sank |
| six | **six** | sees |
| seven | **sept** | seht |
| eight | **huit** | weet |
| nine | **neuf** | nuhf |
| ten | **dix** | dees |

You'll find more to count on in the Numbers chapter.

## When?

| At what time? | **À quelle heure?** | ah kehl ur |
|---------------|---------------------|------------|
| Just a moment. | **Un moment.** | uhn moh-mahn |
| Now. | **Maintenant.** | man-tuh-nahn |
| soon / later | **bientôt / plus tard** | bee-an-toh / plew tar |
| today / tomorrow | **aujourd'hui / demain** | oh-zhoor-dwee / duh-man |

Be creative! You can combine these survival phrases to say: "Two, please," or "No, thank you," or "I'd like a cheap hotel," or "Cheaper, please?" Please is a magic word in any language. If you want something and you don't know the word for it, just point and say, *"S'il vous plaît"* (Please). If you know the word for what you want, such as the bill, simply say, *"L'addition, s'il vous plaît"* (The bill, please).

## Struggling with French:

| | | |
|---|---|---|
| Do you speak English? | **Parlez-vous anglais?** | par-lay-voo ah<u>n</u>-glay |
| A teeny weeny bit? | **Un petit peu?** | uh<u>n</u> puh-tee puh |
| Please speak English. | **Parlez anglais, s'il vous plaît.** | par-lay ah<u>n</u>-glay see voo play |
| You speak English well. | **Vous parlez bien anglais.** | voo par-lay bee-a<u>n</u> ah<u>n</u>-glay |
| I don't speak French. | **Je ne parle pas français.** | zhuh nuh parl pah frah<u>n</u>-say |
| I speak a little French. | **Je parle un petit peu français.** | zhuh parl uh<u>n</u> puh-tee puh frah<u>n</u>-say |
| What is this in French? | **Qu'est-ce que c'est en français?** | kehs kuh say ah<u>n</u> frah<u>n</u>-say |
| Repeat? | **Répétez?** | ray-pay-tay |
| Slowly. | **Lentement.** | lah<u>n</u>-tuh-mah<u>n</u> |
| Do you understand? | **Comprenez-vous?** | koh<u>n</u>-pruh-nay-voo |
| I understand. | **Je comprends.** | zhuh koh<u>n</u>-prah<u>n</u> |
| I don't understand. | **Je ne comprends pas.** | zhuh nuh koh<u>n</u>-prah<u>n</u> pah |
| Write it? | **Ecrivez?** | ay-kree-vay |
| Who speaks English? | **Qui parle anglais?** | kee parl ah<u>n</u>-glay |

To prompt a simple answer, ask, *"Oui ou non?"* (Yes or no?). To turn a word or sentence into a question, ask it in a questioning tone. *"C'est bon"* (It's good) becomes *"C'est bon?"* (Is it good?).

## Handy questions:

| How much? | **Combien?** | kohn-bee-an |
| How long...? | **Combien de temps...?** | kohn-bee-an duh tahn |
| ...is the trip | **...dure le voyage** | dewr luh voy-yahzh |
| Is it far? | **C'est loin?** | say lwan |
| How? | **Comment?** | koh-mahn |
| Is it possible? | **C'est possible?** | say poh-see-bluh |
| Is it necessary? | **C'est nécessaire?** | say nay-suh-sair |
| Can you help me? | **Pouvez-vous m'aider?** | poo-vay-voo may-day |
| What? | **Quoi?** | kwah |
| What is that? | **Qu'est-ce que c'est?** | kehs kuh say |
| When? | **Quand?** | kahn |
| What time is it? | **Quelle heure est-il?** | kehl ur ay-teel |
| At what time? | **À quelle heure?** | ah kehl ur |
| On time? Late? | **A l'heure? En retard?** | ah lur / ahn ruh-tar |
| When does this...? | **Ça... à quelle heure?** | sah... ah kehl ur |
| ...open / close | **...ouvre / ferme** | oo-vruh / fehrm |
| Do you have...? | **Avez-vous...?** | ah-vay-voo |
| Where is...? | **Où est...?** | oo ay |
| Where are...? | **Où sont...?** | oo sohn |
| Where can I find...? | **Où puis-je trouver...?** | oo pwee-zhuh troo-vay |
| Who? | **Qui?** | kee |
| Why? | **Pourquoi?** | poor-kwah |
| Why not? | **Pourquoi pas?** | poor-kwah pah |
| Yes or no? | **Oui ou non?** | wee oo nohn |

## La yin et yang:

| | | |
|---|---|---|
| cheap / expensive | **bon marché / cher** | bohn mar-shay / shehr |
| big / small | **grand / petit** | grahn / puh-tee |
| hot / cold | **chaud / froid** | shoh / frwah |
| open / closed | **ouvert / fermé** | oo-vehr / fehr-may |
| entrance / exit | **entrée / sortie** | ahn-tray / sor-tee |
| arrive / depart | **arriver / partir** | ah-ree-vay / par-teer |
| early / late | **tôt / tard** | toh / tar |
| soon / later | **bientôt / plus tard** | bee-an-toh / plew tar |
| fast / slow | **vite / lent** | veet / lahn |
| here / there | **ici / là-bas** | ee-see / lah-bah |
| near / far | **près / loin** | preh / lwan |
| good / bad | **bon / mauvais** | bohn / moh-vay |
| best / worst | **le meilleur / le pire** | luh meh-yur / luh peer |
| a little / lots | **un peu / beaucoup** | uhn puh / boh-koo |
| more / less | **plus / moins** | plew / mwan |
| easy / difficult | **facile / difficile** | fah-seel / dee-fee-seel |
| left / right | **à gauche / à droite** | ah gohsh / ah dwaht |
| up / down | **en haut / en bas** | ahn oh / ahn bah |
| young / old | **jeune / vieille** | zhuhn / vee-yay-ee |
| new / old | **neuve / vieille** | nuhv / vee-yay-ee |
| heavy / light | **lourd / léger** | loor / lay-zhay |
| dark / light | **sombre / clair** | sohn-bruh / klair |
| beautiful / ugly | **belle / laid** | behl / leh |
| intelligent / stupid | **intelligent / stupide** | an-teh-lee-zhahn / stew-peed |
| vacant / occupied | **libre / occupé** | lee-bruh / oh-kew-pay |
| with / without | **avec / sans** | ah-vehk / sahn |

## Common French expressions:

| | | |
|---|---|---|
| **Ça va?** | sah vah | How are you? (informal) |
| **Ça va.** | sah vah | I'm fine. |
| **D'accord.** | dah-kor | O.K. |
| **Voilà.** | vwah-lah | Here it is. |
| **Bon appétit!** | boh<u>n</u> ah-pay-tee | Enjoy your meal! |

## Big little words:

| | | |
|---|---|---|
| | **je** | zhuh |
| you (formal) | **vous** | voo |
| you (informal) | **tu** | tew |
| we | **nous** | noo |
| he / she | **il / elle** | eel / ehl |
| they | **ils** | eel |
| and | **et** | ay |
| at | **à** | ah |
| because | **parce que** | pars kuh |
| but | **mais** | may |
| by (via) | **par** | par |
| for | **pour** | poor |
| from | **de** | duh |
| here | **ici** | ee-see |
| in | **en** | ah<u>n</u> |
| not | **pas** | pah |
| now | **maintenant** | ma<u>n</u>-tuh-nah<u>n</u> |
| only | **seulement** | suhl-mah<u>n</u> |
| or | **ou** | oo |
| this / that | **ce / cette** | suh / seht |
| to | **à** | ah |
| very | **très** | treh |

## Places in France:

If French clerks at train stations and conductors on trains don't understand your pronunciation of the name of a town, write the name on a piece of paper.

| | |
|---|---|
| **Alsace** | ahl-sahs |
| **Amboise** | ahm-bwahz |
| **Antibes** | ahn-teeb |
| **Arles** | arl |
| **Bayeaux** | bah-yuh |
| **Beaune** | bohn |
| **Bordeaux** | bor-doh |
| **Calais** | kah-lay |
| **Carcassonne** | kar-kah-suhn |
| **Côte d'Azur** | koht dah-zewr |
| **Chamonix** | shah-moh-nee |
| **Chartres** | shart |
| **Cherbourg** | shehr-boor |
| **Dordogne** | dor-dohn-yuh |
| **Grenoble** | gruh-noh-bluh |
| **Le Havre** | luh hah-vruh |
| **Lyon** | lee-ohn |
| **Marseille** | mar-say |
| **Mont Blanc** | mohn blahn |
| **Mont St. Michel** | mohn san mee-shehl |
| **Nantes** | nahnt |
| **Nice** | nees |
| **Paris** | pah-ree |
| **Reims** | rans |
| **Rouen** | roo-ahn |
| **Versailles** | vehr-sī |

# Numbers

| | | |
|---|---|---|
| 1 | **un** | uh<u>n</u> |
| 2 | **deux** | duh |
| 3 | **trois** | twah |
| 4 | **quatre** | kah-truh |
| 5 | **cinq** | sa<u>n</u>k |
| 6 | **six** | sees |
| 7 | **sept** | seht |
| 8 | **huit** | weet |
| 9 | **neuf** | nuhf |
| 10 | **dix** | dees |
| 11 | **onze** | oh<u>n</u>z |
| 12 | **douze** | dooz |
| 13 | **treize** | trehz |
| 14 | **quatorze** | kah-torz |
| 15 | **quinze** | ka<u>n</u>z |
| 16 | **seize** | sehz |
| 17 | **dix-sept** | dee-seht |
| 18 | **dix-huit** | deez-weet |
| 19 | **dix-neuf** | deez-nuhf |
| 20 | **vingt** | va<u>n</u> |
| 21 | **vingt et un** | va<u>n</u>t ay uh<u>n</u> |
| 22 | **vingt-deux** | va<u>n</u>t-duh |
| 23 | **vingt-trois** | va<u>n</u>t-twah |
| 30 | **trente** | trah<u>n</u>t |
| 31 | **trente et un** | trah<u>n</u>t ay uh<u>n</u> |
| 40 | **quarante** | kah-rah<u>n</u>t |
| 41 | **quarante et un** | kah-rah<u>n</u>t ay uh<u>n</u> |
| 50 | **cinquante** | sa<u>n</u>-kah<u>n</u>t |
| 60 | **soixante** | swah-sah<u>n</u>t |

| 70 | **soixante-dix** | swah-sah<u>nt</u>-dees |
| 71 | **soixante et onze** | swah-sah<u>nt</u> ay oh<u>nz</u> |
| 72 | **soixante-douze** | swah-sah<u>nt</u>-dooz |
| 73 | **soixante-treize** | swah-sah<u>nt</u>-trehz |
| 74 | **soixante-quatorze** | swah-sah<u>nt</u>-kah-torz |
| 75 | **soixante-quinze** | swah-sah<u>nt</u>-ka<u>nz</u> |
| 76 | **soixante-seize** | swah-sah<u>nt</u>-sehz |
| 77 | **soixante-dix-sept** | swah-sah<u>nt</u>-dee-seht |
| 78 | **soixante-dix-huit** | swah-sah<u>nt</u>-deez-weet |
| 79 | **soixante-dix-neuf** | swah-sah<u>nt</u>-deez-nuhf |
| 80 | **quatre-vingts** | kah-truh-va<u>n</u> |
| 81 | **quatre-vingt-un** | kah-truh-va<u>n</u>-uh<u>n</u> |
| 82 | **quatre-vingt-deux** | kah-truh-va<u>n</u>-duh |
| 83 | **quatre-vingt-trois** | kah-truh-va<u>n</u>-twah |
| 84 | **quatre-vingt-quatre** | kah-truh-va<u>n</u>-kah-truh |
| 85 | **quatre-vingt-cinq** | kah-truh-va<u>n</u>-sa<u>nk</u> |
| 86 | **quatre-vingt-six** | kah-truh-va<u>n</u>-sees |
| 87 | **quatre-vingt-sept** | kah-truh-va<u>n</u>-seht |
| 88 | **quatre-vingt-huit** | kah-truh-va<u>n</u>-weet |
| 89 | **quatre-vingt-neuf** | kah-truh-va<u>n</u>-nuhf |
| 90 | **quatre-vingt-dix** | kah-truh-va<u>n</u>-dees |
| 91 | **quatre-vingt-onze** | kah-truh-va<u>n</u>-oh<u>nz</u> |
| 92 | **quatre-vingt-douze** | kah-truh-va<u>n</u>-dooz |
| 93 | **quatre-vingt-treize** | kah-truh-va<u>n</u>-trehz |
| 94 | **quatre-vingt-quatorze** | kah-truh-va<u>n</u>-kah-torz |
| 95 | **quatre-vingt-quinze** | kah-truh-va<u>n</u>-ka<u>nz</u> |
| 96 | **quatre-vingt-seize** | kah-truh-va<u>n</u>-sehz |
| 97 | **quatre-vingt-dix-sept** | kah-truh-va<u>n</u>-dee-seht |
| 98 | **quatre-vingt-dix-huit** | kah-truh-va<u>n</u>-deez-weet |
| 99 | **quatre-vingt-dix-neuf** | kah-truh-va<u>n</u>-deez-nuhf |
| 100 | **cent** | sah<u>n</u> |
| 101 | **cent un** | sah<u>n</u> uh<u>n</u> |

| 102 | **cent deux** | sahn duh |
| 200 | **deux cents** | duh sahn |
| 1000 | **mille** | meel |
| 1996 | **mille neuf cent** | meel nuhf sahn |
| | **quatre-vingt-seize** | kah-truh-van-sehz |
| 2000 | **deux mille** | duh meel |
| 10,000 | **dix mille** | dee meel |
| millon | **million** | uhn meel-yohn |
| billion | **milliard** | meel-yar |
| first | **premier** | pruhm-yay |
| second | **deuxième** | duhz-yehm |
| third | **troisième** | twahz-yehm |
| half | **demi** | duh-mee |
| 100% | **cent pourcents** | sahn poor-sahn |
| number one | **numéro un** | new-may-roh uhn |

French numbering is a little quirky from the seventies through the nineties. Let's pretend momentarily that the French speak English. Instead of saying 70, 71, 72, up to 79, the French say "sixty ten," "sixty eleven," "sixty twelve" up to "sixty nineteen." Instead of saying 80, the French say "four twenties." The numbers 81 and 82 are literally "four twenty one" and "four twenty two." It gets stranger. The number 90 is "four twenty ten." To say 91, 92, up to 99, the French say "four twenty eleven," "four twenty twelve" on up to "four twenty nineteen." But take heart. If little French children can learn these numbers, so can you. Besides, didn't Abe Lincoln say, "Four score and seven..."

# Money

| | | |
|---|---|---|
| Can you change dollars? | **Pouvez-vous changer les dollars?** | poo-vay-voo shah<u>n</u>-zhay lay doh-lar |
| What is your exchange rate for dollars...? | **Quel est le cours du dollar...?** | kehl ay luh koor dew doh-lar |
| ...in traveler's checks | **...en chèques de voyage** | ah<u>n</u> shehk duh voy-yahzh |
| What is the commission? | **Quel est la commission?** | kehl ay lah koh-mee-see-oh<u>n</u> |
| Any extra fee? | **Il y a d'autre frais?** | eel yah doh-truh fray |

## Key money words:

| | | |
|---|---|---|
| bank | **banque** | bah<u>n</u>k |
| change money | **changer de l'argent** | shah<u>n</u>-zhay duh lar-zhah<u>n</u> |
| money | **argent** | ar-zhah<u>n</u> |
| large bills | **gros billets** | groh bee-yay |
| small bills | **petits billets** | puh-tee bee-yay |
| coins | **des pièces** | day pee-ehs |
| cashier | **caisse** | kehs |
| credit card | **carte de crédit** | kart duh kray-dee |
| cash advance | **crédit de caisse** | kray-dee duh kehs |
| cash machine | **distributeur de billets** | dee-stree-bew-tur duh bee-yay |
| receipt | **reçu** | ruh-sew |

# Time

| | | |
|---|---|---|
| What time is it? | **Quelle heure est-il?** | kehl ur ay-teel |
| It's... | **Il est...** | eel ay |
| ...8:00. | **...huit heures.** | weet ur |
| ...16:00. | **...seize heures.** | sehz ur |
| ...4:00 in the afternoon. | **...quatre heures de l'après-midi.** | kah-truh ur duh lah-preh-mee-dee |
| ...10:30 (in the evening). | **...dix heures et demie (du soir).** | deez ur ayd-mee (dew swahr) |
| ...a quarter past nine. | **...neuf heures et quart.** | nuhv ur ay kar |
| ...a quarter to eleven. | **...onze heures moins le quart.** | ohnz ur mwan luh kar |
| ...noon / midnight. | **...midi / minuit.** | mee-dee / meen-wee |
| ...sunrise. | **...l'aube.** | lohb |
| ...sunset. | **...le coucher de soleil.** | luh koo-shay duh soh-lay |
| ...early / late. | **...tôt / tard.** | toh / tar |
| ...on time. | **...a l'heure.** | ah lur |

In France, the 24-hour clock (or military time) is used by hotels and stores, and for train, bus, and ferry schedules. Informally, the French use the 24-hour clock and "our clock" interchangeably—17:00 is also *5:00 de l'après-midi* (5:00 in the afternoon). The greeting *"Bonjour"* (Good day) turns to *"Bonsoir"* (Good evening) at sundown.

## Timely words:

| | | |
|---|---|---|
| minute | **minute** | mee-newt |
| hour | **heure** | ur |
| morning | **matin** | mah-tan |
| afternoon | **après-midi** | ah-preh-mee-dee |
| evening | **soir** | swahr |
| night | **nuit** | nwee |
| day | **jour** | zhoor |
| today | **aujourd'hui** | oh-zhoor-dwee |
| yesterday | **hier** | yehr |
| tomorrow | **demain** | duh-man |
| tomorrow morning | **demain matin** | duh-man mah-tan |
| anytime | **n'importe quand** | nan-port kahn |
| immediately | **immédiatement** | ee-may-dee-aht-mahn |
| in one hour | **dans une heure** | dahnz ewn ur |
| every hour | **toutes les heures** | toot layz ur |
| every day | **tous les jours** | too lay zhoor |
| last | **dernier** | dehrn-yay |
| this | **ce** | suh |
| next | **prochain** | proh-shan |
| July 14 | **le quatorze juillet** | luh kah-torz zhwee-yay |

France's biggest holiday is July 14, Bastille Day. Festivities begin on the evening of the 13th and rage throughout the country. Other celebrations include May 1 (Labor Day), May 8 (Liberation Day), and August 15 (Assumption of Mary).

| week | **semaine** | suh-mehn |
| Monday | **lundi** | luhn-dee |
| Tuesday | **mardi** | mar-dee |
| Wednesday | **mercredi** | mehr-kruh-dee |
| Thursday | **jeudi** | zhuh-dee |
| Friday | **vendredi** | vahn-druh-dee |
| Saturday | **samedi** | sahm-dee |
| Sunday | **dimanche** | dee-mahnsh |
| | | |
| month | **mois** | mwah |
| January | **janvier** | zhahn-vee-yay |
| February | **février** | fay-vree-yay |
| March | **mars** | mars |
| April | **avril** | ahv-reel |
| May | **mai** | may |
| June | **juin** | zhwan |
| July | **juillet** | zhwee-yay |
| August | **août** | oot |
| September | **septembre** | sehp-tahn-bruh |
| October | **octobre** | ohk-toh-bruh |
| November | **novembre** | noh-vahn-bruh |
| December | **décembre** | day-sahn-bruh |
| | | |
| year | **année** | ah-nay |
| spring | **printemps** | pran-tahn |
| summer | **été** | ay-tay |
| fall | **automne** | oh-tuhn |
| winter | **hiver** | ee-vehr |

# Transportation

### Trains:

| | | |
|---|---|---|
| Is this the line for...? | **C'est la file pour...?** | say lah feel poor |
| ...tickets | **...les billets** | lay bee-yay |
| ...reservations | **...les réservations** | lay ray-zehr-vah-see-ohn |
| How much is the fare to...? | **C'est combien pour allez à...?** | say kohn-bee-an poor ah-lay ah |
| A ticket to ___. | **Un billet pour ___.** | uhn bee-yay poor |
| When is the next train? | **Le prochain train part á quelle heure?** | luh proh-shan tran par ah kehl ur |
| I'd like to leave... | **Je voudrais partir...** | zhuh voo-dray par-teer |
| I'd like to arrive... | **Je voudrais arriver...** | zhuh voo-dray ah-ree-vay |
| ...by ___. | **...à ___.** | ah |
| ...in the morning. | **...le matin.** | luh mah-tan |
| ...in the afternoon. | **...l'après-midi.** | lah-preh-mee-dee |
| ...in the evening. | **...le soir.** | luh swahr |
| Is there a...? | **Y a-t-il un...?** | ee ah-teel uhn |
| ...earlier train | **...train plus tôt** | tran plew toh |
| ...later train | **...train plus tard** | tran plew tar |
| ..overnight train | **...train de nuit** | tran duh nwee |
| ...supplement | **...supplément** | sew-play-mahn |
| Is there a discount for...? | **Y a-t-il une réduction pour les...?** | ee ah-teel ewn ray-dewk-see-ohn poor lay |
| ...youth | **...jeunes** | zhuhn |
| ...seniors | **...personnes âgée** | pehr-suhn ah-zhay |

| | | |
|---|---|---|
| Is a reservation required? | **Une réservation est-elle nécessaire?** | ewn ray-zehr-vah-see-ohn ay-tehl nay-suh-sair |
| I'd like to reserve... | **Je voudrais réserver...** | zhuh voo-dray ray-zehr-vay |
| ...a seat. | **...une place.** | ewn plahs |
| ...a berth. | **...une couchette.** | ewn koo-sheht |
| ...a sleeper. | **...un compartiment privé.** | uhn kohn-par-tuh-mahn pree-vay |
| Where does (the train) leave from? | **Il part d'où?** | eel par doo |
| What track? | **Quelle voie?** | kehl vwah |
| On time? Late? | **A l'heure? En retard?** | ah lur / ahn ruh-tar |
| When will it arrive? | **Il va arriver à quelle heure?** | eel vah ah-ree-vay ah kehl ur |
| Is it direct? | **C'est direct?** | say dee-rehkt |
| Must I transfer? | **Faut-il prendre une correspondance?** | foh-teel prahn-druh ewn kor-rehs-pohn-dahns |
| When? Where? | **À quelle heure? Où?** | ah kehl ur / oo |
| Which train to...? | **Quel train pour...?** | kehl tran poor |
| Which train car to...? | **Quelle voiture pour...?** | kehl vwah-tewr poor |
| Is (the seat) free? | **C'est libre?** | say lee-bruh |
| That's my seat. | **C'est ma place.** | say mah plahs |
| Save my place? | **Gardez ma place?** | gar-day mah plahs |
| Where are you going? | **Où allez-vous?** | oo ah-lay-voo |
| I'm going to... | **Je vais à...** | zhuh vay ah |
| Tell me when to get off? | **Dites-moi quand je descends?** | deet-mwah kahn zhuh day-sahn |

## *Ticket talk:*

| | | |
|---|---|---|
| ticket | **billet** | bee-yay |
| one way | **aller simple** | ah-lay san-pluh |
| roundtrip | **aller-retour** | ah-lay-ruh-toor |
| first class | **première classe** | pruhm-yenr klahs |
| second class | **deuxième classe** | duhz-yehm klahs |
| reduced fare | **tarif réduit** | tah-reef ray-dwee |
| validate | **composter** | kohn-poh-stay |
| schedule | **horaire** | oh-rair |
| departure | **départ** | day-par |
| direct | **direct** | dee-rehkt |
| connection | **correspondance** | kor-rehs-pohn-dahns |
| reservation | **réservation** | ray-zehr-vah-see-ohn |
| non-smoking | **non fumeur** | nohn few-mur |
| seat... | **place...** | plahs |
| ...by the window | **...à la fenêtre** | ah lah fuh-neh-truh |
| ...on the aisle | **...au couloir** | oh kool-wahr |
| berth... | **couchette...** | koo-sheht |
| ...upper | **...supérieure** | sew-pay-ree-ur |
| ...middle | **...milieu** | meel-yuh |
| ...lower | **...inférieure** | an-fay-ree-ur |
| refund | **remboursement** | rahn-boor-suh-mahn |

## *At the train station:*

| | | |
|---|---|---|
| French State Railways | **SNCF** | S N say F |
| train station | **gare** | gar |
| train information | **renseignements** | rah<u>n</u>-sehn-yuh-mah<u>n</u> |
| train | **train** | tra<u>n</u> |
| high-speed train | **TGV** | tay zhay vay |
| arrival | **arrivée** | ah-ree-vay |
| departure | **départ** | day-par |
| delay | **retard** | ruh-tar |
| waiting room | **salle d'attente** | sahl dah-tah<u>n</u>t |
| lockers | **consigne automatique** | koh<u>n</u>-seen-yuh oh-toh-mah-teek |
| baggage check room | **consigne de bagages** | koh<u>n</u>-seen-yuh duh bah-gahzh |
| lost and found office | **bureau des objets trouvés** | bew-roh dayz ohb-zhay troo-vay |
| tourist information | **office du tourisme** | oh-fees dew too-reez-muh |
| to the platforms | **accès aux quais** | ahk-seh oh kay |
| platform | **quai** | kay |
| track | **voie** | vwah |
| train car | **voiture** | vwah-tewr |
| dining car | **voiture restaurant** | vwah-tewr rehs-toh-rah<u>n</u> |
| sleeper car | **wagon-lit** | vah-goh<u>n</u>-lee |
| conductor | **conducteur** | koh<u>n</u>-dewk-tur |

## *Reading train and bus schedules:*

| | |
|---|---|
| **à, pour** | to |
| **arrivée** | arrival |
| **de** | from |
| **départ** | departure |
| **dimanche** | Sunday |
| **en retard** | late |
| **en semaine** | workdays (Monday-Saturday) |
| **jour férié** | holiday |
| **jours** | days |
| **jusqu'à** | until |
| **la semaine** | weekdays |
| **par** | via |
| **samedi** | Saturday |
| **sauf** | except |
| **seulement** | only |
| **tous** | every |
| **tous les jours** | daily |
| **vacances** | holidays |
| **1-5** | Monday-Friday |
| **6, 7** | Saturday, Sunday |

French schedules use the 24-hour clock. It's like American time until noon. After that, subtract twelve and add p.m. So 13:00 is 1 p.m., 20:00 is 8 p.m., and 24:00 is midnight. If your train is scheduled to depart at 00:01, it'll leave one minute after midnight.

Train schedules show blue (quiet), white (normal), and red (peak and holiday) times. You can save money if you get the blues (travel during off-peak hours).

## Buses and subways:

| | | |
|---|---|---|
| How do I get to...? | **Comment aller à...?** | koh-mah<u>n</u> tah-lay ah |
| Which bus to...? | **Quel bus pour...?** | kehl bews poor |
| Does it stop at...? | **Est-ce qu'il s'arrête à...?** | ehs keel sah-reht ah |
| Which stop for...? | **Quel arrêt pour...?** | kehl ah-reh poor |
| Must I transfer? | **Faut-il prendre une correspondance?** | foh-teel prah<u>n</u>-druh ewn kor-rehs-poh<u>n</u>-dah<u>n</u>s |
| How much is a ticket? | **Combien le ticket?** | koh<u>n</u>-bee-a<u>n</u> luh tee-kay |
| Where can I buy a ticket? | **Où puis-je acheter un ticket?** | oo pwee-zhuh ah-shuh-tay uh<u>n</u> tee-kay |
| When does the... leave? | **Quand est-ce que le... part?** | kah<u>n</u> ehs kuh luh... par |
| ...first | **...premier** | pruhm-yay |
| ..next | **...prochain** | proh-sha<u>n</u> |
| ...last | **...dernier** | dehrn-yay |
| ...bus / subway | **...bus / métro** | bews / may-troh |
| What's the frequency per hour / day? | **Combien de fois par heure / jour?** | koh<u>n</u>-bee-a<u>n</u> duh fwah par ur / zhoor |

## *Key bus and subway words:*

| | | |
|---|---|---|
| ticket | **ticket** | tee-kay |
| city bus | **bus** | bews |
| long-distance bus | **car** | kar |
| bus stop | **arrêt de bus** | ah-reh duh bews |
| bus station | **gare routière** | gar root-yehr |
| subway | **métro** | may-troh |
| subway exit | **sortie** | sor-tee |

## Taxis:

| | | |
|---|---|---|
| Taxi! | **Taxi!** | tahk-see |
| Can you call a taxi? | **Pouvez-vous appeler un taxi?** | poo-vay-vooz ah-puh-lay uhn tahk-see |
| Where is a taxi stand? | **Où est une station de taxi?** | oo ay ewn stah-see-ohn duh tahk-see |
| Are you free? | **Libre?** | lee-bruh |
| Occupied. | **Occupé.** | oh-kew-pay |
| How much will it cost to go to...? | **C'est combien pour aller à...?** | say kohn-bee-an poor ah-lay ah |
| Too much. | **Trop.** | troh |
| Can you take ___ people? | **Pouvez-vous prendre ___ passagers?** | poo-vay-voo prahn-druh ___ pah-sah-zhay |
| Any extra fee? | **Il y a d'autre frais?** | eel yah doh-truh fray |
| The meter, please. | **Le compteur, s'il vous plaît.** | luh kohn-tur see voo play |
| The most direct route. | **La route la plus directe.** | lah root lah plew dee-rehkt |
| Slow down. | **Ralentissez.** | rah-lahn-tee-say |
| If you don't slow down, I'll throw up. | **Si vous ne ralentissez pas, je vais vomir.** | see voo nuh rah-lahn-tee-say pah zhuh vay voh-meer |
| Stop here. | **Arrêtez-vous ici.** | ah-reh-tay-voo ee-see |
| Can you wait? | **Pouvez-vous attendre?** | poo-vay-vooz ah-tahn-druh |
| My change, please. | **La monnaie, s'il vous plaît.** | lah moh-nay see voo play |
| Keep the change. | **Gardez la monnaie.** | gar-day lah moh-nay |

# Rental wheels:

| I'd like to rent... | Je voudrais louer... | zhuh voo-dray loo-ay |
| ...a car. | ...une voiture. | ewn vwah-tewr |
| ...a station wagon. | ...un break. | uhn brayk |
| ...a van. | ...un van. | uhn vahn |
| ...a motorcycle. | ...une motocyclette. | ewn moh-toh-see-kleht |
| ...a motor scooter. | ...un vélomoteur. | uhn vay-loh-moh-tur |
| ...a bicycle. | ...un vélo. | uhn vay-loh |
| ...the Concorde. | ...le Concorde. | luh kohn-kord |
| How much per...? | Combien par...? | kohn-bee-an par |
| ...hour | ...heure | ur |
| ...day | ...jour | zhoor |
| ...week | ...semaine | suh-mehn |
| Unlimited mileage? | Kilométrage illimité? | kee-loh-may-trazh eel-lee-mee-tay |
| I brake for bakeries. | Je m'arrête à chaque boulangerie. | zhuh mah-reht ah shahk boo-lahn-zhuh-ree |
| Is there...? | Est-ce qu'il ya...? | ehs keel yah |
| ...a helmet | ...un casque | uhn kahsk |
| ...a discount | ...une réduction | ewn ray-dewk-see-ohn |
| ...a deposit | ...une caution | ewn koh-see-ohn |
| ...insurance | ...une assurance | ewn ah-sewr-rahns |
| When do I bring it back? | A quelle heure faut-il le ramener? | ah kehl ur foh-teel luh rah-muh-nay |

## Driving:

| gas station | **station service** | stah-see-ohn sehr-vees |
|---|---|---|
| The nearest gas station? | **La plus proche station service?** | lah plew prohsh stah-see-ohn sehr-vees |
| Is it self-service? | **C'est libre service?** | say lee-bruh sehr-vees |
| Fill the tank. | **Faites le plein.** | feht luh plan |
| I need... | **Il me faut...** | eel muh foh |
| ...gas. | **...de l'essence.** | duh leh-sahns |
| ...unleaded. | **...sans plomb.** | sahn plohn |
| ...regular. | **...normale.** | nor-mahl |
| ...super. | **...du super.** | dew sew-pehr |
| ...diesel. | **...gazoil.** | gah-zoyl |
| Check... | **Vérifiez...** | vay-ree-fee-ay |
| ...the oil. | **...l'huile.** | lweel |
| ...the air in the tires. | **...la pression dans les pneus.** | lah pruh-see-ohn dahn lay puh-nuh |
| ...the radiator. | **...le radiateur.** | lah rahd-yah-tur |
| ...the battery. | **...la batterie.** | lah bah-tuh-ree |
| ...the fuses. | **...les bougies.** | lay boo-zhee |
| ...the fanbelt. | **...la courroie du ventilateur.** | lah koor-wah dew vahn-tee-lah-tur |
| ...the brakes. | **...les freins.** | lay fran |
| ...my pulse. | **...mon poul.** | mohn pool |

The cheapest gas in France is sold in *hypermarché* (supermarket) parking lots.

## *Car trouble:*

| | | |
|---|---|---|
| accident | **accident** | ahk-see-dah<u>n</u> |
| breakdown | **en panne** | ah<u>n</u> pahn |
| electrical problem | **problème d'électricité** | proh-blehm day-lehk-tree-see-tay |
| funny noise | **bruit curieux** | brwee kew-ree-uh |
| It won't start. | **Elle ne démarre pas.** | ehl nuh day-mar pah |
| It's overheating. | **Le moteur surchauffe.** | luh moh-tur sewr-shohf |
| This doesn't work. | **Ça ne marche pas.** | sah nuh marsh pah |
| I need a... | **Il me faut un...** | eel muh foh uh<u>n</u> |
| ...tow truck. | **...dépanneur.** | day-pah-nur |
| ...mechanic. | **...mécanicien.** | may-kah-nee-see-a<u>n</u> |
| ...stiff drink. | **...bon coup.** | boh<u>n</u> koo |

## *Parking:*

| | | |
|---|---|---|
| parking garage | **garage** | gah-rahzh |
| Where can I park? | **Où puis-je me garer?** | oo pwee-zhuh muh gah-ray |
| Can I park here? | **Puis-je me garer ici?** | pwee-zhuh muh gah-ray ee-see |
| How long can I park here? | **Je peux me garer ici pour combien de temps?** | zhuh puh muh gah-ray ee-see poor kohn-bee-an duh tahn |
| Must I pay to park here? | **Dois-je payer pour me garer ici?** | dwah-zhuh pay-yay poor muh gah-ray ee-see |
| Is this a safe place to park? | **C'est prudent de se garer ici?** | say prew-dah<u>n</u> duh suh gah-ray ee-see |

## Finding your way:

| | | |
|---|---|---|
| I am going to... | **Je vais à...** | zhuh vay ah |
| How do I get to...? | **Comment aller à...?** | koh-mah<u>n</u> tah-lay ah |
| Do you have...? | **Avez-vous...?** | ah-vay-voo |
| ...a city map | **...un plan de la ville** | uh<u>n</u> plah<u>n</u> duh lah veel |
| ...a road map | **...une carte routière** | ewn kart root-yehr |
| How many minutes...? | **Combien de minutes...?** | koh<u>n</u>-bee-a<u>n</u> duh mee-newt |
| How many hours...? | **Combien d'heures...?** | koh<u>n</u>-bee-a<u>n</u> dur |
| ...on foot | **...à pied** | ah pee-yay |
| ...by bicycle | **...à bicyclette** | ah bee-see-kleht |
| ...by car | **...en voiture** | ah<u>n</u> vwah-tewr |
| How many kilometers to...? | **Combien de kilomètres à...?** | koh<u>n</u>-bee-a<u>n</u> duh kee-loh-meh-truh ah |
| What's the... route to Paris? | **Quelle est la... route pour Paris?** | kehl eh lah... root poor pah-ree |
| ...best | **...meilleure** | meh-yur |
| ...fastest | **...plus directe** | plew dee-rehkt |
| ..most interesting | **...plus intéressante** | plewz a<u>n</u>-tay-reh-sah<u>n</u>t |
| Point it out? | **Montrez-moi?** | moh<u>n</u>-tray mwah |
| I'm lost. | **Je suis perdu.** | zhuh swee pehr-dew |
| Where am I? | **Où suis-je?** | oo swee-zhuh |
| Who am I? | **Qui suis-je?** | kee swee-zhuh |
| Where is...? | **Où est...?** | oo ay |
| The nearest...? | **Le plus proche...?** | luh plew prohsh |
| Where is this address? | **Où se trouve cette adresse?** | oo suh troov seht ah-drehs |

## Key route-finding words:

| city map | **plan de la ville** | plah<u>n</u> duh lah veel |
| road map | **carte routière** | kart root-yehr |
| straight ahead | **tout droit** | too dwah |
| left / right | **à gauche / à droite** | ah gohsh / ah dwaht |
| first / next | **premier / prochain** | pruhm-yay / proh-sha<u>n</u> |
| intersection | **carrefour** | kar-foor |
| stoplight | **feu** | fuh |
| (main) square | **place (principal)** | plahs (pra<u>n</u>-see-pahl) |
| street | **rue** | rew |
| bridge | **pont** | poh<u>n</u> |
| tunnel | **tunnel** | tew-nehl |
| highway | **grande route** | grah<u>n</u>d root |
| national highway | **route nationale** | root nah-see-oh-nahl |
| freeway | **autoroute** | oh-toh-root |
| north / south | **nord / sud** | nor / sewd |
| east / west | **est / ouest** | ehs / wehs |

Along the *autoroute* (freeway), electronic signs flash messages to let you know what's ahead: *bouchon* (traffic jam), *circulation* (traffic), and *fluide* (no traffic). The shortest distance between any two points is the *autoroute*, but the tolls add up. You'll travel cheaper, but slower, on a *route nationale*.

# Sleeping

## Places to stay:

| | | |
|---|---|---|
| hotel | **hôtel** | oh-tehl |
| small hotel | **pension** | pah<u>n</u>-see-oh<u>n</u> |
| room in private home | **chambre d'hôte** | shah<u>n</u>-bruh doht |
| youth hostel | **auberge de jeunesse** | oh-behrzh duh zhuh-nehs |
| country home rental | **gîte** | zheet |
| vacancy | **chambre libre** | shah<u>n</u>-bruh lee-bruh |
| no vacancy | **complet** | koh<u>n</u>-play |

## Reserving a room by phone:

| | | |
|---|---|---|
| Hello. | **Bonjour.** | boh<u>n</u>-zhoor |
| Do you speak English? | **Parlez-vous anglais?** | par-lay-voo ah<u>n</u>-glay |
| Do you have a room...? | **Avez-vous une chambre...?** | ah-vay-voo ewn shah<u>n</u>-bruh |
| ...for one person | **...pour une personne** | poor ewn pehr-suhn |
| ...for two people | **...pour deux personnes** | poor duh pehr-suhn |
| ...for tonight | **...pour ce soir** | poor suh swahr |
| ...for two nights | **...pour deux nuits** | poor duh nwee |
| ...for this Friday | **...pour ce vendredi** | poor suh vah<u>n</u>-druh-dee |
| ...for June 21 | **...pour le vingt et un juin** | poor luh va<u>n</u>t ay uh<u>n</u> zhwa<u>n</u> |
| Yes or no? | **Oui ou non?** | wee oo noh<u>n</u> |

SLEEPING

| I'd like... | **Je voudrais...** | zhuh voo-dray |
| ...a private bathroom. | **...une salle de bains.** | ewn sahl duh ba<u>n</u> |
| ...your cheapest room. | **...la chambre la moins chère.** | lah sha<u>n</u>-bruh lah mwa<u>n</u> shehr |
| ...___ beds for ___ people in ___ rooms. | **...___ lits par ___ personnes dans ___ chambres.** | ___ lee par ___ pehr-suhn dah<u>n</u> ___ sha<u>n</u>-bruh |
| How much is it? | **Combien?** | koh<u>n</u>-bee-a<u>n</u> |
| Anything cheaper? | **Rien de moins cher?** | ree-a<u>n</u> duh mwa<u>n</u> shehr |
| I'll take it. | **Je la prends.** | zhuh lah prah<u>n</u> |
| My name is... | **Je m'appelle...** | zhuh mah-pehl |
| I'll stay... | **Je reste...** | zhuh rehst |
| We'll stay... | **Nous restons...** | noo rehs-toh<u>n</u> |
| ...___ nights. | **...___ nuits.** | ___ nwee |
| I'll come... | **J'arrive...** | zhah-reev |
| We'll come... | **Nous arrivons...** | nooz ah-ree-voh<u>n</u> |
| ...in one hour. | **...dans une heure.** | dah<u>n</u>z ewn ur |
| ...before 16:00. | **...avant seize heures.** | ah-vah<u>n</u> sehz ur |
| ...Friday before 6 p.m. | **...vendredi avant six heures du soir.** | vah<u>n</u>-druh-dee ah-vah<u>n</u> seez ur dew swahr |
| Thank you. | **Merci.** | mehr-see |

Offering some of the best budget beds in Europe, French hotels are rated from one to four stars (check the blue & white plaque by the front door). For budget travelers, one or two stars is the best value.

## Getting specific:

| | | |
|---|---|---|
| I'd like a room... | **Je voudrais une chambre...** | zhuh voo-dray ewn shahn-bruh |
| ...with / without / and | **...avec / sans / et** | ah-vehk / sahn / ay |
| ...toilet | **...WC** | vay say |
| ...sink and toilet | **...cabinet de toilette** | kah-bee-nay duh twah-leht |
| ...shower | **...douche** | doosh |
| ...shower and toilet | **...salle d'eau** | sahl doh |
| ...shower down the hall | **...douche sur le palier** | doosh sewr luh pahl-yay |
| ...bathtub and toilet | **...salle de bain** | sahl duh ban |
| ...double bed | **...grand lit** | grahn lee |
| ...twin beds | **...deux petits lits, lits jumeaux** | duh puh-tee lee, lee zhew-moh |
| ...balcony | **...balcon** | bahl-kohn |
| ...view | **...vue** | vew |
| ...only a sink | **...lavabo seulement** | lah-vah-boh suhl-mahn |
| ...on the ground floor | **...au rez-de-chaussée** | oh ray-duh-shoh-say |
| Is there an elevator? | **Un ascenseur?** | uhn ah-sahn-sur |
| We arrive Monday, depart Wednesday. | **Nous arrivons lundi, nous partons mercredi.** | nooz ah-ree-vohn luhn-dee, noo par-tohn mehr-kruh-dee |
| I have a reservation. | **J'ai une réservation.** | zhay ewn ray-zehr-vah-see-ohn |
| Confirm my reservation? | **Confirmez mes réservations?** | kohn-feer-may may ray-zehr-vah-see-ohn |

**SLEEPING**

## Nailing down the price:

| How much is...? | Combien...? | kohn-bee-an |
| ...a room for ___ people | ...une chambre pour ___ personnes | ewn shahn-bruh poor ___ pehr-suhn |
| ...your cheapest room | ...la chambre la moins chère | lah shahn-bruh lah mwan shehr |
| Is breakfast included? | Petit déjeuner compris? | puh-tee day-zhuh-nay kohn-pree |
| How much without breakfast? | Combien sans le petit déjeuner? | kohn-bee-an sahn luh puh-tee day-zhuh-nay |
| Complete price? | Tout compris? | too kohn-pree |
| Is it cheaper if I stay ___ nights? | C'est moins cher si je reste ___ nuits? | say mwan shehr see zhuh rehst ___ nwee |
| I'll stay ___ nights. | Je vais rester ___ nuits. | zhuh vay rehs-tay ___ nwee |

## Choosing a room:

| Can I see the room? | Puis-je voir la chambre? | pwee-zhuh vwahr lah shahn-bruh |
| Do you have something...? | Avez-vous quelque chose de...? | ah-vay-voo kehl-kuh shohz duh |
| ...larger / smaller | ...plus grand / moins grand | plew grahn / mwan grahn |
| ...better / cheaper | ...meilleur / moins cher | meh-yur / mwan shehr |
| ...brighter | ...plus clair | ploo klair |
| ...quieter | ...plus tranquille | plew trahn-keel |
| Key, please. | Clé, s'il vous plaît. | klay see voo play |

## Hotel help:

| I'd like... | Je voudrais... | zhuh voo-dray |
|---|---|---|
| ...a / another | ...un / un autre | uhn / uhn oh-truh |
| ...towel. | ...serviette de bain. | sehrv-yeht duh ban |
| ...pillow. | ...oreiller. | oh-reh-yay |
| ...clean sheets. | ...draps propres. | drah proh-pruh |
| ...blanket. | ...couverture. | koo-vehr-tewr |
| ...glass. | ...verre. | vehr |
| ...soap. | ...savon. | sah-vohn |
| ...toilet paper. | ...papier hygiénique. | pahp-yay ee-zhay-neek |
| ...crib. | ...berceau. | behr-soh |
| ...roll-away bed. | ...lit pliant. | lee plee-ahn |
| ...different room. | ...autre chambre. | oh-truh shahn-bruh |
| ...silence. | ...silence. | see-lahns |
| Where can I wash / hang my laundry? | Où puis-je faire / étendre ma lessive? | oo pwee-zhuh fair / ay-tahn-druh mah luh-seev |
| I'd like to stay another night. | Je voudrais rester encore une nuit. | zhuh voo-dray rehs-tay ahn-kor ewn nwee |
| Where can I park? | Je me gare où? | zhuh muh gar oo |
| What time do you lock up? | Vous fermez à quelle heure? | voo fehr-may ah kehl ur |
| What time is breakfast? | Le petit déjeuner est servi à quelle heure? | luh puh-tee day-zhuh-nay ay sehr-vee ah kehl ur |
| Please wake me at 7:00. | Réveillez-moi à sept heures, si'l vous plaît. | ray-veh-yay-mwah ah seht ur see voo play |

## Hotel hassles:

| English | French | Pronunciation |
|---|---|---|
| Come with me. | Venez avec moi. | vuh-nay ah-vehk mwah |
| I have a problem in my room. | J'ai un problème dans ma chambre. | zhay uhn proh-blehm dahn mah shahn-bruh |
| Lamp... | Lampe... | lahmp |
| Lightbulb... | Ampoule... | ahn-pool |
| Key... | Clé... | klay |
| Lock... | Serrure... | suh-roor |
| Window... | Fenêtre... | fuh-neh-truh |
| Faucet... | Robinet... | roh-bee-nay |
| Sink... | Lavabo... | lah-vah-boh |
| Toilet... | Toilette... | twah-leht |
| Shower... | Douche... | doosh |
| ...doesn't work. | ...ne marche pas. | nuh marsh pah |
| There is no hot water. | Il n'y a plus d'eau chaude. | eel nee yah plew doh shohd |
| When is the water hot? | L'eau sera chaude à quelle heure? | loh suh-rah shohd ah kehl ur |

## Checking out:

| English | French | Pronunciation |
|---|---|---|
| I leave... | Je parte... | zhuh part |
| We leave... | Nous partons... | noo par-tohn |
| ...today. | ...aujourd'hui. | oh-zhoor-dwee |
| ...tomorrow. | ...demain. | duh-man |
| ...very early. | ...très tôt. | treh toh |

| When is check-out time? | **Quelle est l'heure limite d'occupation?** | kehl ay lur lee-meet doh-kew-pah-see-ohn |
| Can I pay now? | **Puis-je régler la note?** | pwee-zhuh ray-glay lah noht |
| Bill, please. | **Note, s'il vous plaît.** | noht see voo play |
| Credit card O.K.? | **Carte de crédit O.K.?** | kart duh kray-dee "O.K." |
| I slept like a baby. | **J'ai dormi comme un enfant.** | zhay dor-mee kohm uhn ahn-fahn |
| Everything was great. | **C'était super.** | say-tay sew-pehr |
| Will you call my next hotel for me? | **Pouvez-vous contacter mon prochain hôtel pour moi?** | poo-vay-voo kohn-tahk-tay mohn pruh-shan oh-tehl poor mwah |
| Can I...? | **Puis-je...?** | pwee-zhuh |
| Can we...? | **Pouvons-nous...?** | poo-vohn-noo |
| ...leave baggage here until ___ | **...laisser les baggages ici jusqu'à ___** | lay-say lay bah-gahzh ee-see zhews-kah |

SLEEPING

## Camping:

| tent / camping | **tente / camping** | tahnt / kahn-peeng |
| The nearest campground? | **Le plus proche camping?** | luh plew prohsh kahn-peeng |
| Can I...? | **Puis-je...?** | pwee-zhuh |
| Can we...? | **Pouvons-nous...?** | poo-vohn-noo |
| ...camp here for one night | **...camper ici pour une nuit** | kahn-pay ee-see poor ewn nwee |
| Are showers included? | **Les douches sont comprises?** | lay doosh sohn kohn-preez |

# Eating

## Finding a restaurant:

| Where's a good... restaurant? | Où se trouve un bon restaurant...? | oo suh troov uhn bohn rehs-toh-rahn |
| ...cheap | ...bon marché | bohn mar-shay |
| ...local-style | ...cuisine régionale | kwee-zeen ray-zhee-oh-nahl |
| ...untouristy | ...pas touristique | pah too-ree-steek |
| ...Chinese | ...chinois | sheen-wah |
| ...fast food | ...fast food | fahst food |
| ...self-service | ...libre service | lee-bruh sehr-vees |

While the slick self-service restaurants are easy to use, you'll often eat better for the same money in a good little family bistro.

## Getting a table and menu:

| Waiter. | Garçon. | gar-sohn |
| Waitress. | Mademoiselle, Madame. | mahd-mwah-zehl, mah-dahm |
| I'd like... | Je voudrais... | zhuh voo-dray |
| ...a table for one / two. | ...une table pour un / deux. | ewn tah-bluh poor uhn / duh |
| ...non-smoking. | ...non fumeur. | nohn few-mur |
| ...just a drink. | ...une consommation seulement. | ewn kohn-soh-mah-see-ohn suhl-mahn |
| ...a snack. | ...un snack. | uhn snahk |

EATING

| | | |
|---|---|---|
| ...to see the menu. | **...voir la carte.** | vwahr lah kart |
| ...to order. | **...commander.** | koh-mahn-day |
| ...to eat. | **...manger.** | mahn-zhay |
| ...to pay. | **...payer.** | pay-yay |
| ...to throw up. | **...vomir.** | voh-meer |
| What do you recommend? | **Qu'est-ce que vous recommandez?** | kehs kuh voo ruh-koh-mahn-day |
| What's your favorite? | **Quel est votre favorit?** | kehl eh voh-truh fah-voh-ree |
| Is it...? | **C'est...?** | say |
| ...good | **...bon** | bohn |
| ...expensive | **...cher** | shehr |
| ...light | **...léger** | lay-zhay |
| ...filling | **...copieux** | kohp-yuh |
| What's cheap and filling? | **Qu'est-ce qu'il y a de bon marché et de copieux?** | kehs keel yah duh bohn mar-shay ay duh kohp-yuh |
| What is fast? | **Qu'est-ce qui est déjà préparé?** | kehs kee ay day-zhah pray-pah-ray |
| What is local? | **Qu'est-ce que vous avez de la région?** | kehs kuh vooz ah-vay duh lah ray-zhee-ohn |
| What is that? | **Qu'est-ce que c'est?** | kehs kuh say |
| Do you have...? | **Avez-vous...?** | ah-vay-vooz |
| ...an English menu | **...une carte en anglais** | ewn kart ahn ahn-glay |
| ...a children's portion | **...une assiette d'enfant** | ewn ahs-yeht dahn-fahn |

## The menu:

| | | |
|---|---|---|
| menu | **carte** | kart |
| menu of the day | **menu du jour** | muh-new dew zhoor |
| special of the day | **plat du jour** | plah dew zhoor |
| fast service special | **formule rapide** | for-mewl rah-peed |
| tourist menu | **menu touristique** | muh-new too-ree-steek |
| fixed price | **prix fixe** | pree feeks |
| breakfast | **petit déjeuner** | puh-tee day-zhuh-nay |
| lunch | **déjeuner** | day-zhuh-nay |
| dinner | **dîner** | dee-nay |
| specialty of the house | **spécialité de la maison** | spay-see-ah-lee-tay duh lah may-zohn |
| appetizers | **hors-d'oeuvre** | or-duh-vruh |
| bread | **pain** | pan |
| salad | **salade** | sah-lahd |
| soup | **soupe** | soop |
| first course | **entrée** | ahn-tray |
| main course | **plat principal** | plah pran-see-pahl |
| meat | **viande** | vee-ahnd |
| poultry | **volaille** | voh-lī |
| seafood | **fruits de mer** | frwee duh mehr |
| side dishes | **à la carte** | ah lah kart |
| vegetables | **légumes** | lay-gewm |
| cheese | **fromage** | froh-mahzh |
| dessert | **dessert** | duh-sehr |
| beverages | **boissons** | bwah-sohn |
| beer | **bière** | bee-ehr |
| wine | **vin** | van |

EATING

| cover charge | couvert | koo-vehr |
| service included | service compris | sehr-vees kohn-pree |
| service not included | service non compris | sehr-vees nohn kohn-pree |
| with / without | avec / sans | ah-vehk / sahn |
| and / or | et / ou | ay / oo |

In France, a menu is a *carte*, and a fixed-price meal is a *menu*. Many cafés offer fixed-price meals such as a *plat du jour* or *menu touristique*—you'll get your choice of an appetizer, entrée, and dessert at a set price.

## Dietary restrictions:

| I'm allergic to... | Je suis allergique à... | zhuh sweez ah-lehr-zheek ah |
| I cannot eat... | Je ne mange pas de... | zhuh nuh mahnzh pah duh |
| ...dairy products. | ...produits laitiers. | proh-dwee lay-tee-yay |
| ...meat / pork. | ...viande / porc. | vee-ahnd / por |
| ...salt / sugar. | ...sel / sucre. | sehl / sew-kruh |
| I'm a diabetic. | Je suis diabétique. | zhuh swee dee-ah-bay-teek |
| Low cholesterol? | Maigre? Light? | may-gruh / "light" |
| No caffeine. | Décaféiné. | day-kah-fay-nay |
| No alcohol. | Sans alcool. | sahnz ahl-kohl |
| I'm a... | Je suis... | zhuh swee |
| ...male vegetarian. | ...végétarien. | vay-zhay-tah-ree-an |
| ...female vegetarian. | ...végétarienne. | vay-zhay-tah-ree-ehn |
| ...strict vegetarian. | ...végétarien rigoureux. | vay-zhay-tah-ree-an ree-goo-ruh |
| ...carnivore. | ...carnivore. | kar-nee-vor |

## Tableware and condiments:

| plate | **assiette** | ahs-yeht |
| napkin | **serviette** | sehrv-yeht |
| knife | **couteau** | koo-toh |
| fork | **fourchette** | foor-sheht |
| spoon | **cuillère** | kwee-yehr |
| cup | **tasse** | tahs |
| glass | **verre** | vehr |
| carafe | **carafe** | kah-rahf |
| water | **l'eau** | loh |
| bread | **pain** | pan |
| butter | **beurre** | bur |
| margarine | **margarine** | mar-gah-reen |
| salt / pepper | **sel / poivre** | sehl / pwah-vruh |
| sugar | **sucre** | sew-kruh |
| artificial sweetener | **édulcorant** | ay-dewl-koh-rahn |
| honey | **miel** | mee-ehl |
| mustard | **moutarde** | moo-tard |
| mayonnaise | **mayonnaise** | mah-yuh-nehz |
| ketchup | **ketchup** | "ketchup" |

French cuisine is sightseeing for your tastebuds. Restaurants normally serve from 12:00 to 14:00, and from 19:00 until about 22:00. The menu is posted right on the front door or window, and "window shopping" for your meal is a fun, important part of the experience.

EATING

## Restaurant requests and regrets:

| | | |
|---|---|---|
| A little. / More. | **Un peu. / Encore.** | uhn puh / ahn-kor |
| Another. | **Un autre.** | uhn oh-truh |
| The same. | **La même chose.** | lah mehm shohz |
| I did not order this. | **Ce n'est pas ce que j'ai commandé.** | suh nay pah suh kuh zhay koh-mahn-day |
| Is it included with the meal? | **C'est inclus avec le repas?** | say an-kloo ah-vehk luh ruh-pah |
| I'm in a hurry. | **Je suis pressé.** | zhuh swee preh-say |
| I must leave at... | **Je dois partir a...** | zhuh dwah par-teer ah |
| Will the food be ready soon? | **Ce sera prêt bientôt?** | suh suh-rah preh bee-an-toh |
| I've changed my mind. | **J'ai changé d'avis.** | zhay shahn-zhay dah-vee |
| Can I get it "to go?" | **Pour emporter?** | poor ahn-por-tay |
| This is... | **C'est...** | say |
| ...dirty. | **...sale.** | sahl |
| ...greasy. | **...graisseux.** | gray-suh |
| ...too salty. | **...trop salé.** | troh sah-lay |
| ...undercooked. | **...pas assez cuit.** | pah ah-say kwee |
| ...overcooked. | **...trop cuit.** | troh kwee |
| ...cold. | **...froid.** | frwah |
| Heat this up? | **Le chauffage marche?** | luh shoh-fahzh marsh |
| Enjoy your meal! | **Bon appétit!** | bohn ah-pay-tee |
| Enough. | **Assez.** | ah-say |
| Finished. | **Terminé.** | tehr-mee-nay |

| Do any of your customers return? | Avez-vous des clients qui reviennent? | ah-vay-voo day klee-ahn kee ruh-vee-an |
| Yuck! | Pouah! | pwah |
| Delicious! | Délicieux! | day-lee-see-uh |
| Magnificent! | Magnifique! | mahn-yee-feek |
| My compliments to the chef! | Mes compliments au chef! | may kohn-plee-mahn oh shehf |

**EATING**

## Paying for your meal:

| Waiter. | Garçon. | gar-sohn |
| Waitress. | Mademoiselle, Madame. | mahd-mwah-zehl, mah-dahm |
| The bill, please. | L'addition, s'il vous plaît. | lah-dee-see-ohn see voo play |
| Together. | Ensemble. | ahn-sahn-bluh |
| Separate checks. | Notes séparées. | noht say-pah-ray |
| Credit card O.K.? | Carte de crédit O.K.? | kart duh kray-dee "O.K." |
| Any cover charge? | Y a-t-il un couvert? | ee ah-teel uhn koo-vehr |
| Is service included? | Le service est compris? | luh sehr-vees ay kohn-pree |
| This is not correct. | Ce n'est pas exact. | suh nay pah ehg-zahkt |
| Explain this? | Expliquer ça? | ehk-splee-kay sah |
| What if I wash the dishes? | Si je lave la vaisselle moi-même? | see zhuh lahv lah vay-sehl mwah-mehm |
| Keep the change. | Gardez la monnaie. | gar-day lah moh-nay |
| This is for you. | C'est pour vous. | say poor voo |

## Breakfast:

| breakfast | petit déjeuner | puh-tee day-zhuh-nay |
|---|---|---|
| bread | pain | pan |
| roll | petit pain | puh-tee pan |
| toast | toast | tohst |
| butter | beurre | bur |
| jelly | confiture | kohn-fee-tewr |
| pastry | pâtisserie | pah-tee-suh-ree |
| croissant | croissant | kwah-sahn |
| omelet | omelette | oh-muh-leht |
| eggs | des oeufs | dayz uh |
| fried eggs | oeufs au plat | uh oh plah |
| scrambled eggs | oeufs brouillés | uh broo-yay |
| boiled egg... | oeuf à la coque... | uhf ah lah kohk |
| ...soft / hard | ...mollet / dur | moh-lay / dewr |
| ham / cheese | jambon / fromage | zhahn-bohn / froh-mahzh |
| yogurt | yaourt | yah-oort |
| cereal | céréale | say-ray-ahl |
| milk | lait | lay |
| hot chocolate | chocolat chaud | shoh-koh-lah shoh |
| fruit juice | jus de fruit | zhew duh frwee |
| orange juice (fresh) | jus d'orange (frais) | zhew doh-rahnzh (fray) |
| coffee / thé | café / thé | kah-fay / tay |
| Is breakfast included in the room cost? | Est-ce que le petit déjeuner est compris? | ehs kuh luh puh-tee day-zhuh-nay ay kohn-pree |

## Snacks and quick lunches:

| | | |
|---|---|---|
| sandwich | **sandwich** | sah<u>n</u>d-weech |
| crepe | **crêpe** | krehp |
| buckwheat crepe | **galette** | gah-leht |
| omelet | **omelette** | oh-muh-leht |
| quiche... | **quiche...** | keesh |
| ...with cheese | **...au fromage** | oh froh-mahzh |
| ...with ham | **...au jambon** | oh zhah<u>n</u>-boh<u>n</u> |
| ...with mushrooms | **...aux champignons** | oh shah<u>n</u>-peen-yoh<u>n</u> |
| ...with bacon, cheese and onions | **...lorraine** | lor-rehn |
| paté | **pâté** | pah-tay |
| onion tart | **tarte à l'oignon** | tart ah loh-yoh<u>n</u> |
| cheese tart | **tarte au fromage** | tart oh froh-mahzh |
| toasted ham and cheese sandwich | **croque monsieur** | krohk muhs-yur |
| toasted ham, cheese & fried egg sandwich | **croque madame** | krohk mah-dahm |

Light meals are quick and easy at *cafés* and *bars* throughout France. A *sandwich, crêpe, quiche* or *omelette* is a fairly cheap way to fill up, even in Paris. Each can be made with various extras like ham, cheese, mushrooms, and so on. *Crêpes* come in dinner or dessert varieties.

EATING

## Soups and salads:

| | | |
|---|---|---|
| soup (of the day) | **soupe (du jour)** | soop (dew zhoor) |
| broth | **bouillon...** | boo-yoh<u>n</u> |
| ...chicken | **...de poulet** | duh poo-lay |
| ...beef | **...de boeuf** | duh buhf |
| ...with noodles | **...aux nouilles** | oh noo-ee |
| ...with rice | **...au riz** | oh ree |
| thick vegetable soup | **potage de légumes** | poh-tahzh duh lay-gewm |
| onion soup | **soupe à l'oignon** | soop ah lohn-yoh<u>n</u> |
| shellfish chowder | **bisque** | beesk |
| seafood stew | **bouillabaisse** | boo-yah-behs |
| salad... | **salade...** | sah-lahd |
| ...green / mixed | **...verte / mixte** | vehrt / meekst |
| ...of goat cheese | **...au chevre chaud** | oh sheh-vruh shoh |
| ...chef's | **...composée** | koh<u>n</u>-poh-zay |
| ...with ham, cheese, and egg | **...avec jambon, fromage, et oeuf** | ah-vehk zhan-boh<u>n</u>, froh-mahzh, ay uh |
| lettuce | **laitue** | lay-tew |
| tomatoes | **tomates** | toh-maht |
| cucumber | **concombre** | koh<u>n</u>-koh<u>n</u>-bruh |
| oil / vinegar | **huile / vinaigre** | weel / vee-nay-gruh |
| dressing on the side | **la sauce à part** | lah sohs ah par |
| What is in this salad? | **Qu'est-ce qu'il y a dans cette salade?** | kehs keel yah dah<u>n</u> seht sah-lahd |

Salads are usually served with a *vinaigrette* dressing.

## Seafood:

| | | |
|---|---|---|
| seafood | **fruits de mer** | frwee duh mehr |
| assorted sea-food | **assiette de fruits de mer** | ahs-yeht duh frwee duh mehr |
| fish | **poisson** | pwah-sohn |
| cod | **cabillaud** | kah-bee-yoh |
| salty cod | **morue** | moh-rew |
| salmon | **saumon** | soh-mohn |
| trout | **truite** | trweet |
| tuna | **thon** | tohn |
| herring | **hareng** | ah-rahn |
| sardines | **sardines** | sar-deen |
| anchovies | **anchois** | ahn-shwah |
| clams | **palourdes** | pah-loord |
| mussels | **moules** | mool |
| oysters | **huîtres** | wee-truh |
| scallops | **coquilles** | koh-keel |
| shrimp | **crevettes** | kruh-veht |
| prawns | **scampi** | skahn-pee |
| crab | **crabe** | krahb |
| lobster | **homard** | oh-mar |
| squid | **calmar** | kahl-mar |
| Where did this live? | **D'où est-ce que ça vient?** | doo ehs kuh sah vee-an |
| Just the head, please. | **Seulement la tête, s'il vous plaît.** | suhl-mahn lah teht see voo play |

**EATING**

## Poultry and meat:

| | | |
|---|---|---|
| poultry | **volaille** | voh-lī |
| chicken | **poulet** | poo-lay |
| turkey | **dinde** | dan_d |
| duck | **canard** | kah-nar |
| meat | **viande** | vee-ahn_d |
| beef | **boeuf** | buhf |
| roast beef | **rosbif** | rohs-beef |
| beef steak | **bifteck** | beef-tehk |
| veal | **veau** | voh |
| cutlet | **côtelette** | koh-tuh-leht |
| pork | **porc** | por |
| ham | **jambon** | zhahn_-bohn_ |
| sausage | **saucisse** | soh-sees |
| lamb | **agneau** | ahn-yoh |
| bunny | **lapin** | lah-pan_ |
| snails | **escargots** | ehs-kar-goh |
| frog legs | **cuisses de grenouilles** | kwees duh greh-noo-ee |
| brains | **cervelle** | sehr-vehl |
| calf pancreas | **ris de veau** | ree duh voh |
| tongue | **langue** | lahn_g |
| liver | **foie** | fwah |
| tripe | **tripes** | treep |
| horse meat | **viande de cheval** | vee-ahn_d duh shuh-vahl |
| How long has this been dead? | **Il est mort depuis longtemps?** | eel ay mor duh-pwee lohn_-tahn_ |

## How it's prepared:

| | | |
|---|---|---|
| hot / cold | **chaud / froid** | shoh / frwah |
| raw / cooked | **cru / cuit** | krew / kwee |
| assorted | **assiette, variés** | ahs-yeht, vah-ree-ay |
| baked | **cuit au four** | kweet oh foor |
| boiled | **bouilli** | boo-yee |
| fillet | **filet** | fee-lay |
| fresh | **frais** | fray |
| fried | **frit** | free |
| grilled | **grillé** | gree-yay |
| homemade | **fait à la maison** | fay ah lah may-zoh<u>n</u> |
| microwave | **four à micro-ondes** | foor ah mee-kroh-oh<u>n</u>d |
| mild | **doux** | doo |
| mixed | **mixte** | meekst |
| poached | **poché** | poh-shay |
| roasted | **rôti** | roh-tee |
| smoked | **fumé** | few-may |
| spicy hot | **piquant** | pee-kah<u>n</u> |
| steamed | **à la vapeur** | ah lah vah-pur |
| stuffed | **farci** | far-see |
| sweet | **doux** | doo |

## Avoiding mis-steaks:

| | | |
|---|---|---|
| raw (hamburger steak) | **tartare** | tar-tar |
| very rare | **bleu** | bluh |
| rare | **saignant** | sayn-yah<u>n</u> |
| medium | **à point** | ah pwa<u>n</u> |
| well-done | **bien cuit** | bee-a<u>n</u> kwee |
| very well-done | **très bien cuit** | treh bee-a<u>n</u> kwee |

EATING

## Veggies, beans, rice, and pasta:

| | | |
|---|---|---|
| vegetables | **légumes** | lay-gewm |
| mixed vegetables | **légumes variés** | lay-gewm vah-ree-ay |
| with vegetables | **garni** | gar-nee |
| raw veggies | **crudités** | krew-dee-tay |
| artichoke | **artichaut** | ar-tee-shoh |
| asparagus | **aspèrges** | ah-spehrzh |
| beans | **haricots** | ah-ree-koh |
| beets | **betterave** | beh-teh-rahv |
| broccoli | **brocoli** | broh-koh-lee |
| cabbage | **chou** | shoo |
| carrots | **carottes** | kah-roht |
| cauliflower | **chou-fleur** | shoo-flur |
| corn | **maïs** | mah-ees |
| cucumber | **concombre** | koh<u>n</u>-koh<u>n</u>-bruh |
| eggplant | **aubergine** | oh-behr-zheen |
| French fries | **pommes frites** | pohm freet |
| garlic | **ail** | ah-ee |
| green beans | **haricots verts** | ah-ree-koh vehr |
| leeks | **poireaux** | pwah-roh |
| lentils | **lentilles** | lah<u>n</u>-teel |
| mushrooms | **champignons** | shah<u>n</u>-peen-yoh<u>n</u> |
| olives | **olives** | oh-leev |
| onions | **oignons** | oh<u>n</u>-yoh<u>n</u> |
| pasta | **pâtes** | paht |

| peas | **pois** | pwah |
| pepper... | **poivron...** | pwah-vroh<u>n</u> |
| ...green / red / hot | **...vert / rouge / épicé** | vehr / roozh / ay-pee-say |
| pickles | **cornichons** | kor-nee-shoh<u>n</u> |
| potato | **pomme de terre** | pohm duh tehr |
| rice | **riz** | ree |
| spaghetti | **spaghetti** | spah-geh-tee |
| spinach | **épinards** | ay-pee-nar |
| tomatoes | **tomates** | toh-maht |
| zucchini | **courgette** | koor-zheht |

**EATING**

## Say cheese:

| cheese | **fromage** | froh-mahzh |
| mild | **doux** | doo |
| sharp | **fort** | for |
| goat | **chèvre** | sheh-vruh |
| bleu cheese | **fromage bleu** | froh-mahzh bluh |
| cheese with herbs | **fromage aux herbes** | froh-mahzh oh ehrb |
| cream cheese | **fromage à la crème** | froh-mahzh ah lah krehm |
| Swiss cheese | **gruyère, emmenthal** | grew-yehr, eh-mehn-tahl |
| Laughing Cow | **La vache qui rit** | lah vahsh kee ree |
| cheese platter | **le plâteau de fromages** | luh plah-toh duh froh-mahzh |
| May I taste a little? | **Je peux goûter un peu?** | zhuh puh goo-tay uh<u>n</u> puh |

## Fruits and nuts:

| English | French | Pronunciation |
|---|---|---|
| almond | **amande** | ah-mah<u>nd</u> |
| apple | **pomme** | pohm |
| apricot | **abricot** | ah-bree-koh |
| banana | **banane** | bah-nahn |
| berries | **baies** | bay |
| melon | **melon** | muh-loh<u>n</u> |
| cherry | **cerise** | suh-reez |
| chestnut | **marron, chataîgne** | mah-roh<u>n</u>, shah-tayn |
| coconut | **noix de coco** | nwah duh koh-koh |
| date | **datte** | daht |
| fig | **figue** | feeg |
| fruit | **fruit** | frwee |
| grapefruit | **pamplemousse** | pah<u>n</u>-pluh-moos |
| grapes | **raisins** | ray-za<u>n</u> |
| hazelnut | **noisette** | nwah-zeht |
| lemon | **citron** | see-troh<u>n</u> |
| orange | **orange** | oh-rah<u>n</u>zh |
| peach | **pêche** | pehsh |
| peanut | **cacahuete** | kah-kah-weet |
| pear | **poire** | pwahr |
| pineapple | **ananas** | ah-nah-nah |
| pistachio | **pistache** | pee-stahsh |
| plum | **prune** | prewn |
| prune | **pruneau** | prew-noh |
| raspberry | **framboise** | frah<u>n</u>-bwahz |
| strawberry | **fraise** | frehz |
| tangerine | **mandarine** | mah<u>n</u>-dah-reen |
| walnut | **noix** | nwah |
| watermelon | **pastèque** | pah-stehk |

## Just desserts:

| | | |
|---|---|---|
| dessert | **dessert** | duh-sehr |
| cake | **gâteau** | gah-toh |
| ice cream | **glace** | glahs |
| scoop of ice cream | **coupe de glace** | koop du glahs |
| sherbet | **sorbet** | sor-bay |
| fruit cup | **salade de fruits** | sah-lahd duh frwee |
| tart | **tartelette** | tar-tuh-leht |
| pie | **tarte** | tart |
| whipped cream | **crème chantilly** | krehm shahn-tee-yee |
| pastry | **pâtisserie** | pah-tee-suh-ree |
| fruit pastry | **chausson** | shoh-sohn |
| chocolate-filled pastry | **pain au chocolat** | pan oh shoh-koh-lah |
| buttery cake | **madeleine** | mah-duh-lehn |
| crepes | **crèpes** | krehp |
| sweet crepes | **crèpes sucres** | krehp sew-kruh |
| cookies | **petits gâteaux** | puh-tee gah-toh |
| candy | **bonbons** | bohn-bohn |
| low calorie | **bas en calories** | bah ahn kah-loh-ree |
| homemade | **fait à la maison** | fay ah lah may-zohn |
| Exquisite! | **Exquis!** | ehk-skee |

## Crème de la crème:

| | |
|---|---|
| **crème brulée** | rich caramelized cream |
| **crème caramel** | caramel pudding |
| **île flottante** | meringues floating in cream sauce |
| **mille feuille** | light pastry (literally "1000 sheets") |
| **mousse au chocolat** | ultra-chocolate pudding |
| **profitterolle** | cream puff filled with ice cream |
| **tarte tatin** | French apple pie |

# Drinking

### Water, milk, and juice:

| | | |
|---|---|---|
| mineral water... | **eau minérale...** | oh mee-nay-rahl |
| ...carbonated | **...gazuese** | gah-zuhz |
| ...not carbonated | **...non gazeuse** | nohn gah-zuhz |
| tap water | **l'eau du robinet** | loh dew roh-bee-nay |
| whole milk | **lait entier** | lay ahnt-yay |
| skim milk | **lait écrémé** | lay ay-kray-may |
| fresh milk | **lait frais** | lay fray |
| chocolate milk | **lait au chocolat** | lay oh shoh-koh-lah |
| hot chocolate | **chocolat chaud** | shoh-koh-lah shoh |
| fruit juice | **jus de fruit** | zhew duh frwee |
| orange juice | **jus d'orange** | zhew doh-rahnzh |
| apple juice | **jus de pomme** | zhew duh pohm |
| hard apple cider | **cidre** | see-druh |
| with / without.. | **avec / sans...** | ah-vehk / sahn |
| ...ice / sugar | **...glaçons / sucre** | glah-sohn / sew-kruh |
| glass / cup | **verre / tasse** | vehr / tahs |
| small bottle | **petite bouteille** | puh-teet boo-teh-ee |
| large bottle | **grande bouteille** | grahnd boo-teh-ee |
| Is the water safe to drink? | **L'eau est potable?** | loh ay poh-tah-bluh |

To get free tap water at a restaurant, say, *"L'eau du robinet, si'l vous plaît."* The French typically order mineral water (and wine) with their meals. Sold at snack stands, water-bottles with screw tops are light and sturdy—great to pack along and re-use as you travel.

## Coffee and tea:

| | | |
|---|---|---|
| coffee... | **café...** | kah-fay |
| ...black | **...noir** | nwahr |
| ...with milk | **...crème** | krehm |
| ...with lots of milk | **...au lait** | oh lay |
| ...American-style | **...américain** | ah-may-ree-ka<u>n</u> |
| espresso | **express** | "express" |
| instant coffee | **Nescafé** | "Nescafé" |
| decaffeinated, decaf | **décafféiné, déca** | day-kah-fay-nay, day-kah |
| sugar | **sucre** | sew-kruh |
| hot water | **l'eau chaude** | loh shohd |
| tea / lemon | **thé / citron** | tay / see-troh<u>n</u> |
| tea bag | **sachet de thé** | sah-shay duh tay |
| herbal tea | **tisane** | tee-zahn |
| small / big | **petit / grand** | puh-tee / grah<u>n</u> |
| Another cup. | **Encore une tasse.** | ah<u>n</u>-kor ewn tahs |
| Is it the same price if I sit or stand? | **C'est le même prix au bar ou dans la salle?** | say luh mehm pree oh bar oo dah<u>n</u> lah sahl |

Every *café* or *bar* has a complete price list posted. In bigger cities, prices go up when you sit down. It's cheapest to stand at the bar (*au bar* or *au comptoir*), more expensive to sit in the dining room (*la salle*) and most expensive to sit outside (*la terrasse*). Refills aren't free.

EATING

## Wine:

| I would like... | **Je voudrais...** | zhuh voo-dray |
| We would like... | **Nous voudrions...** | noo voo-dree-oh<u>n</u> |
| ...a glass | **...un verre** | uh<u>n</u> vehr |
| ...a carafe | **...une carafe** | ewn kah-rahf |
| ...a half bottle | **...une demi-bouteille** | ewn duh-mee-boo-teh-ee |
| ...a bottle | **...une bouteille** | ewn boo-teh-ee |
| ...of red wine | **...de vin rouge** | duh va<u>n</u> roozh |
| ...of white wine | **...de vin blanc** | duh va<u>n</u> blah<u>n</u> |
| ...the wine list | **...la carte des vins** | lah kart day va<u>n</u> |

### *Wine words:*

| wine | **vin** | va<u>n</u> |
| table wine | **vin de table** | va<u>n</u> duh tah-bluh |
| cheapest house wine | **vin ordinaire** | va<u>n</u> or-dee-nair |
| local | **régional** | ray-zhee-oh-nahl |
| red | **rouge** | roozh |
| white | **blanc** | blah<u>n</u> |
| rosé | **rosé** | roh-zay |
| sparkling | **mousseux** | moo-suh |
| sweet | **doux** | doo |
| medium | **demi-sec** | duh-mee-sehk |
| dry | **sec** | sehk |
| very dry | **brut** | brewt |
| cork | **bouchon** | boo-shoh<u>n</u> |

## Beer:

| | | |
|---|---|---|
| beer | **bière** | bee-ehr |
| from the tap | **a là pression** | ah lah preh-see-oh<u>n</u> |
| bottle | **bouteille** | boo-teh-ee |
| light / dark | **blonde / brune** | bloh<u>n</u>d / brewn |
| local / imported | **régionale / importée** | ray-zhee-oh-nahl / a<u>n</u>-por-tay |
| a small beer | **un demi** | uh<u>n</u> duh-mee |
| a large beer | **une chope** | ewn shohp |
| low calorie beer | **biere "light"** | bee-ehr "light" |
| alcohol-free | **sans alcool** | sah<u>n</u>z ahl-kohl |
| cold / colder | **fraîche / plus fraîche** | fraysh / plew fraysh |

## Bar talk:

| | | |
|---|---|---|
| What would you like? | **Qu'est-ce que vous prenez?** | kehs kuh voo pruh-nay |
| What is the local specialty? | **Quelle est la spécialité régionale?** | kehl ay lah spay-see-ah-lee-tay ray-zhee-oh-nahl |
| Straight. | **Sec.** | sehk |
| With / Without... | **Avec / Sans...** | ah-vehk / sah<u>n</u> |
| ...alcohol. | **...alcool.** | ahl-kohl |
| ...ice. | **...glaçons.** | glah-soh<u>n</u> |
| One more. | **Encore une.** | ah<u>n</u>-kor ewn |
| Cheers! | **Santé!** | sah<u>n</u>-tay |
| To your health! | **À votre santé!** | ah voh-truh sah<u>n</u>-tay |
| Long live France! | **Vive la France!** | veev lah frah<u>n</u>s |

EATING

# Picnicking

## At the market:

| | | |
|---|---|---|
| Is it self-service? | **C'est libre service?** | say lee-bruh sehr-vees |
| Ripe for today? | **Pour manger aujourd'hui?** | poor mahn-zhay oh-joord-wee |
| Does it need to be cooked? | **Est'ce qu'il faut le faire cuire?** | ehs keel foh luh fair kweer |
| May I taste a little? | **Je peux goûter un peu?** | zhuh puh goo-tay uhn puh |
| Fifty grams. | **Cinquante grammes.** | san-kahnt grahm |
| One hundred grams. | **Cent grammes.** | sahn grahm |
| More. / Less. | **Plus. / Moins.** | plew / mwan |
| A piece. | **Un morceau.** | uhn mor-soh |
| A slice. | **Une tranche.** | ewn trahnsh |
| Sliced. | **Tranché.** | trahn-shay |
| Can you make me a sandwich? | **Pouvez-vous me faire un sandwich?** | poo-vay-voo muh fair uhn sahnd-weech |
| To take out. | **Pour emporter.** | poor ahn-por-tay |
| Is there a park nearby? | **Il y a un parc près d'ici?** | eel yah uhn park preh dee-see |
| Is it O.K. to picnic here? | **Est-ce qu'on peut pique-niquer ici?** | ehs kohn puh peek-nee-kay ee-see |
| Enjoy your meal! | **Bon appétit!** | bohn ah-pay-tee |

Ask if there's an open air market (*marché*) nearby. These lively markets offer the best selection and ambience.

## Handy picnic words:

| | | |
|---|---|---|
| open air market | **marché** | mar-shay |
| grocery store | **épicerie** | ay-pee-suh-ree |
| supermarket | **supermarché** | sew-pehr-mar-shay |
| super-duper market | **hypermarché** | ee-pehr-mar-shay |
| picnic | **pique-nique** | peek-neek |
| sandwich | **sandwich** | sah<u>nd</u>-weech |
| (whole wheat) bread | **pain (complet)** | pa<u>n</u> (koh<u>n</u>-play) |
| roll | **petit pain** | puh-tee pa<u>n</u> |
| ham | **jambon** | zhahn-boh<u>n</u> |
| sausage | **saucisse** | soh-sees |
| cheese | **fromage** | froh-mahzh |
| mustard in a tube | **moutarde in tube** | moo-tard een tewb |
| mayonnaise in a tube | **mayonnaise in tube** | mah-yuh-nehz een tewb |
| yogurt | **yaourt** | yah-oort |
| fruit | **fruit** | frwee |
| box of juice | **boîte de jus** | bwaht duh zhew |
| cold drinks | **boissons fraîches** | bwah-soh<u>n</u> fraysh |
| spoon / fork... | **cuillère / fourchette...** | kwee-yehr / foor-sheht |
| ...made of plastic | **...en plastique** | ah<u>n</u> plah-steek |
| cup / plate... | **timbale / assiette...** | ta<u>n</u>-bahl / ahs-yeht |
| ...made of paper | **...en papier** | ah<u>n</u> pahp-yay |

While you can opt for a *supermarché*, it's more fun to visit the small shops: a *boulangerie* for bread, a *charcuterie* for meat, a *fromagerie* for cheese, and a *pâtisserie* for dessert. Order meat and cheese by the gram. A hundred grams is about ¼ pound, enough for two sandwiches.

# French-English Menu Decoder

This handy decoder won't list every word on the menu, but it'll help you get *riz et veau* (rice and veal) instead of *ris de veau* (calf pancreas).

**à la carte**  side dishes
**abricot**  apricot
**agneau**  lamb
**ail**  garlic
**aïoli**  garlic mayonnaise
**alcool**  alcohol
**amande**  almond
**ananas**  pineapple
**anchois**  anchovies
**Anglaise**  boiled
**artichaut**  artichoke
**aspèrges**  asparagus
**assiette**  plate
**aubergine**  eggplant
**avec**  with
**baguette**  bread
**baies**  berries
**banane**  banana
**Béarnaise**  sauce of egg and wine
**betterave**  beets
**beurre**  butter
**bière**  beer
**bifteck**  beef steak
**bisque**  shellfish chowder
**blanc**  white
**blonde**  light
**boeuf**  beef

**boissons**  beverages
**bon**  good
**bonbons**  candy
**bouillabaisse**  seafood stew
**bouilli**  boiled
**bouillon**  broth
**Bourguignon**  cooked in red wine
**bouteille**  bottle
**brocoli**  broccoli
**brouillés**  scrambled
**brune**  dark
**brut**  very dry
**cabillaud**  cod
**cacahuete**  peanut
**café**  coffee
**calmar**  squid
**canard**  duck
**carafe**  carafe
**carottes**  carrots
**carte des vins**  wine list
**carte**  menu
**cassoulet**  bean and meat stew
**cerise**  cherry
**cervelle**  brains
**champignons**  mushrooms
**chataîgne**  chestnut
**chaud**  hot

**chausson** fruit pastry
**cheval** horse
**chèvre** goat
**chinois** Chinese
**chocolat** chocolate
**chope** large beer
**chou** cabbage
**chou-fleur** cauliflower
**cidre** hard apple cider
**citron** lemon
**complet** whole, full
**compris** included
**concombre** cucumber
**confiture** jelly
**consommé** broth
**copieux** filling
**coq** chicken
**cornichon** pickle
**côtelette** cutlet
**coupe** scoop
**courgette** zucchini
**couvert** cover charge
**crabe** crab
**crème** cream
**crème chantilly** whipped cream
**crêpe** crepe
**crêpes forment** buckwheat crepes
**crevettes** shrimp
**croque madame** ham, cheese, & egg sandwich
**croque monsieur** ham & cheese sandwich

**cru** raw
**crudités** raw vegetables
**cuisses de grenouilles** frog legs
**cuit** cooked
**cuit au four** baked
**datte** date
**déjeuner** lunch
**demi** half, small beer
**demi-bouteille** half bottle
**demi-sec** medium dry
**dinde** turkey
**dîner** dinner
**doux** mild, sweet
**eau** water
**entier** whole
**entrecôte** rib steak
**entrée** first course
**épinards** spinach
**escargots** snails
**et** and
**express** espresso
**farci** stuffed
**faux-filet** flank steak
**figue** fig
**filet** fillet
**flambée** flaming
**foie** liver
**forestière** with mushrooms
**frais** fresh
**fraise** strawberry
**framboise** raspberry
**frit** fried
**froid** cold

**fromage** cheese
**fruit** fruit
**fruits de mer** seafood
**fumé** smoked
**galette** buckwheat crepe
**garni** with vegetables
**gâteau** cake
**gazeuse** carbonated
**glace** ice cream
**glaçons** ice
**grand** large
**gras** fat
**gratinée** topped with cheese
**grenouille** frog
**grillades** mixed grill
**grillé** grilled
**gruyère** Swiss cheese
**hareng** herring
**haricots** beans
**hollandaise** sauce of egg and
  butter
**homard** lobster
**hors-d'oeuvre** appetizers
**huile** oil
**huîtres** oysters
**importée** imported
**jambon** ham
**jardinière** with vegetables
**jus** juice
**lait** milk
**laitue** lettuce
**langue** tongue
**lapin** bunny

**léger** light
**légumes** vegetables
**light** light
**madeleine** buttery cake
**maïs** corn
**maison** house
**mandarine** tangerine
**marron** chestnut
**melon** canteloupe
**menu du jour** menu of the day
**meunière** fried in butter
**micro-ondes** microwave
**miel** honey
**mixte** mixed
**morceau** piece
**morue** salty cod
**moules** mussels
**mousseux** sparkling
**moutarde** mustard
**noir** black
**noisette** hazelnut
**noix** walnut
**noix de coco** coconut
**non** not
**nouvelle** new
**oeufs** eggs
**oignon** onion
**olives** olives
**orange** orange
**ou** or
**pain** bread
**pamplemousse** grapefruit
**pastèque** watermelon

**pâté** paté
**pâtes** pasta
**pâtisserie** pastry
**pêche** peach
**petit** small
**petit déjeuner** breakfast
**petits gâteaux** cookies
**piquant** spicy hot
**plat principal** main course
**plat du jour** special of the day
**plâteau** platter
**poché** poached
**poire** pear
**poireaux** leeks
**pois** peas
**poisson** fish
**poivre** pepper
**poivron** bell pepper
**pomme** apple
**pomme de terre** potato
**pommes frites** French fries
**porc** pork
**potage** soup
**poulet** chicken
**pour emporter** "to go"
**pression** draft (beer)
**prix fixe** fixed price
**provençale** with garlic and tomatoes
**prune** plum
**pruneau** prune
**ragoût** meat stew
**raisins** grapes

**ratatouille** eggplant casserole
**régionale** local
**ris de veau** calf pancreas
**riz** rice
**rosbif** roast beef
**rosé** rosé
**rôti** roasted
**rouge** red
**saignant** rare
**salade** salad
**sans** without
**saucisse** sausage
**saumon** salmon
**scampi** prawns
**sec** dry
**sel** salt
**service compris** service included
**service non compris** service not included
**sliced** tranché
**sorbet** sherbet
**soupe** soup
**spécialité** specialty
**steak tartare** raw hamburger
**sucre** sugar
**tartare** raw
**tarte** pie
**tartelette** tart
**tasse** cup
**terrine** paté
**thè** tea
**thon** tuna
**tisane** herbal tea

**tournedos**  prime cut steak
**tranche**  slice
**tripes**  tripe
**truffes**  truffles (earthy mushrooms)
**truite**  trout
**vapeur**  steamed
**variés**  assorted
**veau**  veal

**végétarien**  vegetarian
**verre**  glass
**vert**  green
**viande**  meat
**vin**  wine
**vinaigre**  vinegar
**volaille**  poultry
**yaourt**  yogurt

# Sightseeing

| Where is...? | Où est...? | oo ay |
|---|---|---|
| ...the best view | ...la meilleure vue | lah meh-yur vew |
| ...the main square | ...la place principale | lah plahs pran-see-pahl |
| ...the old town center | ...la vieille ville | lah vee-yay-ee veel |
| ...the museum | ...le musée | luh mew-zay |
| ...the castle | ...le château | luh shah-toh |
| ...the palace | ...le palais | luh pah-lay |
| ...the ruins | ...les ruines | lay rween |
| ...a festival | ...une fête | ewn feht |
| ...the tourist information office | ...l'office du tourisme | loh-fees dew too-reez-muh |
| Do you have...? | Avez-vous...? | ah-vay-voo |
| ...a map | ...une carte | ewn kart |
| ...information | ...renseignements | rahn-sehn-yuh-mahn |
| ...a guidebook | ...une guide | ewn geed |
| ...a tour | ...une visite guidée | ewn vee-zeet gee-day |
| ...in English | ...en anglais | ahn ahn-glay |
| When is the next tour? | La prochaine visite sera à quelle heure? | lah proh-shehn vee-zeet suh-rah ah kehl ur |
| Is it free? | Est-ce gratuit? | ehs grah-twee |
| How much is it? | Combien? | kohn-bee-an |
| Is there a discount for...? | Y a-t-il une réduction pour...? | ee ah-teel ewn ray-dewk-see-ohn poor |
| ...youth | ...les jeunes gens | lay zhuhn zhahn |
| ...students | ...les étudiants | layz ay-tew-dee-ahn |
| ...seniors | ...les personnes âgée | lay pehr-suhn ah-zhay |

ACTIVITIES

# Shopping

## Names of French shops:

| | | |
|---|---|---|
| antiques | **antiquités** | ahn-tee-kee-tay |
| bakery | **boulangerie** | boo-lahn-zhuh-ree |
| barber shop | **coiffeur** | kwah-fur |
| beauty salon | **coiffeur pour dames** | kwah-fur poor dahm |
| book shop | **librairie** | lee-bray-ree |
| camera shop | **boutique photographique** | boo-teek foh-toh-grah-feek |
| cheese shop | **fromagerie** | froh-mah-zhay-ree |
| department store | **grand magasin** | grahn mah-gah-zan |
| flea market | **marché aux puces** | mar-shay oh pews |
| flower market | **marché aux fleurs** | mar-shay oh flur |
| grocery store | **épicerie** | ay-pee-suh-ree |
| jewelry shop | **bijouterie** | bee-zhoo-tuh-ree |
| laundromat | **laverie** | lah-vuh-ree |
| newsstand | **maison de la presse** | meh-zohn duh lah prehs |
| office supplies | **papeterie** | pah-pay-tuh-ree |
| open air market | **marché en plein air** | mar-shay ahn plan air |
| optician | **opticien** | ohp-tee-see-an |
| pharmacy | **pharmacie** | far-mah-see |
| supermarket | **supermarché** | sew-pehr-mar-shay |
| toy store | **magasin de jouets** | mah-gah-zan duh zhway |
| travel agency | **agence de voyages** | ah-zhahns duh voy-yahzh |

## Shop till you drop:

| sale | **solde** | sohld |
|---|---|---|
| How much is it? | **Combien?** | kohn-bee-an |
| I'm just browsing. | **Je regarde.** | zhuh ruh-gard |
| We're just browsing. | **Nous regardons.** | noo ruh-gar-dohn |
| I'd like... | **Je voudrais...** | zhuh voo-dray |
| Do you have...? | **Avez-vous...?** | ah-vay-voo |
| ...something cheaper | **...quelque chose de moins cher** | kehl-kuh shohz duh mwan shehr |
| Can I see more? | **Puis-je en voir d'autres?** | pwee zhuh ahn vwahr doh-truh |
| Can I try it on? | **Je peux l'essayer?** | zhuh puh leh-say-yay |
| A mirror? | **Un miroir?** | uhn meer-wahr |
| Too... | **Trop...** | troh |
| ...big. | **...grand.** | grahn |
| ...small. | **...petit.** | puh-tee |
| ...expensive. | **...cher.** | shehr |
| Credit card O.K.? | **Carte de crédit O.K.?** | kart duh kray-dee "O.K." |
| I'll think about it. | **Je vais y penser.** | zhuh vay ee pahn-say |
| Is that your lowest price? | **C'est votre prix le plus bas?** | say voh-truh pree luh plew bah |
| My last offer. | **Ma dernière offre.** | mah dehrn-yehr oh-fruh |
| I'm nearly broke. | **Je suis presque fauché.** | zhuh swee prehsk foh-shay |

# Entertainment

| | | |
|---|---|---|
| What's happening tonight? | **Qu'est-ce qui ce passe ce soir?** | kehs kee suh pahs suh swahr |
| What do you recommend? | **Qu'est-ce que vous recommandez?** | kehs kuh voo ruh-koh-mah<u>n</u>-day |
| Is it free? | **C'est gratuit?** | say grah-twee |
| Where can I buy a ticket? | **Où puis-je acheter un billet?** | oo pwee-zhuh ah-shuh-tay uh<u>n</u> bee-yay |
| When does it start? | **Ça commence à quelle heure?** | sah koh-mah<u>n</u>s ah kehl ur |
| When does it end? | **Ça se termine à quelle heure?** | sah suh tehr-meen ah kehl ur |

## What's happening:

| | | |
|---|---|---|
| movie... | **film...** | feelm |
| ..original version | **...version originale (V.O.)** | vehr-see-oh<u>n</u> oh-ree-zhee-nahl |
| ...in English | **...en anglais** | ah<u>n</u> ah<u>n</u>-glay |
| ...with subtitles | **...avec sous-titres** | ah-vehk soo-tee-truh |
| music... | **musique...** | mew-zeek |
| ...live | **...en directe** | ah<u>n</u> dee-rehkt |
| ...classical | **...classique** | klahs-seek |
| ...folk | **...folklorique** | fohk-loh-reek |
| old rock | **rock classique** | rohk klah-seek |
| jazz / blues | **jazz / blues** | zhazz / "blues" |
| concert | **concert** | koh<u>n</u>-sehr |
| dancing | **danse** | dah<u>n</u>s |
| cover charge | **couvert** | koo-vehr |

# Phoning

| The nearest phone? | **Le plus proche téléphone?** | luh plew prohsh tay-lay-fohn |
| Where's the post office? | **Où est la Poste?** | oo ay lah pohst |
| I'd like to telephone... | **Je voudrais téléphoner...** | zhuh voo-dray tay-lay-foh-nay |
| ...the U.S.A. | **...aux U.S.A.** | ohz ew ehs ah |
| What is the cost per minute? | **C'est combien par minute?** | say kohn-bee-an par mee-newt |
| I'd like to make a... call. | **Je voudrais faire un appel...** | zhuh voo-dray fair uhn ah-pehl |
| ...local | **...local.** | loh-kahl |
| ...collect | **...en P.C.V.** | ahn pay say vay |
| ...credit card | **...avec une carte de crédit.** | ah-vehk ewn kart duh kray-dee |
| ...long distance (within France) | **...interurbain.** | an-tehr-ewr-ban |
| ...international | **...international.** | an-tehr-nah-see-oh-nahl |
| It doesn't work. | **Il ne marche pas.** | eel nuh marsh pah |
| May I use your phone? | **Puis-je téléphoner?** | pwee-zhuh tay-lay-foh-nay |
| Can you dial for me? | **Pouvez-vous composer le numéro?** | poo-vay-voo kohn-poh-zay luh new-may-roh |
| Can you talk for me? | **Pouvez-vous parler pour moi?** | poo-vay-voo par-lay poor mwah |
| It's busy. | **C'est occupé.** | say oh-kew-pay |

| Will you try again? | **Essayez de nouveau?** | eh-say-yay duh noo-voh |
| Hello. (on phone) | **Âllo.** | ah-loh |
| My name is... | **Je m'appelle...** | zhuh mah-pehl |
| My number is... | **Mon numéro est...** | mohn new-may-roh ay |
| Speak slowly. | **Parlez lentement.** | par-lay lahn-tuh-mahn |
| Wait a moment. | **Un moment.** | uhn moh-mahn |
| Don't hang up. | **Ne racrochez pas.** | nuh rah-kroh-shay pah |

## Key telephone words:

| telephone | **téléphone** | tay-lay-fohn |
| telephone card | **télécarte** | tay-lay-kart |
| post office | **Poste** | pohst |
| operator | **standardiste** | stahn-dar-deest |
| international assis-<br>tance | **renseignements<br>internationaux** | rahn-sehn-yuh-mahn<br>an-tehr-nah-see-oh-noh |
| country code | **code international** | kohd an-tehr-nah-see-oh-nahl |
| area code | **code régional** | kohd ray-zhee-oh-nahl |
| telephone book | **bottin, annuaire** | boh-tan, ahn-new-air |
| yellow pages | **pages jaunes** | pahzh zhohn |
| toll-free | **gratuit** | grah-twee |
| out of service | **hors service** | or sehr-vees |

French post offices often have metered phones. It's also easy to make a call with a handy *télécarte* (phone card), available at post offices, train stations and *tabacs* (tobacco shops). Insert the card into a phone and call anywhere in the world. For more tips, see "Let's Talk Telephones" later in this book.

# Mailing

| Where is the post office? | **Où est la Poste?** | oo ay luh pohst |
| Which window for...? | **Quel guichet pour...?** | kehl gee-shay poor |
| ...stamps | **...les timbres** | lay tan-bruh |
| ...packages | **...les colis** | lay koh-lee |
| To the United States... | **Aux Etats-Unis...** | ohz ay-tah-zew-nee |
| ...by air mail. | **...par avion.** | par ah-vee-ohn |
| ...by surface mail. | **...par surface.** | par sewr-fahs |

## Licking the postal code:

| post office | **La Poste** | lah pohst |
| stamp | **timbre** | tan-bruh |
| postcard | **carte postale** | kart poh-stahl |
| letter | **lettre** | leht-ruh |
| envelope | **enveloppe** | ahn-vuh-lohp |
| package | **colis** | koh-lee |
| box | **boîte en carton** | bwaht ahn kar-tohn |
| string | **ficelle** | fee-sehl |
| tape | **bolduc** | bohl-dewk |
| mailbox | **boîte aux lettres** | bwaht oh leht-truh |
| air mail | **par avion** | par ah-vee-ohn |
| surface (slow & cheap) | **surface** | sewr-fahs |
| book rate | **tarif des livres** | tah-reef day lee-vruh |

# Help!

| Help! | **Au secours!** | oh suh-koor |
| Help me! | **A l'aide!** | ah layd |
| Call a doctor! | **Appelez un docteur!** | ah-play uhn dohk-tur |
| ambulance | **ambulance** | ahn-bew-lahns |
| accident | **accident** | ahk-see-dahn |
| injured | **blessé** | bleh-say |
| emergency | **urgence** | ewr-zhahns |
| fire | **feu** | fuh |
| police | **police** | poh-lees |
| thief | **voleur** | voh-lur |
| pick-pocket | **pickpocket** | peek-poh-keht |
| I've been ripped off. | **On m'a volé.** | ohn mah voh-lay |
| I've lost... | **J'ai perdu...** | zhay pehr-dew |
| ...my passport. | **...mon passeport.** | mohn pah-spor |
| ...my ticket. | **...mon billet.** | mohn bee-yay |
| ...my baggage. | **...mes bagages.** | may bah-gahzh |
| ...my purse. | **...mon sac.** | mohn sahk |
| ...my wallet. | **...mon portefeuille.** | mohn por-tuh-fuh-ee |
| ...my faith in humankind. | **...ma foi en l'humanité.** | mah fwah ahn lew-mah-nee-tay |
| I'm lost. | **Je suis perdu.** | zhuh swee pehr-dew |

In a medical emergency, the French call *SOS médecins*, doctors who make emergency house-calls. If you need help, someone will call an *SOS médicin* for you.

## Help for women:

| | | |
|---|---|---|
| Leave me alone. | **Laissez-moi tranquille.** | lay-say-mwah trahn-keel |
| I *vant* to be alone. | **Je veux être seule.** | zhuh vuh eh-truh suhl |
| I'm not interested. | **Ça ne m'intéresse pas.** | sah nuh man-tay-rehs pah |
| I'm married. | **Je suis mariée.** | zhuh swee mah-ree-ay |
| I'm a lesbion. | **Je suis lesbienne.** | zhuh swee lehz-bee-ehn |
| I have a contagious disease. | **J'ai une maladie contagieuse.** | zhay ewn mah-lah-dee kohn-tah-zhuhz |
| Don't touch me. | **Ne me touchez pas.** | nuh muh too-shay pah |
| You're disgusting. | **Vous êtes dégoutant.** | vooz eht day-goo-tahn |
| Stop following me. | **Arrêtez de me suivre.** | ah-reh-tay duh muh swee-vruh |
| This man is bothering me. | **Cet homme m'embête.** | seht ohm mahn-beht |
| Enough! | **Ça suffit!** | sah sew-fee |
| Get lost! | **Dégagez!** | day-gah-zhay |
| Drop dead! | **Fous-moi la paix!** | foo-mwah lah pay |
| I'll call the police. | **J'appelle la police.** | zhah-pehl lah poh-lees |

# Health

| | | |
|---|---|---|
| I feel sick. | **Je me sens malade.** | zhuh muh sah<u>n</u> mah-lahd |
| I need a doctor... | **Il me faut un docteur...** | eel muh foh uh<u>n</u> dohk-tur |
| ...who speaks English. | **...qui parle anglais.** | kee parl ah<u>n</u>-glay |
| It hurts here. | **Ça me fait mal ici.** | sah muh fay mahl ee-see |
| I'm allergic to... | **Je suis allergique à...** | zhuh sweez ah-lehr-zheek ah |
| ...penicillin. | **...la pénicilline.** | lah pay-nee-see-leen |
| I am diabetic. | **Je suis diabétique.** | zhuh swee dee-ah-bay-teek |
| I've missed a period. | **J'ai du retard dans mes règles.** | zhay dew ruh-tar dah<u>n</u> may reh-gluh |
| I have... | **J'ai...** | zhay |
| ...a burn. | **...une brûlure.** | ewn brew-lewr |
| ...chest pains. | **...mal à la poitrine.** | mahl ah lah pwah-treen |
| ...a cold. | **...un rhume.** | uh<u>n</u> rewm |
| ...constipation. | **...la constipation.** | lah koh<u>n</u>-stee-pah-see-oh<u>n</u> |
| ...a cough. | **...une toux.** | ewn too |
| ...diarrhea. | **...la diarrhée.** | lah dee-ah-ray |
| ...a fever. | **...une fièvre.** | ewn fee-eh-vruh |
| ...the flu. | **...la grippe.** | lah greep |
| ...the giggles. | **...le fou rire.** | luh foo reer |
| ...a headache. | **...mal à la tête.** | mahl ah lah teht |
| ...hemorrhoids. | **...hémorroïdes.** | ay-mor-wahd |
| ...indigestion. | **...une indigestion.** | ewn a<u>n</u>-dee-zhuh-stee-oh<u>n</u> |

| | | |
|---|---|---|
| ...an infection. | ...une infection. | ewn an-fehk-see-ohn |
| ...nausea. | ...la nausée. | lah noh-zay |
| ...a rash. | ...des boutons. | day boo-tohn |
| ...a sore throat. | ...mal à la gorge. | mahl ah lah gorzh |
| ...a stomach ache. | ...mal à l'estomac. | mahl ah luh-stoh-mah |
| ...a swelling. | ...une enflure. | ewn ahn-flewr |
| ...a toothache. | ...mal aux dents. | mahl oh dahn |
| ...worms. | ...des vers. | day vehr |
| I have body odor. | Je sens mauvais. | zhuh sahn moh-vay |
| Is it serious? | C'est sérieux? | say say-ree-uh |

## Handy health words:

| | | |
|---|---|---|
| doctor | docteur | dohk-tur |
| dentist | dentiste | dahn-teest |
| health insurance | assurance maladie | ah-sew-rahns mah-lah-dee |
| hospital | hôpital | oh-pee-tahl |
| pharmacy | pharmacie | far-mah-see |
| bandage | bandage | bahn-dahzh |
| medicine | médicaments | may-dee-kah-mahn |
| aspirin | aspirine | ah-spee-reen |
| non-aspirin substitute | Tylenol | tee-luh-nohl |
| cough drops | pastilles pour la toux | pah-steel poor lah too |
| cold medicine | remède contre le rhume | ruh-mehd kohn-truh luh rewm |
| antibiotic | antibiotique | ahn-tee-bee-oh-teek |
| pain killer | calmant | kahl-mahn |
| prescription | ordonnance | or-duh-nahns |

HEALTH

# Chatting

| My name is... | **Je m'appelle...** | zhuh mah-pehl |
| What's your name? | **Quel est votre nom?** | kehl ay voh-truh noh<u>n</u> |
| Where are you from? | **D'où venez-vous?** | doo vuh-nay-voo |
| I'm a... | **Je suis...** | zhuh swee |
| ...male American. | **...américain.** | zah-may-ree-ka<u>n</u> |
| ...female American. | **...américaine.** | zah-may-ree-kehn |
| ...male Canadian. | **...canadien.** | kah-nah-dee-a<u>n</u> |
| ...female Canadian. | **...canadienne.** | kah-nah-dee-ehn |
| I'm... years old. | **J'ai... ans.** | zhay... ah<u>n</u> |
| How old are you? | **Quel âge avez-vous?** | kehl ahzh ah-vay-voo |
| I'm rich and single. | **Je suis riche et célibataire.** | zhuh swee reesh ay say-lee-bah-tair |
| I'm married. | **Je suis marié.** | zhuh swee mah-ree-ay |
| Are you married? | **Êtes-vous marié?** | eht voo mah-ree-ay |
| Do you have children? | **Avez-vous des enfants?** | ah-vay-voo dayz ah<u>n</u>-fah<u>n</u> |

## The right thing to say:

| Beautiful child! | **Bel enfant!** | behl ah<u>n</u>-fah<u>n</u> |
| Beautiful children! | **Beaux enfants!** | bohz ah<u>n</u>-fah<u>n</u> |
| Great! | **Formidable!** | for-mee-dah-bluh |
| Well done! | **Bien joué!** | bee-a<u>n</u> zhoo-ay |
| Congratulations! | **Félicitations!** | fay-lee-see-tah-see-oh<u>n</u> |
| You're welcome. | **Je vous en prie.** | zhuh vooz ah<u>n</u> pree |
| Bless you! (sneeze) | **À vos souhaits!** | ah voh sway |
| Excuse me. | **Pardon.** | par-doh<u>n</u> |

## Travel talk:

| | | |
|---|---|---|
| I am / Are you...? | **Je suis / Êtes-vous...?** | zhuh sweez / eht-vooz |
| ...on vacation | **...en vacances** | ahn vah-kahns |
| ...on business | **...en voyage d'affaires** | ahn voy-yahzh dah-fair |
| How long have you been traveling? | **Il y a longtemps que vous voyagez?** | eel yah lohn-tahn kuh voo voy-yah-zhay |
| day / week | **jour / semaine** | zhoor / suh-mehn |
| month / year | **mois / année** | mwah / ah-nay |
| Where are you going? | **Où allez-vous?** | oo ah-lay-voo |
| Where have you traveled? | **Où êtes-vous allé?** | oo eht-vooz ah-lay |
| Where would you like to go? | **Où voulez-vous aller?** | oo voo-lay-vooz ah-lay |
| When are you going home? | **Quand allez-vous rentrer?** | kahn ah-lay-voo rahn-tray |
| I've traveled to... | **J'ai visité...** | zhay vee-zee-tay |
| Next I'll go to... | **Je veux visiter...** | zhuh vuh vee-zee-tay |
| This is my first time in... | **C'est la première fois que je visite...** | say lah pruhm-yehr fwah kuh zhuh vee-zeet |
| I'm happy here. (male / female) | **Je suis content / contente ici.** | zhuh swee kohn-tahn / kohn-tahnt ee-see |
| The French are friendly. | **Les Français sont gentils.** | lay frahn-say sohn zhahn-tee |
| France is wonderful. | **La France est magnifique.** | lah frahns ay mahn-yee-feek |
| Have a good trip! | **Bon voyage!** | bohn voy-yahzh |

**CHAT**

## Profanity and other animal noises:

In case you're wondering what the more colorful locals are saying...

| Damn! (Good God!) | **Bon Dieu!** | bohn dee-uh |
| bastard / bitch | **salaud / salope** | sah-loh / sah-lohp |
| breasts (colloq.) | **tétons** | tay-tohn |
| big breasts | **grands tétons** | grahn tay-tohn |
| penis (colloq.) | **bite** | beet |
| butthole | **sale con** | sahl kohn |
| shit | **merde** | mehrd |
| idiot | **idiot** | ee-dee-oh |
| imbecile | **imbécile** | an-bay-seel |
| jerk | **connard** | kuh-nar |
| Did someone...? | **Est-ce que quelqu'un à...?** | ehs kuh kehl-kuhn ah |
| ...burp / fart | **...roter / péter** | roh-tay / pay-tay |

## *Conversing with French animals:*

| rooster / cock-a-doodle-doo | **coq / cocorico** | kohk / koh-koh-ree-koh |
| bird / tweet tweet | **oiseau / cui cui** | wah-zoh / kwee kwee |
| cat / meow | **chat / miaou** | shah / mee-ah-oo |
| dog / woof woof | **chien / ouah ouah** | shee-an / wah wah |
| duck / quack quack | **canard / coin coin** | kah-nar / kwan kwan |
| cow / moo | **vache / meu** | vahsh / muh |
| pig / oink oink | **cochon / groin groin** | koh-shohn / grwan grwan |

# ITALIAN

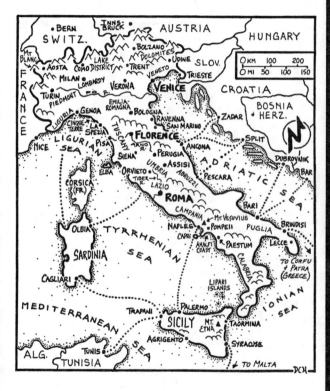

# Getting Started

### User-friendly Italian

...is easy to get the hang of. Some Italian words are so familiar, you'd think they were English. If you can say *pizza, lasagna,* and *spaghetti,* you can speak Italian.

There are a few unusual twists to its pronunciation:

*C* usually sounds like C in cat.
  But *C* followed by *E* or *I* sounds like CH in chance.
*CH* sounds like C in cat.
*E* often sounds like AY in play.
*G* usually sounds like G in get.
  But *G* followed by *E* or *I* sounds like G in gentle.
*GH* sounds like G in *spaghetti.*
*GLI* sounds like LI in million. The G is silent.
*GN* sounds like GN in *lasagna.*
*H* is never pronounced.
*I* sounds like EE in seed.
*R* is rolled as in *brrravo!*
*SC* usually sounds like SK in skip.
  But *SC* followed by *E* or *I* sounds like SH in shape.
*Z* usually sounds like TS in hits, and sometimes like the
  sound of DZ in kids.

Have you ever noticed that most Italian words end in a vowel? It's *o* if the word is masculine and *a* if it's feminine. So a *bambino* gets blue and a *bambina* gets pink. A man is *generoso* (generous), a woman is *generosa.* In the

Italian section of this book, we show gender-bender words like this: *generoso[a]*. If you are speaking of a woman (which includes women speaking about themselves), use the *a* ending. It's always pronounced "ah."

Italians usually pronounce every letter in a word, so *due* (two) is **doo**-ay. Sometimes two vowels share one syllable. *Piano* sounds like peeah-noh. The "peeah" is one syllable. When one vowel in a pair should be emphasized, it will appear in bold letters: *italiano* is ee-tah-lee**ah**-noh.

Here's a guide to the phonetics we've used in the Italian section of this book:

| | |
|---|---|
| ah | like A in father. |
| ay | like AY in play. |
| eh | like E in let. |
| ee | like EE in seed. |
| ehı | sounds like "air." |
| g | like G in go. |
| o | like O in cost. |
| oh | like O in note. |
| oo | like OO in too. |
| or | like OR in core. |
| ow | like OW in cow. |
| s | like S in sun. |
| ts | like TS in hits. It's a small explosive sound. Think of *pizza* (pee-tsah). |

Be confident and have fun communicating in Italian. The Italians really do want to understand you, and are forgiving of a yankee-fied version of their language.

# Italian Basics

## Greeting and meeting Italians:

| | | |
|---|---|---|
| Good day. | **Buon giorno.** | bwohn **jor**-noh |
| Good morning. | **Buon giorno.** | bwohn **jor**-noh |
| Good evening. | **Buona sera.** | **bwoh**-nah **say**-rah |
| Good night. | **Buona notte.** | **bwoh**-nah **not**-tay |
| Hi / Bye. (informal) | **Ciao.** | chow |
| Mr. / Mrs. | **Signor / Signora** | **seen**-yor / seen-**yoh**-rah |
| Miss | **Signorina** | seen-yoh-**ree**-nah |
| How are you? | **Come sta?** | **koh**-may stah |
| Very well, thanks. | **Molto bene, grazie.** | **mohl**-toh **behn**-ay **graht**-seeay |
| And you? | **E lei?** | ay lehee |
| My name is... | **Mi chiamo...** | mee **keeah**-moh |
| What's your name? | **Come si chiama?** | **koh**-may see **keeah**-mah |
| Pleased to meet you. | **Piacere.** | peeah-**chay**-ray |
| Where are you from? | **Di dove è?** | dee **doh**-vay eh |
| I am / Are you...? | **Sono / È...?** | **soh**-noh / eh |
| ...on vacation | **...in vacanza** | een vah-**kahnt**-sah |
| ...on business | **...qui per lavoro** | kwee pehr lah-**voh**-roh |
| See you later. | **A più tardi.** | ah pew **tar**-dee |
| Goodbye. | **Arrivederci.** | ah-ree-vay-**dehr**-chee |
| Good luck! | **Buona fortuna!** | **bwoh**-nah for-**too**-nah |
| Have a good trip! | **Buon viaggio!** | bwohn veeah-joh |

## Survival phrases

In 800, Charlemagne traveled to Rome and became the Holy Roman Emperor using only these phrases. They are repeated on your tear-out cheat sheet later in this book.

### The essentials:

| | | |
|---|---|---|
| Good day. | **Buon giorno.** | bwohn **jor**-noh |
| Do you speak English? | **Parla inglese?** | **par**-lah een-**glay**-zay |
| Yes. / No. | **Si. / No.** | see / noh |
| I don't speak Italian. | **Non parlo l'italiano.** | nohn **par**-loh lee-tah-leeah-noh |
| I'm sorry. | **Mi dispiace.** | mee dee-speeah-chay |
| Please. | **Per favore.** | pehr fah-**voh**-ray |
| Thank you. | **Grazie.** | **graht**-seeay |
| It's (not) a problem. | **(Non) c'è problema.** | (nohn) cheh proh-**blay**-mah |
| It's good. | **Va bene.** | vah **behn**-ay |
| You are very kind. | **Lei è molto gentile.** | **lehee** eh **mohl**-toh jayn-**tee**-lay |
| Goodbye! | **Arrivederci!** | ah-ree-vay-**dehr**-chee |

### Where?

| | | |
|---|---|---|
| Where is...? | **Dov'è...?** | doh-**veh** |
| ...a hotel | **...un hotel** | oon oh-**tehl** |
| ...a youth hostel | **...un ostello della gioventù** | oon oh-**stehl**-loh **day**-lah joh-vehn-**too** |
| ...a restaurant | **...un ristorante** | oon ree-stoh-**rahn**-tay |

| ...a supermarket | ...un supermercado | oon soo-pehr-mehr-**kah**-doh |
| ...a pharmacy | ...una farmacia | **oo**-nah far-mah-**chee**-ah |
| ...a bank | ...una banca | **oo**-nah **bahn**-kah |
| ...the train station | ...la stazione | lah staht-see**oh**-nay |
| ...tourist information | ...informazioni per turisti | een-for-maht-see**oh**-nee pehr too-**ree**-stee |
| ...the toilet | ...la toilette | lah twah-**leht**-tay |
| men | uomini, signori | **woh**-mee-nee, seen-**yoh**-ree |
| women | donne, signore | **don**-nay, seen-**yoh**-ray |

## How much?

| How much is it? | Quanto costa? | **kwahn**-toh **kos**-tah |
| Write it? | Lo scrive? | loh **skree**-vay |
| Cheap(er). | (Più) economico. | (pew) ay-koh-**noh**-mee-koh |
| Cheapest. | Il più economico. | eel pew ay-koh-**noh**-mee-koh |
| Is it free? | È gratis? | eh **grah**-tees |
| Is it included? | È incluso? | eh een-**kloo**-zoh |
| Do you have...? | Ha...? | ah |
| I would like... | Vorrei.... | vor-**rehee** |
| We would like... | Vorremo... | vor-**ray**-moh |
| ...this. | ...questo. | **kway**-stoh |
| ...just a little. | ...un pochino. | oon poh-**kee**-noh |
| ...more. | ...di più. | dee pew |
| ...a ticket. | ...un biglietto. | oon beel-**yay**-toh |
| ...a room. | ...una camera. | **oo**-nah **kah**-may-rah |
| ...the bill. | ...il conto. | eel **kohn**-toh |

## How many?

| one | **uno** | **oo**-noh |
| two | **due** | **doo**-ay |
| three | **tre** | tray |
| four | **quattro** | **kwah**-troh |
| five | **cinque** | **cheeng**-kway |
| six | **sei** | sehee |
| seven | **sette** | **seht**-tay |
| eight | **otto** | **ot**-toh |
| nine | **nove** | **nov**-ay |
| ten | **dieci** | deeay-chee |
| hundred | **cento** | **chehn**-toh |
| thousand | **mille** | **mee**-lay |

## When?

| At what time? | **A che ora?** | ah kay **oh**-rah |
| Just a moment. | **Un momento.** | oon moh-**mayn**-toh |
| Now. | **Adesso.** | ah-**dehs**-soh |
| soon / later | **presto / tardi** | **prehs**-toh / tar-dee |
| today / tomorrow | **oggi / domani** | **oh**-jee / doh-**mah**-nee |

Experiment! You can combine these survival phrases to say: "Two, please," or "No, thank you," or "I'd like a cheap hotel," or "Cheaper, please?" Please is a magic word in any language. If you want something and you don't know the word for it, just point and say *"Per favore"* (Please). If you know the word for what you want, such as the bill, simply say, *"Il conto, per favore"* (The bill, please).

## Struggling with Italian:

| | | |
|---|---|---|
| Do you speak English? | **Parla inglese?** | **par**-lah een-**glay**-zay |
| Even a teeny weeny bit? | **Nemmeno un pochino?** | nehm-**may**-noh oon poh-**kee**-noh |
| Please speak English. | **Parli inglese, per favore.** | **par**-lee een-**glay**-zay pehr fah-**voh**-ray |
| You speak English well. | **Lei parla l'inglese bene.** | lehee **par**-lah leen-**glay**-zay **behn**-ay |
| I don't speak Italian. | **Non parlo l'italiano.** | nohn **par**-loh lee-tah-leeah-noh |
| I speak a little Italian. | **Parlo un po' d'italiano.** | **par**-loh oon poh dee-tah-leeah-noh |
| What is this in Italian? | **Come si dice questo in italiano?** | **koh**-may see **dee**-chay **kway**-stoh een ee-tah-leeah-noh |
| Repeat? | **Ripeta?** | ree-**pay**-tah |
| Slowly. | **Lentamente.** | layn-tah-**mayn**-tay |
| Do you understand? | **Capisce?** | kah-**pee**-shay |
| I understand. | **Capisco.** | kah-**pee**-skoh |
| I don't understand. | **Non capisco.** | nohn kah-**pee**-skoh |
| Write it? | **Lo scrive?** | loh **skree**-vay |
| Who speaks English? | **Chi parla inglese?** | kee **par**-lah een-**glay**-zay |

To prompt a simple answer, ask, *"Si o no?"* (Yes or no?). To turn a word or sentence into a question, ask it in a questioning tone. An easy way to say, "Where is the toilet?" is to ask, *"Toilette?"*

## Common questions:

| | | |
|---|---|---|
| How much? | **Quanto?** | kwahn-toh |
| How long...? | **Quanto tempo...?** | kwahn-toh tehm-poh |
| ...is the trip | **...ci vuole il viaggio** | chee vwah-lay eel veeah-joh |
| How far? | **Quanto dista?** | kwahn-toh dee-stah |
| How? | **Come?** | koh-may |
| Is it possible? | **È possibile?** | eh poh-see-bee-lay |
| Is it necessary? | **È necessario?** | eh nay-say-sah-reeoh |
| Can you help me? | **Può aiutarmi?** | pwoh ah-yoo-tar-mee |
| What? | **Che cosa?** | kay koh-zah |
| What is that? | **Che cos'è quello?** | kay koh-zeh kway-loh |
| When? | **Quando?** | kwahn-doh |
| What time is it? | **Che ora è?** | kay oh-rah eh |
| At what time? | **A che ora?** | ah kay oh-rah |
| When does this...? | **A che ora...?** | ah kay oh-rah |
| ...open | **...aprite** | ah-pree-tay |
| ...close | **...chiudete** | keeoo-day-tay |
| Do you have...? | **Ha...?** | ah |
| Where is...? | **Dov'è...?** | doh-veh |
| Where are...? | **Dove sono...?** | doh-vay soh-noh |
| Who? | **Chi?** | kee |
| Why? | **Perchè?** | pehr-keh |
| Why not? | **Perchè no?** | pehr-keh noh |
| Yes or no? | **Si o no?** | see oh noh |

## Yin and yang:

| cheap / expensive | economico / caro | ay-koh-noh-mee-koh / kah-roh |
| --- | --- | --- |
| big / small | grande / piccolo | grahn-day / pee-koh-loh |
| hot / cold | caldo / freddo | kahl-doh / fray-doh |
| open / closed | aperto / chiuso | ah-pehr-toh / keeoo-zoh |
| entrance / exit | entrata / uscita | ayn-trah-tah / oo-shee-tah |
| arrive / depart | arrivare / partire | ah-ree-vah-ray / par-tee-ray |
| early / late | presto / più tardi | prehs-toh / pew tar-dee |
| soon / later | presto / tardi | prehs-toh / tar-dee |
| fast / slow | veloce / lento | vay-loh-chay / lehn-toh |
| here / there | qui / lì | kwee / lee |
| near / far | vicino / lontano | vee-chee-noh / lohn-tah-noh |
| good / bad | buono / cattivo | bwoh-noh / kah-tee-voh |
| a little / lots | poco / tanto | poh-koh / tahn-toh |
| more / less | più / meno | pew / may-noh |
| easy / difficult | facile / difficile | fah-chee-lay / dee-fee-chee-lay |
| left / right | sinistra / destra | see-nee-strah / dehs-trah |
| young / old | giovane / anziano | joh-vah-nay / ahnt-see-ah-noh |
| new / old | nuovo / vecchio | nwoh-voh / vehk-eeoh |
| heavy / light | pesante / leggero | pay-zahn-tay / lay-jay-roh |
| beautiful / ugly | bello / brutto | behl-loh / broo-toh |
| intelligent / stupid | intelligente / stupido | een-tehl-ee-jayn-tay / stoo-pee-doh |

BASICS

| vacant / occupied | **libero / occupato** | lee-bay-roh / oh-koo-**pah**-toh |
| with / without | **con / senza** | kohn / **sehn**-sah |

## Big little words:

| I | **io** | eeoh |
| you (formal) | **Lei** | lehee |
| you (informal) | **tu** | too |
| we | **noi** | nohee |
| he | **lui** | lwee |
| she | **lei** | lehee |
| they | **loro** | .loh-roh |
| and | **e** | ay |
| at | **a** | ah |
| because | **perchè** | pehr-**keh** |
| but | **ma** | mah |
| by (via) | **in** | een |
| for | **per** | pehr |
| from | **da** | dah |
| here | **qui** | kwee |
| in | **in** | een |
| not | **non** | nohn |
| now | **adesso** | ah-**dehs**-soh |
| only | **solo** | **soh**-loh |
| or | **o** | oh |
| this / that | **questo / quello** | **kway**-stoh / **kway**-loh |
| to | **a** | ah |
| very | **molto** | **mohl**-toh |

*Prego* is an all-purpose Italian word that means: Can I help you? All right. Thanks. You're welcome.

# Numbers

| 1  | uno        | **oo**-noh            |
|----|------------|-----------------------|
| 2  | due        | **doo**-ay            |
| 3  | tre        | tray                  |
| 4  | quattro    | **kwah**-troh         |
| 5  | cinque     | **cheeng**-kway       |
| 6  | sei        | sehee                 |
| 7  | sette      | **seht**-tay          |
| 8  | otto       | **ot**-toh            |
| 9  | nove       | **nov**-ay            |
| 10 | dieci      | deeay-chee            |
| 11 | undici     | **oon**-dee-chee      |
| 12 | dodici     | **doh**-dee-chee      |
| 13 | tredici    | **tray**-dee-chee     |
| 14 | quattordici| kwah-**tor**-dee-chee |
| 15 | quindici   | **kween**-dee-chee    |
| 16 | sedici     | **say**-dee-chee      |
| 17 | diciassette| dee-chahs-**seht**-tay|
| 18 | diciotto   | dee-**choh**-toh      |
| 19 | diciannove | dee-chahn-**nov**-ay  |
| 20 | venti      | **vayn**-tee          |
| 21 | ventuno    | vayn-**too**-noh      |
| 22 | ventidue   | vayn-tee-**doo**-ay   |
| 23 | ventitrè   | vayn-tee-**tray**     |
| 30 | trenta     | **trayn**-tah         |
| 31 | trentuno   | trayn-**too**-noh     |

| | | |
|---|---|---|
| 40 | **quaranta** | kwah-**rahn**-tah |
| 41 | **quarantuno** | kwah-rahn-**too**-noh |
| 50 | **cinquanta** | cheeng-**kwahn**-tah |
| 60 | **sessanta** | say-**sahn**-tah |
| 70 | **settanta** | say-**tahn**-tah |
| 80 | **ottanta** | ot-**tahn**-tah |
| 90 | **novanta** | noh-**vahn**-tah |
| 100 | **cento** | **chehn**-toh |
| 101 | **centouno** | chehn-toh-**oo**-noh |
| 102 | **centodue** | chehn-toh-**doo**-ay |
| 200 | **duecento** | doo-ay-**chehn**-toh |
| 1000 | **mille** | **mee**-lay |
| 1996 | **millenovecento novantasei** | **mee**-lay-nov-ay-**chehn**-toh-noh-vahn-tah-**sehee** |
| 2000 | **duemila** | doo-ay-**mee**-lah |
| 10,000 | **diecimila** | dee**ay**-chee-**mee**-lah |
| million | **milione** | mee-lee**oh**-nay |
| billion | **miliardo** | meel-**yar**-doh |
| first | **primo** | **pree**-moh |
| second | **secondo** | say-**kohn**-doh |
| third | **terzo** | **tehrt**-soh |
| half | **mezzo** | **mehd**-zoh |
| 100% | **cento per cento** | **chehn**-toh pehr **chehn**-toh |
| number one | **numero uno** | **noo**-may-roh **oo**-noh |

# Money

| Can you change dollars? | Può cambiare dollari? | pwoh kahm-bee**ah**-ray **dol**-lah-ree |
| What is your exchange rate for dollars...? | Qual'è il cambio del dollari...? | kwah-**leh** eel **kahm**-beeoh dayl **dol**-lah-ree |
| ...in traveler's checks | ...per traveler's checks | pehr "traveler's checks" |
| What is the commission? | Quant'è la commissione? | kwahn-**teh** lah koh-mee-seeo**h**-nay |
| Any extra fee? | C'è un sovrapprezzo? | cheh oon soh-vrah-**preht**-soh |

## Key money words:

| bank | banca | **bahn**-kah |
| change money | cambiare dei soldi | kahm-beea**h**-ray dehee **sohl**-dee |
| money | soldi, denaro | **sohl**-dee, day-**nah**-roh |
| large bills | banconote di grosso taglio | bahn-koh-**noh**-tay dee **groh**-soh **tahl**-yoh |
| small bills | banconote di piccolo taglio | bahn-koh-**noh**-tay dee **pee**-koh-loh **tahl**-yoh |
| coins | monete | moh-**nay**-tay |
| cashier | cassiere | kah-see**eay**-ray |
| credit card | carta di credito | **kar**-tah dee **kray**-dee-toh |
| cash advance | prelievo | pray-lee**eay**-voh |
| cash machine | cassa automatica | **kah**-sah ow-toh-**mah**-tee-kah |
| receipt | ricevuta | ree-chay-**voo**-tah |

# Time

| | | |
|---|---|---|
| What time is it? | **Che ore sono?** | kay **oh**-ray **soh**-noh |
| It's... | **È...** | eh |
| ...8:00. | **...le otto.** | lay **ot**-toh |
| ...16:00. | **...le sedici.** | lay **say**-dee-chee |
| ...4:00 in the afternoon. | **...le quattro del pomeriggio.** | lay **kwah**-troh dayl poh-may-**ree**-joh |
| ...10:30 (in the evening). | **...le dieci e trenta (di sera).** | lay deeay-chee ay **trayn**-tah (dee **say**-rah) |
| ...a quarter past nine. | **...le nove e un quarto.** | lay **nov**-ay ay oon **kwar**-toh |
| ...a quarter to eleven. | **...le undici meno un quarto.** | lay **oon**-dee-chee **may**-noh oon **kwar**-toh |
| ...noon. | **...mezzogiorno.** | mehd-zoh-**jor**-noh |
| ...midnight. | **...mezzanotte.** | mehd-zah-**not**-tay |
| ...sunrise / sunset. | **...alba / tramonto.** | **ahl**-bah / trah-**mohn**-toh |
| ...early / late. | **...presto / tardi.** | **prehs**-toh / **tar**-dee |
| ...on time. | **...puntuale.** | poon-too**ah**-lay |

NUMBERS, MONEY, TIME

In Italy, the 24-hour clock (or military time) is used by hotels and stores, and for train, bus, and ferry schedules. Friends use the same "12-hour clock" we do. You'd meet a friend at 3:00 in the afternoon (*3:00 del pomeriggio*) to catch a train that leaves at 15:15. The greeting *"Buon giorno"* (Good day) turns to *"Buona sera"* (Good evening) as the sun sets.

## Timely words:

| | | |
|---|---|---|
| minute | **minuto** | mee-**noo**-toh |
| hour | **ora** | **oh**-rah |
| morning | **mattina** | mah-**tee**-nah |
| afternoon | **pomeriggio** | poh-may-**ree**-joh |
| evening | **sera** | **say**-rah |
| night | **notte** | **not**-tay |
| day | **giorno** | **jor**-noh |
| today | **oggi** | **oh**-jee |
| yesterday | **ieri** | **yay**-ree |
| tomorrow | **domani** | doh-**mah**-nee |
| tomorrow morning | **domani mattina** | doh-**mah**-nee mah-**tee**-nah |
| day after tomorrow | **dopodomani** | doh-poh-doh-**mah**-nee |
| anytime | **a qualsiasi ora** | ah kwahl-seeah-zee **oh**-rah |
| immediately | **immediatamente** | ee-may-deeah-tah-**mayn**-tay |
| in one hour | **tra un'ora** | trah oon-**oh**-rah |
| every hour | **ogni ora** | **ohn**-yee **oh**-rah |
| every day | **ogni giorno** | **ohn**-yee **jor**-noh |
| last | **passato** | pah-**sah**-toh |
| this | **questo** | **kway**-stoh |
| next | **prossimo** | **pros**-see-moh |
| May 15 | **il quindici di maggio** | eel **kween**-dee-chee dee **mah**-joh |

| week | settimana | say-tee-**mah**-nah |
| Monday | lunedì | loo-nay-**dee** |
| Tuesday | martedì | mar-tay-**dee** |
| Wednesday | mercoledì | mehr-koh-lay-**dee** |
| Thursday | giovedì | joh-vay-**dee** |
| Friday | venerdì | vay-nehr-**dee** |
| Saturday | sabato | **sah**-bah-toh |
| Sunday | domenica | doh-**may**-nee-kah |
| | | |
| month | mese | **may**-zay |
| January | gennaio | jay-**nah**-yoh |
| February | febbraio | fay-**brah**-yoh |
| March | marzo | **mart**-soh |
| April | aprile | ah-**pree**-lay |
| May | maggio | **mah**-joh |
| June | giugno | **joon**-yoh |
| July | luglio | **lool**-yoh |
| August | agosto | ah-**goh**-stoh |
| September | settembre | say-**tehm**-bray |
| October | ottobre | oh-**toh**-bray |
| November | novembre | noh-**vehm**-bray |
| December | dicembre | dee-**chehm**-bray |
| | | |
| year | anno | **ahn**-noh |
| spring | primavera | pree-mah-**vay**-rah |
| summer | estate | ay-**stah**-tay |
| fall | autunno | ow-**too**-noh |
| winter | inverno | een-**vehr**-noh |

# Transportation

## Trains:

| Is this the line for...? | Questa è la fila per...? | kway-stah eh lah fee-lah pehr |
| ...tickets | ...biglietti | beel-yay-tee |
| ...reservations | ...prenotazioni | pray-noh-taht-seeoh-nee |
| How much is the fare to...? | Quant'è la tariffa per...? | kwahn-teh lah tah-ree-fah pehr |
| A ticket to ___. | Un biglietto per ___. | oon beel-yay-toh pehr |
| When is the next train? | Quando è il prossimo treno? | kwahn-doh eh eel pros-see-moh tray-noh |
| I'd like to leave... | Vorrei partire... | vor-rehee par-tee-ray |
| I'd like to arrive... | Vorrei arrivare... | vor-rehee ah-ree-vah-ray |
| ...by ___. | ...per le ___. | pehr lay |
| ...in the morning. | ...la mattina. | lah mah-tee-nah |
| ...in the afternoon. | ...il pomeriggio. | eel poh-may-ree-joh |
| ...in the evening. | ...la sera. | lah say-rah |
| Is there a...? | C'è un...? | cheh oon |
| ...earlier train | ...treno prima | tray-noh pree-mah |
| ...later train | ...treno più tardi | tray-noh pew tar-dee |
| ...overnight train | ...treno notturno | tray-noh noh-toor-noh |
| ...supplement | ...supplemento | soo-play-mayn-toh |
| Any discount for...? | Fate sconti per...? | fah-tay skohn-tee pehr |
| ...youths / seniors | ...giovani / anziani | joh-vah-nee / ahnt-seeah-nee |

| | | |
|---|---|---|
| Is a reservation required? | **Ci vuole la prenotazione?** | chee **vwoh**-lay lah pray-noh-taht-see**oh**-nay |
| I'd like to reserve... | **Vorrei prenotare...** | vor-**rehee** pray-noh-**tah**-ray |
| ...a seat. | **...un posto.** | oon **poh**-stoh |
| ...a berth. | **...una cuccetta.** | **oo**-nah koo-**chay**-tah |
| ...a sleeper. | **...un posto in vagone letto.** | oon **poh**-stoh een vah-**goh**-nay **leht**-toh |
| Where does (the train) leave from? | **Da dove parte?** | dah **doh**-vay **par**-tay |
| What track? | **Quale binario?** | **kwah**-lay bee-**nah**-reeoh |
| On time? | **Puntuale?** | poon-too**ah**-lay |
| Late? | **In ritardo?** | een ree-**tar**-doh |
| When will it arrive? | **Quando arriva?** | **kwahn**-doh ah-**ree**-vah |
| Is it direct? | **È diretto?** | eh dee-**reht**-toh |
| Must I transfer? | **Devo cambiare?** | **day**-voh kahm-beeah-ray |
| When? Where? | **Quando? Dove?** | **kwahn**-doh / **doh**-vay |
| Which train to...? | **Quale treno per....?** | **kwah**-lay **tray**-noh pehr |
| Which train car to...? | **Quale vagone per....?** | **kwah**-lay vah-**goh**-nay pehr |
| Is this (seat) free? | **È libero?** | eh **lee**-bay-roh |
| It's my seat. | **È il mio posto.** | eh eel **mee**-oh **poh**-stoh |
| Save my place? | **Mi tenga il posto?** | mee **tayn**-gah eel **poh**-stoh |
| Where are you going? | **Dove va?** | **doh**-vay vah |
| I'm going to... | **Vado a...** | **vah**-doh ah |
| Tell me when to get off? | **Mi dica quando devo scendere?** | mee **dee**-kah **kwahn**-doh **day**-voh **shehn**-day-ray |

## *Ticket talk:*

| | | |
|---|---|---|
| ticket | **biglietto** | beel-**yay**-toh |
| one way | **andata** | ahn-**dah**-tah |
| roundtrip | **ritorno** | ree-**tor**-noh |
| first class | **prima classe** | **pree**-mah **klah**-say |
| second class | **seconda classe** | say-**kohn**-dah **klah**-say |
| reduced fare | **tariffa ridotta** | tah-**ree**-fah ree-**doh**-tah |
| validate | **convalidare** | kohn-vah-lee-**dah**-ray |
| schedule | **orario** | oh-**rah**-reeoh |
| departure | **partenza** | par-**tehnt**-sah |
| direct | **diretto** | dee-**reht**-toh |
| connection | **coincidenza** | koh-een-chee-**dehnt**-sah |
| reservation | **prenotazione** | pray-noh-taht-seeoh-nay |
| non-smoking | **non fumare** | nohn foo-**mah**-ray |
| seat | **posto** | **poh**-stoh |
| seat by... | **posto vicino...** | **poh**-stoh vee-**chee**-noh |
| ...the window | **...al finestrino** | ahl fee-nay-**stree**-noh |
| ...the aisle | **...al corridoio** | ahl kor-ree-**doh**-yoh |
| berth... | **cuccetta...** | koo-**chay**-tah |
| ...upper | **...di sopra** | dee **soh**-prah |
| ...middle | **...in mezzo** | een **mehd**-zoh |
| ...lower | **...di sotto** | dee **soh**-toh |
| refund | **rimborso** | reem-**bor**-soh |

Italian train stations have wonderful (and fun) new schedule computers. Once you've mastered these (start by punching the "English" button), you'll save lots of time figuring out the right train connections.

## *At the train station:*

| | | |
|---|---|---|
| Italian State Railways | **Ferrovie dello Stato (FS)** | fay-**roh**-veeay **day**-loh **stah**-toh |
| train station | **stazione** | staht-seeoh-nay |
| train information | **informazioni sui treni** | een-for-maht-seeoh-nee **sooee** tray-nee |
| train | **treno** | **tray**-noh |
| high speed train | **inter-city (IC, EC)** | "inter-city" |
| arrival | **arrivo** | ah-**ree**-voh |
| departure | **partenza** | par-**tehnt**-sah |
| delay | **ritardo** | ree-**tar**-doh |
| waiting room | **sala di attesa, sala d'aspetto** | **sah**-lah dee ah-**tay**-zah, **sah**-lah dah-**spay**-toh |
| lockers | **armadietti** | ar-mah-deeay-tee |
| baggage check room | **sala di controllo, consegna** | **sah**-lah dee kohn-**troh**-loh, kohn-**sayn**-yah |
| lost and found office | **ufficio oggetti smarriti** | oo-**fee**-choh oh-**jeht**-tee smah-**ree**-tee |
| tourist information | **informazioni per turisti** | een-for-maht-seeoh-nee pehr too-**ree**-stee |
| to the trains | **ai treni** | ahee **tray**-nee |
| track or platform | **binario** | bee-**nah**-reeoh |
| train car | **vagone** | vah-**goh**-nay |
| dining car | **carrozza ristorante** | kar-**rot**-sah ree-stoh-**rahn**-tay |
| sleeper car | **carrozza letto** | kar-**rot**-sah **leht**-toh |
| conductor | **conduttore** | kohn-doo-**toh**-ray |

*Reading train schedules:*

| | |
|---|---|
| a | to |
| arrivo | arrival (abbreviated "a") |
| da | from |
| domenica | Sunday |
| eccetto | except |
| feriali | weekdays including Saturday |
| ferma a tutte le stazione | stops at all the stations |
| festivi | Sundays and holidays |
| fino | until |
| giorni | days |
| giornaliero | daily |
| in ritardo | late |
| non ferma a... | doesn't stop in... |
| ogni | every |
| partenza | departure (abbreviated "p") |
| per | for |
| sabato | Saturday |
| solo | only |
| tutti i giorni | daily |
| vacanza | holiday |
| 1-5 | Monday-Friday |
| 6, 7 | Saturday, Sunday |

Italian schedules use the 24-hour clock. It's like American time until noon. After that, subtract twelve and add p.m. So 13:00 is 1 p.m., 20:00 is 8 p.m., and 24:00 is midnight. If your train is scheduled to depart at 00:01, it'll leave one minute after midnight.

## Buses and subways:

| How do I get to...? | Come si va a...? | koh-may see vah ah |
| Which bus to...? | Quale autobus per....? | kwah-lay ow-toh-boos pehr |
| Does it stop at...? | Si ferma a...? | see fehr-mah ah |
| Which metro stop for...? | A quale stazione scendo per...? | ah kway-lay staht-seeoh-nay shehn-doh pehr |
| Must I transfer? | Devo cambiare? | day-voh kahm-beeah-ray |
| How much is a ticket? | Quanto costa un biglietto? | kwahn-toh kos-tah oon beel-yay-toh |
| Where can I buy a ticket? | Dove posso comprare un biglietto? | doh-vay pos-soh kohm-prah-ray oon beel-yay-toh |
| When is the...? | Quando parte...? | kwahn-doh par-tay |
| ...first / next / last | ...primo / prossimo / ultimo | pree-moh / pros-see-moh / ool-tee-moh |
| ...bus / subway | ...autobus / metropolitana | ow-toh-boos / may-troh-poh-lee-tah-nah |
| What's the frequency per hour / day? | Quante volte passa all'ora / al giorno? | kwahn-tay vohl-tay pah-sah ahl-loh-rah / ahl jor-noh |

### Key bus and subway words:

| ticket | biglietto | beel-yay-toh |
| city bus | autobus | ow-toh-boos |
| long-distance bus | pullman | pool-mahn |
| bus stop | fermata | fehr-mah-tah |
| bus station | stazione degli autobus | staht-seeoh-nay dayl-yee ow-toh-boos |
| subway | metropolitana | may-troh-poh-lee-tah-nah |
| subway exit | uscita | oo-shee-tah |

## Taxis:

| | | |
|---|---|---|
| Taxi! | **Taxi!** | **tahk**-see |
| Can you call a taxi? | **Può chiamare un taxi?** | pwoh kee-ah-**mah**-ray oon **tahk**-see |
| Where is a taxi stand? | **Dov'è una fermata dei taxi?** | doh-**veh oo**-nah fehr-**mah**-tah deh-ee **tahk**-see |
| Are you free? | **È libero?** | eh **lee**-bay-roh |
| Occupied. | **Occupato.** | oh-koo-**pah**-toh |
| How much will it cost to go to...? | **Quanto per andare a...?** | **kwahn**-toh pehr ahn-**dah**-ray ah |
| Too much. | **Troppo.** | **trop**-poh |
| Can you take ___ people? | **Può portar ___ persone?** | pwoh **por**-tar ___ pehr-**soh**-nay |
| Any extra fee? | **C'è un sovrapprezzo?** | cheh oon soh-vrah-**preht**-soh |
| The meter, please. | **Il tassametro, per favore.** | eel tah-sah-**may**-troh pehr fah-**voh**-ray |
| The most direct route. | **Il percorso più breve.** | eel pehr-**kor**-soh pew **bray**-vay |
| Slow down. | **Rallenti.** | rah-**lehn**-tee |
| If you don't slow down, I'll throw up. | **Se non rallenta, vomito.** | say nohn rah-**lehn**-tah, **voh**-mee-toh |
| Stop here. | **Si fermi qui.** | see **fehr**-mee kwee |
| Can you wait? | **Può aspettare?** | pwoh ah-spay-**tah**-ray |
| My change, please. | **Il resto, per favore.** | eel **rehs**-toh pehr fah-**voh**-ray |
| Keep the change. | **Tenga il resto.** | **tayn**-gah eel **rehs**-toh |

## Rental wheels:

| I'd like to rent... | Vorrei affittare... | vor-**rehee** ah-feet-**tah**-ray |
| ...a car. | ...una macchina. | **oo**-nah **mah**-kee-nah |
| ...a station wagon. | ...una station wagon. | **oo**-nah **staht**-see-ohn **wah**-gohn |
| ...a van. | ...un pulmino. | oon pool-**mee**-noh |
| ...a motorcycle. | ...una motocicletta. | **oo**-nah moh-toh-chee-**klay**-tah |
| ...a motor scooter. | ...un motorino. | oon moh-toh-**ree**-noh |
| ...a bicycle. | ...una bicicletta. | **oo**-nah bee-chee-**klay**-tah |
| How much...? | Quanto...? | **kwahn**-toh |
| ...per hour | ...all'ora | ah-**loh**-rah |
| ...per day | ...al giorno | ahl **jor**-noh |
| ...per week | ...alla settimana | **ah**-lah say-tee-**mah**-nah |
| Unlimited mileage? | Chilometraggio illimitato? | kee-loh-may-**trah**-joh eel-lee-mee-**tah**-toh |
| I brake for bakeries. | Mi fermo ad ogni pasticceria. | mee **fehr**-moh ahd **ohn**-yee pah-stee-chay-**ree**-ah |
| Is there...? | C'è...? | cheh |
| ...a helmet | ...un casco | oon **kah**-skoh |
| ...a discount | ...uno sconto | **oo**-noh **skohn**-toh |
| ...a deposit | ...un deposito | oon day-**poh**-zee-toh |
| ...insurance | ...l'assicurazione | lah-see-koo-raht-see**oh**-nay |
| When do I bring it back? | Quando lo riporto indietro? | **kwahn**-doh loh ree-**por**-toh een-**deeay**-troh |

## Driving:

| | | |
|---|---|---|
| gas station | **benzinaio** | baynd-zee-**nah**-yoh |
| The nearest gas station? | **Il benzinaio più vicino?** | eel baynd-zee-**nah**-yoh pew vee-**chee**-noh |
| Self-service? | **Self-service?** | "self service" |
| Fill the tank. | **Il pieno.** | eel peeay-noh |
| I need... | **Ho bisogno di...** | oh bee-**zohn**-yoh dee |
| ...gas. | **...benzina.** | baynd-**zee**-nah |
| ...unleaded. | **...benzina verde.** | baynd-**zee**-nah **vehr**-day |
| ...regular. | **...normale.** | nor-**mah**-lay |
| ...super. | **...super.** | **soo**-pehr |
| ...diesel. | **...gasolio.** | gah-**zoh**-leeoh |
| Check... | **Controlli...** | kohn-**troh**-lee |
| ...the oil. | **...l'olio.** | **loh**-leeoh |
| ...the tires. | **...le gomme.** | lay **goh**-may |
| ...the radiator. | **...il radiatore.** | eel rah-deeah-**toh**-ray |
| ...the battery. | **...la batteria.** | lah bah-tay-**ree**-ah |
| ...the fuses. | **...i fusibili.** | ee foo-**zee**-bee-lee |
| ...the fanbelt. | **...la cinghia del ventilatore.** | lah **cheen**-geeah dayl vehn-tee-lah-**toh**-ray |
| ...the brakes. | **...i freni.** | ee **fray**-nee |
| ...my pulse. | **...il mio battito cardiaco.** | eel **mee**-oh bah-**tee**-toh kar-deeah-koh |

The freeway rest stops and city *automat* gas pumps are the only places that sell gas during the afternoon siesta hours.

## *Car trouble:*

| | | |
|---|---|---|
| accident | **incidente** | een-chee-**dehn**-tay |
| breakdown | **guasto** | gooah-stoh |
| funny noise | **rumore strano** | roo-**moh**-ray **strah**-noh |
| My car won't start. | **La mia macchina non parte.** | lah **mee**-ah mah-kee-nah nohn **par**-tay |
| It's overheating. | **Si sta surriscaldando.** | see stah soo-ree-skahl-**dahn**-doh |
| This doesn't work | **Non funziona.** | nohn foont-seeoh-nah |
| I need... | **Ho bisogno di...** | oh bee-**zohn**-yoh dee |
| ...a tow truck. | **...un carro attrezzi.** | oon **kar**-roh ah-**trayt**-see |
| ...a mechanic. | **...un meccanico.** | oon may-**kah**-nee-koh |
| ...a stiff drink. | **...whiskey.** | "whiskey" |

## *Parking:*

| | | |
|---|---|---|
| parking garage | **garage** | gah-**rahj** |
| Where can I park? | **Dove posso parcheggiare?** | **doh**-vay **pos**-soh par-kay-**jah**-ray |
| Can I park here? | **Posso parcheggiare qui?** | **pos**-soh par-kay-**jah**-ray kwee |
| How long can I park here? | **Per quanto tempo posso parcheggiare qui?** | pehr **kwahn**-toh **tehm**-poh **pos**-soh par-kay-**jah**-ray kwee |
| Must I pay to park here? | **È a pagamento questo parcheggio?** | eh ah pah-gah-**mayn**-toh **kway**-stoh par-**kay**-joh |
| Is this a safe place to park? | **È sicuro parcheggiare qui?** | eh see-**koo**-roh par-kay-**jah**-ray kwee |

## Finding your way:

| | | |
|---|---|---|
| I am going to... | Vado a... | **vah**-doh ah |
| How do I get to...? | Come si va a...? | **koh**-may see vah ah |
| Is there a map? | C'e una cartina? | cheh **oo**-nah kar-**tee**-nah |
| How many minutes...? | Quanti minuti...? | **kwahn**-tee mee-**noo**-tee |
| How many hours...? | Quante ore...? | **kwahn**-tay oh-ray |
| ...on foot | ...a piedi | ah peeay-dee |
| ...by bicycle | ...in bicicletta | een bee-chee-**klay**-tah |
| ...by car | ...in macchina | een **mah**-kee-nah |
| How many kilometers to...? | Quanti chilometri per...? | **kwahn**-tee kee-**loh**-may-tree pehr |
| What is the... route to Rome? | Qual'è la strada... per andare a Roma? | kwah-**leh** lah **strah**-dah... pehr ahn-**dah**-ray ah **roh**-mah |
| ...best | ...migliore | meel-**yoh**-ray |
| ...fastest | ...più veloce | pew vay-**loh**-chay |
| ...most interesting | ...più interessante | pew een-tay-ray-**sahn**-tay |
| Point it out? | Me lo mostri? | may loh **mohs**-tree |
| I'm lost. | Mi sono perso[a]. | mee **soh**-noh **pehr**-soh |
| Where am I? | Dove sono? | **doh**-vay **soh**-noh |
| Who am I? | Chi sono? | kee **soh**-noh |
| Where is...? | Dov'è...? | doh-**veh** |
| The nearest...? | Il più vicino...? | eel pew vee-**chee**-noh |
| Where is this address? | Dov'è questo indirizzo? | doh-**veh kway**-stoh een-dee-**reet**-soh |

## *Key route-finding words:*

| | | |
|---|---|---|
| map | **cartina** | kar-**tee**-nah |
| road map | **cartina stradale** | kar-**tee**-nah strah-**dah**-lay |
| straight ahead | **sempre diritto** | **sehm**-pray dee-**ree**-toh |
| left / right | **sinistra / destra** | see-**nee**-strah / **dehs**-trah |
| first / next | **prima / prossima** | **pree**-mah / **pros**-see-mah |
| intersection | **intersezione** | een-tehr-seht-seeoh-nay |
| stoplight | **semaforo** | say-mah-**foh**-roh |
| (main) square | **piazza (principale)** | peeaht-sah (preen-chee-**pah**-lay) |
| street | **strada, via** | **strah**-dah, **vee**-ah |
| bridge | **ponte** | **pohn**-tay |
| tunnel | **tunnel** | **toon**-nel |
| highway | **autostrada** | ow-toh-**strah**-dah |
| freeway | **superstrada** | soo-pehr-**strah**-dah |
| north / south | **nord / sud** | nord / sood |
| east / west | **est / ovest** | ayst / **oh**-vehst |

**TRANSPORTATION**

The flashing lights of a patrol car are a sure sign that someone's in trouble. If it's you, say: *"Mi dispiace, sono un turista."* (Sorry, I'm a tourist.) Or, for the adventurous: *"Se non le piace come guido, si tolga dal marciapiede."* (If you don't like how I drive, stay off the sidewalk.)

# Sleeping

## Places to stay:

| | | |
|---|---|---|
| hotel | **hotel, albergo** | **oh**-tehl, ahl-**behr**-goh |
| small hotel (usually family-run) | **pensione, locanda** | payn-seeoh-nay, loh-**kahn**-dah |
| room in private home | **camera in affitto** | **kah**-may-rah een ah-**fee**-toh |
| youth hostel | **ostello della gioventù** | oh-**stehl**-loh **day**-lah joh-vehn-**too** |
| vacancy | **camere libere** | **kah**-may-rah **lee**-bay-ray |
| no vacancy | **completo** | kohm-**play**-toh |

## Reserving a room by phone:

| | | |
|---|---|---|
| Hello. | **Buon giorno.** | bwohn **jor**-noh |
| Do you speak English? | **Parla inglese?** | **par**-lah een-**glay**-zay |
| Do you have a room...? | **Avete una camera...?** | ah-**vay**-tay **oo**-nah **kah**-may-rah |
| ...for one person | **...per una persona** | pehr **oo**-nah pehr-**soh**-nah |
| ...for two people | **...per due persone** | pehr **doo**-ay pehr-**soh**-nay |
| ...for tonight | **...per stanotte** | pehr stah-**not**-tay |
| ...for two nights | **...per due notti** | pehr **doo**-ay **not**-tee |
| ...for this Friday | **...per venerdì** | pehr vay-nehr-**dee** |
| ...for June 21 | **...per ventuno giugno** | pehr vayn-**too**-noh **joon**-yoh |
| Yes or no? | **Sì o no?** | see oh noh |

| I'd like... | Vorrei... | vor-**rehee** |
|---|---|---|
| ...a private bathroom. | ...un bagno completo. | oon **bahn**-yoh kohm-**play**-toh |
| ...your cheapest room. | ...la camera più economico. | lah **kah**-may-rah pew ay-koh-**noh**-mee-koh |
| ...___ bed (beds) | ...___ letto (letti) | ___ **leht**-toh (**leht**-tee) |
| for ___ people | per ___ persone | pehr ___ pehr-**soh**-nay |
| in ___ room (rooms). | nella ___ camera (camere). | **nay**-lah ___ **kah**-may-rah (**kah**-may-ray) |
| How much is it? | Quanto costa? | **kwahn**-toh **kos**-tah |
| Anything cheaper? | Niente di più economico? | nee-**ehn**-tay dee pew ay-koh-**noh**-mee-koh |
| I'll take it. | La prendo. | lah **prehn**-doh |
| My name is... | Mi chiamo... | mee keeah-moh |
| I'll stay for... | Starò per... | stah-**roh** pehr |
| We'll stay for... | Staremo per... | stah-**ray**-moh pehr |
| ...___ night (nights). | ...___ notte (notti). | ___ **not**-tay (**not**-tee) |
| I'll come... | Arriverò... | ah-ree-vay-**roh** |
| We'll come... | Arriveremo... | ah-ree-vay-**ray**-moh |
| ...in one hour. | ...tra un'ora. | trah oon-**oh**-rah |
| ...before 16:00. | ...prima delle sedici. | **pree**-mah **day**-lay say-dee-chee |
| ...Friday before 6 p.m. | ...venerdí prima le sei di sera. | vay-nehr-**dee pree**-mah lay sehee dee **say**-rah |
| Thank you. | Grazie. | **graht**-seeay |

Italian hotels almost always have larger rooms to fit three to six people. Your price per person plummets as you pack more into a room.

SLEEPING

## Getting specific:

| | | |
|---|---|---|
| I'd like a room... | **Vorrei una camera...** | vor-**rehee** **oo**-nah **kah**-may-rah |
| ...with / without / and | **...con / senza / e** | kohn / **sehn**-sah / ay |
| ...toilet | **...toilette** | twah-**leht**-tay |
| ...shower | **...doccia** | **doh**-chah |
| ...shower down the hall | **...doccia in fondo al corridoio** | **doh**-chah een **fohn**-doh ahl kor-ree-**doh**-yoh |
| ...bathtub | **...vasca da bagno** | **vah**-skah dah **bahn**-yoh |
| ...double bed | **...letto matrimoniale** | **leht**-toh mah-tree-moh-**neeah**-lay |
| ...twin beds | **...letti singoli** | **leht**-tee **seeng**-goh-lee |
| ...balcony | **...balcone** | bahl-**koh**-nay |
| ...view | **...vista** | **vee**-stah |
| ...only a sink | **...solo un lavandino** | **soh**-loh oon lah-vahn-**dee**-noh |
| ...on the ground floor | **...al piano terreno** | ahl **peeah**-noh tay-**ray**-noh |
| Is there an elevator? | **Un ascensore?** | oon ah-shayn-**soh**-ray |
| We arrive Monday, depart Wednesday. | **Arriviamo lunedì, ripartiamo mercoledì.** | ah-ree-veeah-moh loo-nay-**dee**, ree-par-teeah-moh mehr-koh-lay-**dee** |
| I have a reservation. | **Ho una prenotazione.** | oh **oo**-nah pray-noh-taht-**seeoh**-nay |
| Confirm my reservation? | **Confermi la mia prenotazione?** | kohn-**fehr**-mee lah **mee**-ah pray-noh-taht-see**oh**-nay |

## Nailing down the price:

| How much is...? | Quanto costa...? | kwahn-toh kos-tah |
| ...a room for ___ people | ...una camera per ___ persone | oo-nah kah-may-rah pehr ___ pehr-soh-nay |
| ...your cheapest room | ...la camera più economica | lah kah-may-rah pew ay-koh-noh-mee-kah |
| Is breakfast included? | La colazione è inclusa? | lah koh-laht-seeoh-nay eh een-kloo-zah |
| How much without breakfast? | Quant'è senza la colazione? | kwahn-teh sehn-sah lah koh-laht-seeoh-nay |
| Complete price? | Prezzo completo? | preht-soh kohm-play-toh |
| Is it cheaper if I stay ___ nights? | È più economico se mi fermo ___ notti? | eh pew ay-koh-noh-mee-koh say mee fehr-moh ___ not-tee |
| I'll stay ___ nights. | Mi fermo ___ notti. | mee fehr-moh ___ not-tee |

## Choosing a room:

| Can I see the room? | Posso vedere la camera? | pos-soh vay-day-ray lah kah-may-rah |
| Do you have something...? | Avete qualcosa...? | ah-vay-tay kwahl-koh-zah |
| ...larger / smaller | ...di più grande / di più piccolo | dee pew grahn-day / dee pew pee-koh-loh |
| ...better / cheaper | ...di meglio / più economico | dee mehl-yoh / pew ay-koh-noh-mee-koh |
| ...quieter | ...di più tranquillo | dee pew trahn-kwee-loh |
| Key, please. | Chiave, per favore. | keeah-vay pehr fah-voh-ray |

## Hotel help:

| | | |
|---|---|---|
| I'd like... | Vorrei... | vor-**rehee** |
| ...a / another | ...un / un altro | oon / oon **ahl**-troh |
| ...towel. | ...asciugamano. | ah-shoo-gah-**mah**-noh |
| ...pillow. | ...cuscino. | koo-**shee**-noh |
| ...clean sheets. | ...lenzuola pulite. | lehnt-so**ooh**-lah poo-**lee**-tay |
| ...blanket. | ...coperta. | koh-**pehr**-tah |
| ...glass. | ...bicchiere. | bee-kee**ay**-ray |
| ...soap. | ...sapone. | sah-**poh**-nay |
| ...toilet paper. | ...carta igienica. | **kar**-tah ee-**jay**-nee-kah |
| ...crib. | ...culla. | **koo**-lah |
| ...small extra bed. | ...extra letto singolo. | **ehk**-strah **leht**-toh **seeng**-goh-loh |
| ...different room. | ...altra camera. | **ahl**-trah kah-**may**-rah |
| ...silence. | ...silenzio. | see-**lehnt**-seeoh |
| Where can I wash / hang my laundry? | Dove posso fare del / stendere il bucato? | **doh**-vay **pos**-soh **fah**-ray dayl / **stehn**-day-ray eel boo-**kah**-toh |
| I'd like to stay another night. | Vorrei fermarmi un'altra notte. | vor-**rehee** fehr-**mar**-mee oo-**nahl**-trah **not**-tay |
| Where can I park? | Dove posso parcheggiare? | **doh**-vay **pos**-soh par-kay-**jah**-ray |
| When do you lock up? | A che ora chiude? | ah kay **oh**-rah kee**oo**-day |
| What time is breakfast? | A che ora è la colazione? | ah kay **oh**-rah eh lah koh-laht-see**oh**-nay |
| Please wake me at 7:00. | Mi svegli alle sette, per favore. | mee **zvayl**-yee **ah**-lay **seht**-tay pehr fah-**voh**-ray |

## Hotel hassles:

| | | |
|---|---|---|
| Come with me. | **Venga con me.** | **vayn**-gah kohn may |
| I have a problem in my room. | **Ho un problema con la mia camera.** | oh oon proh-**blay**-mah kohn lah **mee**-ah **kah**-may-rah |
| Lamp... | **Lampada...** | lahm-**pah**-dah |
| Lightbulb... | **Lampadina...** | lahm-pah-**dee**-nah |
| Key... | **Chiave...** | keeah-**vay** |
| Lock... | **Serratura...** | say-rah-**too**-rah |
| Window... | **Finestra...** | fee-**nay**-strah |
| Faucet... | **Rubinetto...** | roo-bee-**nay**-toh |
| Sink... | **Lavabo...** | **lah**-vah-boh |
| Toilet... | **Toilette...** | twah-**leht**-tay |
| Shower... | **Doccia...** | **doh**-chah |
| ...doesn't work. | **...non funziona.** | nohn foont-seeoh-nah |
| There is no hot water. | **Non c'è acqua calda.** | nohn cheh **ah**-kwah **kahl**-dah |
| When is the water hot? | **A che ora è calda l'acqua?** | ah kay **oh**-rah eh **kahl**-dah **lah**-kwah |

## Checking out:

| | | |
|---|---|---|
| I'll leave / We'll leave... | **Parto / Partiamo...** | **par**-toh / par-teeah-moh |
| ...today / tomorrow. | **...oggi / domani.** | **oh**-jee / doh-**mah**-nee |
| ...very early. | **...molto presto.** | **mohl**-toh **prehs**-toh |
| When is check-out time? | **A che ora devo lasciare la camera?** | ah kay **oh**-rah **day**-voh lah-**shah**-ray lah **kah**-may-rah |

| Can I pay now? | Posso pagare subito? | **pos**-soh pah-**gah**-ray soo-bee-toh |
| The bill, please. | Il conto, per favore. | eel **kohn**-toh pehr fah-**voh**-ray |
| Credit card O.K.? | Carta di credito è O.K.? | **kar**-tah dee **kray**-dee-toh eh "O.K." |
| I slept like a rock. | Ho dormito come un sasso. | oh dor-**mee**-toh **koh**-may oon **sah**-soh |
| Everything was great. | Tutto magnifico. | **too**-toh mahn-**yee**-fee-koh |
| Will you call my next hotel for me? | Può telefonare a questo altro albergo per me? | pwoh tay-lay-foh-**nah**-ray ah **kway**-stoh **ahl**-troh ahl-**behr**-goh pehr may |
| Can I / Can we...? | Posso / Possiamo...? | **pos**-soh / pos-seeah-moh |
| ...leave baggage here until ___ | ...lasciare il bagaglio qui fino a ___ | lah-**shah**-ray eel bah-**gahl**-yoh kwee **fee**-noh ah |

## Camping:

| tent | tenda | **tayn**-dah |
| camping | campeggio | kahm-**pay**-joh |
| Where is the nearest campground? | Dov'è il campeggio più vicino? | doh-**veh** eel kahm-**pay**-joh pew vee-**chee**-noh |
| Can I / Can we...? | Posso / Possiamo...? | **pos**-soh / pos-seeah-moh |
| ...camp here for the night | ...campeggiare qui per la notte | kahm-pay-**jah**-ray kwee pehr lah **not**-tay |
| Do showers cost extra? | Costano extra le docce? | koh-**stah**-noh **ehk**-strah lay **doh**-chay |

# Eating

## Finding a restaurant:

| Where's a good... restaurant? | Dov'è un buon ristorante...? | doh-**veh** oon bwohn ree-stoh-**rahn**-tay |
| --- | --- | --- |
| ...cheap | ...economico | ay-koh-**noh**-mee-koh |
| ...local-style | ...con cucina casereccia | kohn koo-**chee**-nah kah-zay-**ray**-chah |
| ...untouristy | ...non per turisti | nohn pehr too-**ree**-stee |
| ...Chinese | ...cinese | chee-**nay**-zay |
| ...fast food (Italian-style) | ...tavola calda | **tah**-voh-lah **kahl**-dah |
| ...cafeteria | ...self-service | "self-service" |
| with a salad bar | con un banco delle insalate | kohn oon **bahn**-koh **day**-lay een-sah-**lah**-tay |

## Getting a table and menu:

| Waiter. | Cameriere. | kah-may-reeay-ray |
| --- | --- | --- |
| Waitress. | Cameriera. | kah-may-reeay-rah |
| I'd like... | Vorrei... | vor-**rehee** |
| ...a table for one / two. | ...un tavolo per uno[a] / due. | oon **tah**-voh-loh pehr **oo**-noh / **doo**-ay |
| ...non-smoking. | ...non fumatori. | nohn foo-mah-**toh**-ree |
| ...just a drink. | ...soltanto qualcosa da bere. | sohl-**tahn**-toh kwahl-**koh**-zah dah **bay**-ray |
| ...a snack. | ...un spuntino. | oon spoon-**tee**-noh |
| ...only a first course (pasta dish). | ...solo un primo piatto. | **soh**-loh oon **pree**-moh peeah-toh |
| ...to see the menu. | ...vedere il menù. | vay-**day**-ray eel may-**noo** |

| | | |
|---|---|---|
| ...to order. | **...ordinare.** | or-dee-**nah**-ray |
| ...to eat. | **...mangiare.** | mahn-**jah**-ray |
| ...to pay. | **...pagare.** | pah-**gah**-ray |
| ...to throw up. | **...vomitare.** | voh-mee-**tah**-ray |
| What do you recommend? | **Che cosa raccomanda?** | kay **koh**-zah rah-koh-**mahn**-dah |
| What's your favorite? | **Qual'è il suo preferito?** | kwah-**leh** eel **soo**-oh pray-fay-**ree**-toh |
| Is it good? | **È buono?** | eh **bwoh**-noh |
| Is it expensive? | **È caro?** | eh **kah**-roh |
| Is it light? | **È leggero?** | eh lay-**jay**-roh |
| Is it filling? | **È sostanzioso?** | eh soh-stahnt-see**oh**-zoh |
| What is...? | **Che cosa c'è...?** | kay **koh**-zah cheh |
| ...that | **...quello** | **kway**-loh |
| ...local | **...di locale** | dee loh-**kah**-lay |
| ...fast | **...di veloce** | dee vay-**loh**-chay |
| ...cheap and filling | **...di economico e sostanzioso** | dee ay-koh-**noh**-mee-koh ay soh-stahnt-see**oh**-zoh |
| Do you have...? | **Avete...?** | ah-**vay**-tay |
| ...an English menu | **...un menù in inglese** | oon may-**noo** een een-**glay**-zay |
| ...children's portions | **...le porzioni per bambini** | lay port-see**oh**-nee pehr bahm-**bee**-nee |

A *menù del giorno* (menu of the day) offers you a choice of appetizer, entrée, and dessert (or wine) at a fixed price, usually with cover and service charges included.

## The menu:

| | | |
|---|---|---|
| menu | **menù** | may-**noo** |
| menu of the day | **menù del giorno** | may-**noo** dayl **jor**-noh |
| tourist menu | **menù turistico** | may-**noo** too-**ree**-stee-koh |
| specialty of the house | **specialità della casa** | spay-chah-lee-**tah day**-lah **kah**-zah |
| chef's speciality | **capricciosa** | kah-pree-**choh**-zah |
| breakfast | **colazione** | koh-laht-seeoh-nay |
| lunch | **pranzo** | **prahnt**-soh |
| dinner | **cena** | **chay**-nah |
| appetizers | **antipasti** | ahn-tee-**pah**-stee |
| bread | **pane** | **pah**-nay |
| salad | **insalata** | een-sah-**lah**-tah |
| soup | **minestra, zuppa** | mee-**nehs**-trah, **tsoo**-pah |
| first course (pasta, soup) | **primo piatto** | **pree**-moh peeah-toh |
| main course (meat, fish) | **secondo piatto** | say-**kohn**-doh peeah-toh |
| meat | **carni** | **kar**-nee |
| poultry | **pollame** | poh-**lah**-may |
| seafood | **frutti di mare** | **froo**-tee dee **mah**-ray |
| side dishes | **contorni** | kohn-**tor**-nee |
| vegetables | **legumi** | lay-**goo**-mee |
| cheeses | **formaggi** | for-**mah**-jee |
| desserts | **dolci** | **dohl**-chee |
| beverages | **bevande, bibite** | bay-**vahn**-day, **bee**-bee-tay |

| beer | birra | **beer**-rah |
| wines | vini | **vee**-nee |
| cover charge | coperto | koh-**pehr**-toh |
| service (not) included | servizio (non) incluso | sehr-**veet**-seeoh (nohn) een-**kloo**-zoh |
| with / without | con / senza | kohn / **sehn**-sah |
| and / or | e / o | ay / oh |

## Dietary restrictions:

| I'm allergic to... | **Sono allergico[a] al...** | **soh**-noh ahl-**lehr**-jee-koh ahl |
| I cannot eat... | **Non posso mangiare...** | nohn **pos**-soh mahn-**jah**-ray |
| ...dairy products. | **...prodotti casearei.** | proh-**dot**-tee kah-zay-ah-**rayee** |
| ...meat / pork. | **...carne / maiale.** | **car**-nay / mah-**yah**-lay |
| ...salt / sugar. | **...sale / zucchero.** | **sah**-lay / **tsoo**-kay-roh |
| I am diabetic. | **Ho il diabete.** | oh eel deeah-**bay**-tay |
| Low cholesterol? | **Basso colesterolo?** | **bah**-soh koh-lay-stay-**roh**-loh |
| No caffeine. | **Senza caffeina.** | **sehn**-sah kah-fay**ee**-nah |
| No alcohol. | **Niente alcool.** | nee**ehn**-tay **ahl**-kohl |
| I am a... | **Sono un...** | **soh**-noh oon |
| ...vegetarian. | **...vegetariano[a].** | vay-jay-tah-ree**ah**-noh |
| ...strict vegetarian. | **...strettamente vegetariano[a].** | stray-tah-**mayn**-tay vay-jay-tah-ree**ah**-noh |
| ...carnivore. | **...carnivoro[a].** | kar-**nee**-voh-roh |

EATING

## Tableware and condiments:

| | | |
|---|---|---|
| plate | **piatto** | peeah-toh |
| napkin | **tovagliolo** | toh-vahl-**yoh**-loh |
| knife | **coltello** | kohl-**tehl**-loh |
| fork | **forchetta** | for-**kay**-tah |
| spoon | **cucchiaio** | koo-keeah-yoh |
| cup | **tazza** | taht-sah |
| glass | **bicchiere** | bee-keeay-ray |
| carafe | **caraffa** | kah-**rah**-fah |
| water | **acqua** | ah-kwah |
| bread | **pane** | pah-nay |
| breadsticks | **grissini** | gree-**see**-nee |
| butter | **burro** | boo-roh |
| margarine | **margarina** | mar-gah-**ree**-nah |
| salt / pepper | **sale / pepe** | **sah**-lay / **pay**-pay |
| sugar | **zucchero** | tsoo-kay-roh |
| artificial sweetener | **dolcificante** | dohl-chee-fee-**kahn**-tay |
| honey | **miele** | meeay-lay |
| mustard | **senape** | **say**-nah-pay |
| mayonnaise | **maionese** | mah-yoh-**nay**-zay |

## Restaurant requests and regrets:

| | | |
|---|---|---|
| A little. | **Un po.'** | oon poh |
| More. | **Un altro po.'** | oon **ahl**-troh poh |
| Another. | **Un altro.** | oon **ahl**-troh |
| The same. | **Uguale.** | oo-**gwah**-lay |
| I did not order this. | **Io questo non l'ho ordinato.** | eeoh **kway**-stoh nohn loh or-dee-**nah**-toh |

| Is it included with the meal? | È incluso nel pasto questo? | eh een-**kloo**-zoh nayl **pah**-stoh **kway**-stoh |
| I'm in a hurry. | Sono di fretta. | **soh**-noh dee **fray**-tah |
| I must leave by... | Devo anare via alle... | **day**-voh ah-**nah**-ray **vee**-ah ah-lay |
| When will the food be ready? | Tra quanto è pronto il cibo? | trah **kwahn**-toh eh **pron**-toh eel **chee**-boh |
| I've changed my mind. | Ho cambiato idea. | oh kahm-beeah-toh ee-**day**-ah |
| Can I get it "to go"? | Da portar via? | dah **por**-tar **vee**-ah |
| This is... | Questo è... | **kway**-stoh eh |
| ...dirty / greasy. | ...sporco / grasso. | **spor**-koh / **grah**-soh |
| ...too salty. | ...troppo salato. | **trop**-poh sah-**lah**-toh |
| ...undercooked. | ...troppo crudo. | **trop**-poh **kroo**-doh |
| ...overcooked. | ...troppo cotto. | **trop**-poh **kot**-toh |
| ...cold. | ...freddo. | **fray**-doh |
| Heat it up? | Lo può scaldare? | loh pwoh skahl-**dah**-ray |
| Enjoy your meal! | Buon appetito! | bwohn ah-pay-**tee**-toh |
| Enough. | Basta. | **bah**-stah |
| Finished. | Finito. | fee-**nee**-toh |
| Do any of your customers return? | Ritornano i vostri clienti? | ree-**tor**-nah-noh ee **voh**-stree klee-**ehn**-tee |
| Yuck! | Che schifo! | kay **skee**-foh |
| Delicious! | Delizioso! | day-leet-seeoh-zoh |
| Divinely good! | Una vera bontà! | **oo**-nah **vay**-rah bohn-**tah** |
| My compliments to the chef! | Complimenti al cuoco! | kohm-plee-**mayn**-tee ahl **koooh**-koh |

EATING

## Paying for your meal:

| | | |
|---|---|---|
| Waiter. | **Cameriere.** | kah-may-ree**ay**-ray |
| Waitress. | **Cameriera.** | kah-may-ree**ay**-rah |
| The bill, please. | **Il conto,** **per favore.** | eel **kohn**-toh pehr fah-**voh**-ray |
| Together. | **Conto unico.** | **kohn**-toh oo-nee-koh |
| Separate checks. | **Conto separato.** | **kohn**-toh say-pah-**rah**-toh |
| Credit card O.K.? | **Carta di credito è** **O.K.?** | **kar**-tah dee **kray**-dee-toh eh "O.K." |
| Is there a cover charge? | **Si paga per il** **coperto?** | see **pah**-gah pehr eel koh-**pehr**-toh |
| Is service included? | **È incluso il servizio?** | eh een-**kloo**-zoh eel sehr-**veet**-seeoh |
| This is not correct. | **Questo non è giusto.** | **kway**-stoh nohn eh **joo**-stoh |
| Can you explain it? | **Lo può spiegare?** | loh pwoh speeay-**gah**-ray |
| What if I wash the dishes? | **E se lavassi i piatti?** | ay say lah-**vah**-see ee **peeah**-tee |
| Keep the change. | **Tenga il resto.** | **tayn**-gah eel **rehs**-toh |
| This is for you. | **Questo è per lei.** | **kway**-stoh eh pehr **lehee** |

In Italian bars and freeway rest stops, pay first at the *cassa* (cash register), then take your receipt to the counter to get your food. In restaurants, you'll get *il conto* (the bill) only when you ask for it. Most menus clearly list the *coperto* (cover charge) and the *servizio* (service charge). If the *servizio* is *incluso* (included), an extra tip is not expected, but it's polite to leave some coins.

## Breakfast:

| breakfast | colazione | koh-laht-seeoh-nay |
| bread | pane | pah-nay |
| roll | brioche | bree-osh |
| toast / butter | toast / burro | tost / boo-roh |
| jelly | gelatina | jay-lah-tee-nah |
| pastry | pasticcini | pah-stee-chee-nee |
| croissant | cornetto | kor-nay-toh |
| omelet | omelette, frittata | oh-may-leht-tay, free-tah-tah |
| eggs... | uova... | woh-vah |
| ...fried / scrambled | ...fritte / strapazzate | free-tay / strah-paht-sah-tay |
| boiled egg... | uovo alla coque... | woh-voh ah-lah kok |
| ...soft / hard | ...molle / sodo | mol-lay / soh-doh |
| ham | prosciutto cotto | proh-shoo-toh kot-toh |
| cheese | formaggio | for-mah-joh |
| yogurt | yogurt | yoh-goort |
| cereal (any kind) | corn flex | korn flehx |
| milk | latte | lah-tay |
| hot chocolate | cioccolata calda | choh-koh-lah-tah kahl-dah |
| fruit juice | succo di frutta | soo-koh dee froo-tah |
| fresh orange juice | spremuta di arancia | spray-moo-tah dee ah-rahn-chah |
| coffee / tea | caffè / tè | kah-feh / teh |
| Is breakfast included (in the room cost)? | La colazione è inclusa? | lah koh-laht-seeoh-nay eh een-kloo-zah |

EATING

## Appetizers and snacks:

| | |
|---|---|
| **antipasto misto** | mixed appetizers (usually meat) |
| **bruschetta** | toast with tomatoes and garlic |
| **crostini Fiorentina** | toast with liver paté |
| **crostini Napoletana** | toast with cheese |
| **formaggi misti** | assorted cheeses |
| **panini** | sandwiches |
| **prosciutto e melone** | cured ham with melon |
| **salame** | cured pork sausage |
| **toast al prosciutto e formaggio** | toast with ham and cheese |
| **tramezzini vari** | assorted small sandwiches |

## Italian specialties:

| | |
|---|---|
| **cozze ripiene** | mussels stuffed with bread, cheese, garlic, and tomatoes |
| **focaccia** | flat bread with herbs |
| **insalata caprese** | salad of fresh mozzarella, basil, and tomatoes |
| **pancetta** | thick bacon |
| **polenta** | moist cornmeal (Venice) |
| **ribollita** | cabbage and bean soup (Tuscany) |
| **risotto** | saffron rice dish with meat, seafood, or vegetables (Northern Italy) |
| **saltimbocca** | veal wrapped in ham (Rome) |
| **tramezzini** | crustless filled sandwiches |

## Pizza and quick meals:

For fresh, fast, and frugal pizza, *Pizza Rustica* shops offer the cheapest hot meal in any Italian town, selling pizza by the slice (*pezzo*) or weight (*etto* = 100 grams, around a quarter pound). *Due etti* (200 grams) make a good light lunch. You can eat your pizza on the spot, or order it *"Da portar via"* (for the road). For handier pizza, nearly any bar has lousy, microwavable pizza snacks. To get cold pizza warmed up, say, *"Calda"* (hot) or *"Più calda"* (hotter) and throw in *"per favore"* (please). To get an extra plate, ask for a *"piatto extra."* Pizza words include:

| | |
|---|---|
| acciughe | anchovies |
| calzone | folded pizza with various fillings |
| capricciosa | chef's specialty |
| carciofini | artichokes |
| funghi | mushrooms |
| Margherita | cheese and tomato sauce |
| Napoletana | cheese, anchovies, and tomato sauce |
| peperoni | green or red peppers (not sausage!) |
| prosciutto | cured ham |
| Quattro Stagioni | 4 toppings on separate quarters of a pizza |
| salamino piccante | pepperoni |

For other quick, tasty meals, drop by a *Rosticceria*—a deli where you'll find a cafeteria-style display of reasonably priced food. Get it "to go" or take a seat and eat.

## Soups and salads:

| | | |
|---|---|---|
| soup | **minestra, zuppa** | mee-**nehs**-trah, **tsoo**-pah |
| soup of the day | **zuppa del giorno** | **tsoo**-pah dayl **jor**-noh |
| broth... | **brodo...** | **brod**-oh |
| ...chicken | **...di pollo** | dee **poh**-loh |
| ...beef | **...di carne** | dee **kar**-nay |
| ...vegetable | **...di verdura** | dee vehr-**doo**-rah |
| ...with noodles | **...con pastina** | kohn pah-**stee**-nah |
| ...with rice | **...con riso** | kohn **ree**-zoh |
| vegetable soup | **minestrone** | mee-nay-**stroh**-nay |
| green salad | **insalata verde** | een-sah-**lah**-tah **vehr**-day |
| mixed salad | **insalata mista** | een-sah-**lah**-tah **mee**-stah |
| seafood salad | **insalata di mare** | een-sah-**lah**-tah dee **mah**-ray |
| chef's salad... | **insalata dello chef...** | een-sah-**lah**-tah **day**-loh shehf |
| ...with ham, cheese, and egg | **...con prosciutto, formaggio, e uova** | kohn proh-**shoo**-toh, for-**mah**-joh, ay **woh**-vah |
| lettuce | **lattuga** | lah-**too**-gah |
| tomatoes | **pomodori** | poh-moh-**doh**-ree |
| cucumber | **cetrioli** | chay-treeoh-lee |
| oil / vinegar | **olio / aceto** | **oh**-leeoh / ah-**chay**-toh |
| What is in this salad? | **Che cosa c'è in questa insalata?** | kay **koh**-zah cheh een **kway**-stah een-sah-**lah**-tah |

In Italian restaurants, salad dressing is normally just the oil and vinegar at the table. Salad bars at fast food restaurants and *autostrada* rest stops can be a good budget bet.

## Pasta:

Italy is the land of *pasta*. You can taste over 500 types! While there are a few differences in ingredients, the big deal is basically the shape. Watch for *rigatone* (little tubes), *canneloni* (big tubes), *fettucine* (flat noodles), *farfalline* (butterfly-shaped pasta), *gnocchi* (shell-shaped noodles made from potatoes), *linguine* (thin, flat noodles), *penne* (angle-cut tubes), *rotelline* (wheel-shaped pasta), *tagliatelle* (short, flat noodles), *toscanini* (slender conductor), and *tortellini* (pasta "doughnuts" filled with meat or cheese), and surprise...*spaghetti*. Pasta can be stuffed *ravioli*-style with various meats, cheeses, herbs, and spices. Pasta sauces and styles include:

| | |
|---|---|
| **amatriciana** | Roman-style with bacon, tomato, and spices |
| **bolognese** | meat and tomato sauce |
| **carbonara** | bacon, egg, cream, and pepper |
| **genovese** | pesto |
| **in brodo** | in broth |
| **marinara** | tomato and garlic |
| **panna** | cream |
| **pescatora** | seafood |
| **pesto** | olive oil, garlic, basil, and pine nuts |
| **pomodoro** | tomato only |
| **quattro formaggi** | four cheeses |
| **ragù** | meaty tomato sauce |
| **sugo** | sauce, usually tomato |
| **vongole** | with clams and spices |

## Seafood:

| | | |
|---|---|---|
| seafood | **frutti di mare** | **froo**-tee dee **mah**-ray |
| assorted seafood | **misto di frutti di mare** | **mee**-stoh dee **froo**-tee dee **mah**-ray |
| fish | **pesce** | **pay**-shay |
| cod | **merluzzo** | mehr-**loot**-soh |
| salmon | **salmone** | sahl-**moh**-nay |
| sole | **sogliola** | sohl-**yoh**-lah |
| trout | **trota** | **trot**-ah |
| tuna | **tonno** | **toh**-noh |
| herring | **aringa** | ah-**reeng**-gah |
| sardines | **sarde** | **sar**-day |
| anchovies | **acciughe** | ah-**choo**-gay |
| clams | **vongole** | **vohn**-goh-lay |
| mussels | **cozze** | **kot**-say |
| oysters | **ostriche** | **os**-tree-kay |
| shrimp | **gamberetti** | gahm-bay-**ray**-tee |
| prawns | **scampi** | **skahm**-pee |
| crab | **granchione** | grahn-keeoh-nay |
| lobster | **aragosta** | ah-rah-**goh**-stah |
| squid | **calamari** | kah-lah-**mah**-ree |
| Where did this live? | **Da dove viene questo?** | dah **doh**-vay veeay-nay **kway**-stoh |
| Just the head, please. | **Solo la testa, per favore.** | **soh**-loh lah **tehs**-tah pehr fah-**voh**-ray |

## Poultry and meat:

| | | |
|---|---|---|
| poultry | **pollame** | poh-**lah**-may |
| chicken | **pollo** | **poh**-loh |
| turkey | **tacchino** | tah-**kee**-noh |
| duck | **anatra** | **ah**-nah-trah |
| meat | **carne** | **kar**-nay |
| beef | **manzo** | **mahnd**-zoh |
| roast beef | **roast beef** | "roast beef" |
| beef steak | **bistecca di manzo** | bee-**stay**-kah dee **mahnd**-zoh |
| veal | **vitello** | vee-**tehl**-loh |
| thin-sliced veal | **scaloppine** | skah-loh-**pee**-nay |
| cutlet (veal) | **cotoletta** | koh-toh-**lay**-tah |
| pork | **maiale** | mah-**yah**-lay |
| cured ham | **prosciutto** | proh-**shoo**-toh |
| sausage | **salsiccia** | sahl-**see**-chah |
| lamb | **agnello** | ahn-**yehl**-loh |
| bunny | **coniglio** | koh-**neel**-yoh |
| brains | **cervello** | chehr-**vehl**-loh |
| sweetbreads | **animelle di vitello** | ah-nee-**mehl**-lay dee vee-**tehl**-loh |
| tongue | **lingua** | **leeng**-gwah |
| liver | **fegato** | **fay**-gah-toh |
| tripe | **trippa** | **tree**-pah |
| horse meat | **carne di cavallo** | **kar**-nay dee kah-**vah**-loh |
| How long has this been dead? | **Da quanto tempo è morto questo?** | dah **kwahn**-toh **tehm**-poh eh **mor**-toh **kway**-stoh |

EATING

## How it's prepared:

| | | |
|---|---|---|
| hot / cold | **caldo / freddo** | **kahl**-doh / **fray**-doh |
| raw / cooked | **crudo / cotto** | **kroo**-doh / **kot**-toh |
| assorted | **assortiti, misto** | ah-sor-**tee**-tee, **mee**-stoh |
| baked | **al forno** | ahl **for**-noh |
| boiled | **bollito** | boh-**lee**-toh |
| fillet | **filetto** | fee-**lay**-toh |
| fresh | **fresco** | **fray**-skoh |
| fried | **fritto** | **free**-toh |
| grilled | **alla griglia** | **ah**-lah **greel**-yah |
| homemade | **casalingo** | kah-zah-**leen**-goh |
| in cream sauce | **con panna** | kohn **pah**-nah |
| microwave | **forno a micro onde** | **for**-noh ah **mee**-kroh **ohn**-day |
| mild | **saporito** | sah-poh-**ree**-toh |
| poached | **affogato** | ah-foh-**gah**-toh |
| roasted | **arrosto** | ah-**roh**-stoh |
| sautéed | **saltato in padella** | sahl-**tah**-toh een pah-**dehl**-lah |
| smoked | **affumicato** | ah-foo-mee-**kah**-toh |
| spicy hot | **piccante** | pee-**kahn**-tay |
| steamed | **al vapore** | ahl vah-**poh**-ray |
| stuffed | **ripieno** | ree-peeay-noh |
| sweet | **dolce** | **dohl**-chay |

## Avoiding mis-steaks:

| | | |
|---|---|---|
| raw | **crudo** | **kroo**-doh |
| rare | **al sangue** | ahl **sahn**-gway |
| medium | **cotto** | **kot**-toh |
| well done | **ben cotto** | bayn **kot**-toh |
| almost burnt | **quasi bruciato** | **kwah**-zee broo-**chah**-toh |

## Veggies, beans, and rice:

| | | |
|---|---|---|
| vegetables | **legumi, verdure** | lay-**goo**-mee, vehr-**doo**-ray |
| mixed vegetables | **misto di verdure** | **mee**-stoh dee vehr-**doo**-ray |
| artichoke | **carciofo** | kar-**choh**-foh |
| asparagus | **asparagi** | ah-spah-**rah**-jee |
| beans | **fagioli** | fah-**joh**-lee |
| beets | **barbabietole** | bar-bah-beeay-**toh**-lay |
| broccoli | **broccoli** | **brok**-koh-lee |
| cabbage | **verza** | **vehrt**-sah |
| carrots | **carote** | kah-**rot**-ay |
| cauliflower | **cavolfiore** | kah-vohl-feeoh-ray |
| corn | **granturco** | grahn-**toor**-koh |
| cucumber | **cetrioli** | chay-treeoh-lee |
| eggplant | **melanzana** | may-lahnt-**sah**-nah |
| French fries | **patate fritte** | pah-**tah**-tay **free**-tay |
| garlic | **aglio** | **ahl**-yoh |
| green beans | **fagiolini** | fah-joh-**lee**-nee |
| lentils | **lenticchie** | lehn-**tee**-keeay |
| mushrooms | **funghi** | **foong**-gee |
| olives | **olive** | oh-**lee**-vay |
| onions | **cipolle** | chee-**poh**-lay |
| peas | **piselli** | pee-**zehl**-lee |
| peppers... | **peperoni...** | pay-pay-**roh**-nee |
| ...green / red | **...verdi / rossi** | **vehr**-dee / **roh**-see |
| pickles | **cetriolini** | chay-treeoh-**lee**-nee |

| potatoes | **patate** | pah-**tah**-tay |
| rice | **riso** | **ree**-zoh |
| spinach | **spinaci** | spee-**nah**-chee |
| tomatoes | **pomodori** | poh-moh-**doh**-ree |
| zucchini | **zucchine** | tsoo-**kee**-nay |

## Say cheese:

| cheese | **formaggio** | for-**mah**-joh |
| mild and soft | **fresco** | **fray**-skoh |
| sharp and hard | **stagionato** | stah-joh-**nah**-toh |
| mozzarella | **mozzarella** | moht-sah-**ray**-lah |
| small mozzarella balls | **latticini** | lah-tee-**chee**-nee |
| goat | **di capra** | dee **kah**-prah |
| sheep cheese | **pecorino** | pay-koh-**ree**-noh |
| bleu cheese | **gorgonzola** | gor-gohnd-**zoh**-lah |
| cream cheese | **formaggio** **philadelphia** | for-**mah**-joh fee-lah-**dehl**-feeah |
| Swiss cheese | **groviera,** **emmenthal** | groh-vee**ay**-rah, ehm-mehn-**tahl** |
| parmesan | **parmigiano** | par-mee-**jah**-noh |
| a soft white cheese | **Bel Paese** | behl pah-**ay**-zay |
| a tasty spreadable cheese | **stracchino** | strah-**kee**-noh |
| A little taste? | **Un assaggio?** | oon ah-**sah**-joh |

## Fruits and nuts:

| | | |
|---|---|---|
| almond | **mandorle** | mahn-**dor**-lay |
| apple | **mela** | **may**-lah |
| apricot | **albicocca** | ahl-bee-**koh**-kah |
| banana | **banana** | bah-**nah**-nah |
| berries | **frutti di bosco** | **froo**-tee dee **bos**-koh |
| canteloupe | **melone** | may-**loh**-nay |
| cherry | **ciliegia** | chee-lee**ay**-jah |
| chestnut | **castagne** | kah-**stahn**-yay |
| coconut | **noce di cocco** | **noh**-chay dee **koh**-koh |
| dates | **datteri** | **dah**-tay-ree |
| fig | **fico** | **fee**-koh |
| fruit | **frutta** | **froo**-tah |
| grapefruit | **pompelmo** | pohm-**payl**-moh |
| grapes | **uva** | **oo**-vah |
| hazelnut | **nocciola** | noh-**choh**-lah |
| lemon | **limone** | lee-**moh**-nay |
| orange | **arancia** | ah-**rahn**-chah |
| peach | **pesca** | **pehs**-kah |
| peanut | **noccioline** | noh-choh-**lee**-nay |
| pear | **pera** | **pay**-rah |
| pineapple | **ananas** | **ah**-nah-nahs |
| plum | **susina** | soo-**zee**-nah |
| prune | **prugna** | **proon**-yah |
| raspberry | **lampone** | lahm-**poh**-nay |
| strawberry | **fragola** | **frah**-goh-lah |
| tangerine | **mandarino** | mahn-dah-**ree**-noh |
| walnut | **noce** | **noh**-chay |
| watermelon | **cocomero** | koh-koh-**may**-roh |

## Just desserts:

| | | |
|---|---|---|
| dessert | **dolci** | **dohl**-chee |
| cake | **torta** | **tor**-tah |
| ice cream | **gelato** | jay-**lah**-toh |
| sherbet | **sorbetto** | sor-**bay**-toh |
| fruit cup | **coppa di frutta** | **kop**-pah dee **froo**-tah |
| tart | **tartina** | tar-**tee**-nah |
| pie | **torte** | **tor**-tay |
| whipped cream | **panna** | **pah**-nah |
| chocolate mousse | **mousse** | moos |
| pudding | **budino** | boo-**dee**-noh |
| pastry | **pasticcini** | pah-stee-**chee**-nee |
| strudel | **strudel** | **stroo**-dehl |
| cookies | **biscotti** | bee-**skot**-tee |
| candy | **caramelle** | kah-rah-**mehl**-lay |
| low calorie | **poche calorie** | **poh**-kay kah-loh-**ree**-ay |
| homemade | **casalingo** | kah-zah-**leen**-goh |
| Exquisite. | **Squisito.** | skwee-**zee**-toh |
| Sinfully good. (a sin of the throat) | **Un peccato di gola.** | oon pay-**kah**-toh dee **goh**-lah |
| So good I even licked my moustache. | **Così buono che mi sono leccato[a] anche i baffi.** | koh-**zee** bwoh-noh kay mee **soh**-noh lay-**kah**-toh **ahn**-kay ee **bah**-fee |

## Gelati talk:

| | | |
|---|---|---|
| ice cream | **gelato** | jay-**lah**-toh |
| cone | **cono** | **koh**-noh |
| cup | **coppa** | **kop**-pah |
| one scoop | **una pallina** | **oo**-nah pah-**lee**-nah |
| two scoops | **due palline** | **doo**-ay pah-**lee**-nay |
| with whipped cream | **con panna** | kohn **pah**-nah |
| A little taste? | **Un assaggio?** | oon ah-**sah**-joh |
| How many flavors can I get per scoop? | **Quanti gusti posso avere per pallina?** | **kwahn**-tee **goo**-stee **pos**-soh ah-**vay**-ray pehr pah-**lee**-nah |

## More Italian treats:

| | |
|---|---|
| **bignole con crema** | cream puffs (Florence) |
| **cassata** | ice cream, sponge cake, ricotta cheese, fruit, and pistachios (Sicily) |
| **granita** | snow-cone |
| **panforte** | dense fruit and nut cake (Siena) |
| **tartufo** | super-chocolate ice cream (Rome) |
| **tiramisú** | espresso-soaked cake with chocolate, cream, and brandy |
| **zabaglione** | delicious egg and liquor cream |
| **zuppa inglese** | rum-soaked cake with whipped cream |

# Drinking

## Water, milk, and juice:

| | | |
|---|---|---|
| mineral water... | **acqua minerale...** | **ah**-kwah mee-nay-**rah**-lay |
| ...carbonated | **...gassata** | gah-**sah**-tah |
| ...not carbonated | **...non gassata** | nohn gah-**sah**-tah |
| tap water | **acqua del rubinetto** | **ah**-kwah dayl roo-bee-**nay**-toh |
| | | |
| milk... | **latte...** | **lah**-tay |
| ...whole | **...intero** | een-**tay**-roh |
| ...skim | **...magro** | **mah**-groh |
| ...fresh | **...fresco** | **fray**-skoh |
| milk shake | **frappè** | frah-**peh** |
| orange soda | **aranciata** | ah-rahn-**chah**-tah |
| lemon soda | **limonata** | lee-moh-**nah**-tah |
| juice... | **succo...** | **soo**-koh |
| ...fruit | **...di frutta** | dee **froo**-tah |
| ...apple | **...di mela** | dee **may**-lah |
| ...orange | **...di arancia** | dee ah-**rahn**-chah |
| with / without... | **con / senza...** | kohn / **sehn**-sah |
| ...ice | **...ghiaccio** | geeah-choh |
| ...sugar | **...zucchero** | **tsoo**-kay-roh |
| glass / cup | **bicchiere / tazza** | bee-**keeay**-ray / **taht**-sah |
| bottle... | **bottiglia...** | boh-**teel**-yah |
| ...small / large | **...piccola / grande** | **pee**-koh-lah / **grahn**-day |
| Is this water safe to drink? | **È potabile quest'acqua?** | eh poh-**tah**-bee-lay kway-**stah**-kwah |

## Coffee and tea:

| | | |
|---|---|---|
| coffee... | **caffè...** | kah-**feh** |
| ...with water | **...lungo** | **loon**-goh |
| ...with a little milk | **...macchiato** | mah-keeah-toh |
| ...with milk | **...latte** | **lah**-tay |
| ...iced | **...freddo** | **fray**-doh |
| ...instant | **...solubile** | soo-**loo**-bee-lay |
| ...American-style | **...Americano** | ah-may-ree-**kah**-noh |
| coffee with foamy milk | **cappuccino** | kah-poo-**chee**-noh |
| decaffeinated | **decaffeinato, Hag** | day-kah-fay-**nah**-toh, hahg |
| black | **nero** | **nay**-roh |
| milk... | **latte...** | **lah**-tay |
| ...with a little coffee | **...macchiato** | mah-keeah-toh |
| sugar | **zucchero** | **tsoo**-kay-roh |
| hot water | **acqua calda** | **ah**-kwah **kahl**-dah |
| tea / lemon | **tè / limone** | teh / lee-**moh**-nay |
| tea bag | **bustina di tè** | boo-**stee**-nah dee teh |
| herbal tea (decaf) | **tè decaffeinato** | teh day-kah-fay-**nah**-toh |
| iced tea | **tè freddo** | teh **fray**-doh |
| small / large | **piccola / grande** | **pee**-koh-lah / **grahn**-day |
| Another cup. | **Un'altra tazza.** | oo-**nahl**-trah **taht**-sah |
| Same price if I sit or stand? | **Costa uguale al tavolo o al banco?** | **kos**-tah oo-**gwah**-lay ahl **tah**-voh-loh oh ahl **bahn**-koh |

If you ask for just plain *caffè,* you'll get espresso in a teeny tiny cup.

# Wine:

| | | |
|---|---|---|
| I would like... | **Vorrei....** | vor-**rehee** |
| We would like... | **Vorremo...** | vor-**ray**-moh |
| ...a glass | **...un bicchiere** | oon bee-keeay-ray |
| ...a quarter of a liter | **...un quarto litro** | oon **kwar**-toh **lee**-troh |
| ...a half liter | **...un mezzo litro** | oon **mehd**-zoh **lee**-troh |
| ...a carafe | **...una caraffa** | **oo**-nah kah-**rah**-fah |
| ...a half bottle | **...una mezza bottiglia** | **oo**-nah **mehd**-zah boh-**teel**-yah |
| ...a bottle | **...una bottiglia** | **oo**-nah boh-**teel**-yah |
| ...of red wine | **...di rosso** | dee **roh**-soh |
| ...of white wine | **...di bianco** | dee beeahn-koh |
| ...the wine list | **...la lista dei vini** | lah **lee**-stah **dehee vee**-nee |

## *Wine words:*

| | | |
|---|---|---|
| wine / wines | **vino / vini** | **vee**-noh / **vee**-nee |
| house wine | **vino della casa** | **vee**-noh **day**-lah **kah**-zah |
| local | **locale** | loh-**kah**-lay |
| red | **rosso** | **roh**-soh |
| white | **bianco** | beeahn-koh |
| rosé | **rosato** | roh-**zah**-toh |
| sparkling | **frizzante** | freet-**sahn**-tay |
| sweet | **dolce, abbocato** | **dohl**-chay, ah-boh-**kah**-toh |
| medium | **medio** | **may**-deeoh |
| dry | **secco** | **say**-koh |
| very dry | **molto secco** | **mohl**-toh **say**-koh |
| cork | **tappo** | **tah**-poh |

## Beer:

| | | |
|---|---|---|
| beer | **birra** | **bee**-rah |
| from the tap | **alla spina** | **ah**-lah **spee**-nah |
| bottle | **bottiglia** | boh-**teel**-yah |
| light / dark | **chiara / scura** | keeah-rah / **skoo**-rah |
| local / imported | **locale / importata** | loh-**kah**-lay / eem-por-**tah**-tah |
| small / large | **piccola / grande** | **pee**-koh-lah / **grahn**-day |
| alcohol-free | **analcolica** | ahn-ahl-**koh**-lee-kah |
| cold | **fredda** | **fray**-dah |
| colder | **più fredda** | pew **fray**-dah |

**EATING**

## Bar talk:

| | | |
|---|---|---|
| What would you like? | **Che cosa prende?** | kay **koh**-zah **prehn**-day |
| What is the local specialty? | **Qual'è la specialità locale?** | kwah-**leh** lah spay-chah-lee-**tah** loh-**kah**-lay |
| Straight. | **Liscio.** | **lee**-shoh |
| With / Without... | **Con / Senza...** | kohn / **sehn**-sah |
| ...alcohol. | **...alcool.** | **ahl**-kohl |
| ...ice. | **...ghiaccio.** | geeah-**choh** |
| One more. | **Un altro.** | oon **ahl**-troh |
| Cheers! | **Cin cin!** | cheen cheen |
| To your health! | **Salute!** | sah-**loo**-tay |
| Long life! | **Lunga vita!** | **loong**-gah **vee**-tah |
| Long live Italy! | **Viva l'Italia!** | **vee**-vah lee-**tahl**-yah |

# Picnicking

## At the market:

| | | |
|---|---|---|
| Is it self service? | **È self-service?** | eh "self-service" |
| Ripe for today? | **Per mangiare oggi?** | pehr mahn-**jah**-ray **oh**-jee |
| Does it need to be cooked? | **Bisogna cucinarlo prima di mangiarlo?** | bee-**zohn**-yah koo-chee-**nar**-loh **pree**-mah dee mahn-**jar**-loh |
| A little taste? | **Un assaggio?** | oon ah-**sah**-joh |
| Fifty grams. | **Cinquanta grammi.** | cheeng-**kwahn**-tah **grah**-mee |
| One hundred grams. | **Un etto.** | oon **eht**-toh |
| More. / Less. | **Più. / Meno.** | pew / **may**-noh |
| A piece. | **Un pezzo.** | oon **peht**-soh |
| A slice. | **Una fettina.** | **oo**-nah fay-**tee**-nah |
| Sliced. | **Tagliato a fettine.** | tahl-**yah**-toh ah fay-**tee**-nay |
| Can you make me a sandwich? | **Mi può fare un panino?** | mee pwoh **fah**-ray oon pah-**nee**-noh |
| To take out. | **Da portar via.** | dah **por**-tar **vee**-ah |
| Is there a park nearby? | **C'è un parco qui vicino?** | cheh oon **par**-koh kwee vee-**chee**-noh |
| May we picnic here? | **Va bene fare un picnic qui?** | vah **behn**-nay **fah**-ray oon **peek**-neek kwee |
| Enjoy your meal! | **Buon appetito!** | bwohn ah-pay-**tee**-toh |

## Picnic prose:

| | | |
|---|---|---|
| open air market | **mercato** | mehr-**kah**-toh |
| grocery store | **alimentari** | ah-lee-mayn-**tah**-ree |
| supermarket | **supermercato** | soo-pehr-mehr-**kah**-toh |
| picnic | **picnic** | **peek**-neek |
| sandwich or roll | **panino** | pah-**nee**-noh |
| bread | **pane** | **pah**-nay |
| cured ham | **prosciutto** | proh-**shoo**-toh |
| sausage | **salsiccia** | sahl-**see**-chah |
| cheese | **formaggio** | for-**mah**-joh |
| mustard... | **senape...** | **say**-nah-pay |
| mayonnaise... | **maionese...** | mah-yoh-**nay**-zay |
| ...in a tube | **...in tubetto** | een too-**bay**-toh |
| yogurt | **yogurt** | **yoh**-goort |
| fruit | **frutta** | **froo**-tah |
| box of juice | **cartoccio di succo di frutta** | kar-**toh**-choh dee **soo**-koh dee **froo**-tah |
| spoon / fork... | **cucchiaio / forchetta...** | koo-keeah-yoh / for-**kay**-tah |
| ...made of plastic | **...di plastica** | dee **plah**-stee-kah |
| cup / plate... | **bicchiere / piatto...** | bee-keeay-ray / peeah-toh |
| ...made of paper | **...di carta** | dee **kar**-tah |

You can shop at a lively *mercato*, sleepy *alimentari*, or industrial-size *supermercato*. Order meat and cheese by the gram. One hundred grams (what the Italians call an *etto*) is about a quarter pound, enough for two sandwiches.

# Italian-English Menu Decoder

This handy decoder won't list every word on the menu, but it'll get you *trota* (trout) instead of *trippa* (tripe).

**abbocato** sweet
**acciughe** anchovies
**aceto** vinegar
**acqua minerale** mineral water
**affogato** poached
**affumicato** smoked
**aglio** garlic
**agnello** lamb
**al forno** baked
**albicocca** apricot
**alcool** alcohol
**amatriciana** with bacon, tomato, & spices
**ananas** pineapple
**anatra** duck
**antipasti** appetizers
**aragosta** lobster
**arancia** orange
**aranciata** orange soda
**aringa** herring
**arrosto** roasted
**asparagi** asparagus
**assortiti** assorted
**bacio** chocolate hazelnut
**barbabietole** beets
**bevande** beverages
**bianco** white
**bibite** beverages

**bicchiere** glass
**birra** beer
**biscotti** cookies
**bistecca** beef steak
**bistecca Fiorentina** T-bone steak
**bollito** boiled
**bolognese** meat & tomato sauce
**bottiglia** bottle
**brioche** roll
**brodo** broth
**bruschetta** toast with tomatoes
**budino** pudding
**burro** butter
**caffè** coffee
**calamari** squid
**caldo** hot
**calzone** folded pizza
**cannelloni** large tube-shaped noodles
**cappuccino** coffee with foam
**capra** goat
**caprese** mozzarella & tomato salad
**capricciosa** chef's specialty
**caraffa** carafe
**caramelle** candy
**carbonara** with meat sauce
**carciofo** artichoke
**carne** meat

**carote** carrots
**casa** house
**casalingo** homemade
**castagne** chestnut
**cavolfiore** cauliflower
**cena** dinner
**cervello** brains
**cetrioli** cucumber
**cetriolini** pickles
**cibo** food
**ciliegia** cherry
**cinese** Chinese
**cioccolata** chocolate
**cipolle** onions
**cocomero** watermelon
**colazione** breakfast
**con** with
**coniglio** rabbit
**cono** cone
**contorni** side dishes
**coperto** cover charge
**coppa** small bowl
**coretto** coffee & firewater
**cornetto** croissant
**cotoletta** cutlet
**cotto** cooked
**cozze** mussels
**crema** vanilla
**crudo** raw
**cucina** cuisine
**cuoco** chef
**da portar via** "to go"
**datteri** dates

**del giorno** of the day
**della casa** of the house
**di** of
**digestivo** after-dinner drink
**dolce** sweet
**dolci** desserts
**e** and
**emmenthal** Swiss cheese
**entrecote** sirloin steak
**etto** one hundred grams
**fagioli** beans
**fagiolini** green beans
**farfalline** butterfly-shaped pasta
**fatto in casa** homemade
**fegato** liver
**fettina** slice
**fettucine** flat noodles
**fico** fig
**filetto** fillet
**focaccia** flat bread
**formaggio** cheese
**fragola** strawberry
**frappè** milkshake
**freddo** cold
**fresco** fresh
**frittata** omelet
**fritto** fried
**frizzante** sparkling
**frutta** fruit
**frutti di mare** seafood
**frutti di bosco** berries
**funghi** mushrooms
**gamberetti** shrimp

**gassata** carbonated
**gelatina** jelly
**gelato** Italian ice cream
**genovese** with pesto sauce
**ghiaccio** ice
**giorno** day
**gnocchi** potato noodles
**gorgonzola** bleu cheese
**granchione** crab
**grande** large
**granita** snow-cone
**granturco** corn
**grappa** firewater
**griglia** grilled
**grissini** breadsticks
**groviera** Swiss cheese
**gusti** flavors
**importata** imported
**incluso** included
**insalata** salad
**lampone** raspberry
**latte** milk
**latticini** small mozzarella balls
**lattuga** lettuce
**leggero** light
**legumi** vegetables
**limonata** lemon soda
**limone** lemon
**lingua** tongue
**locale** local
**maiale** pork
**maionese** mayonnaise
**mandarino** tangerine

**mandorle** almond
**manzo** beef
**margarina** margarine
**marmellata** jam
**mela** apple
**melanzana** eggplant
**melone** canteloupe
**menta** mint
**menù turistico** fixed-price menu
**menù del giorno** menu of the day
**mercato** open air market
**merluzzo** cod
**mezzo** half
**miele** honey
**Milanese** fried in breadcrumbs
**minerale, acqua** mineral water
**minestra** soup
**minestrone** vegetable soup
**mirtillo** blueberry
**misto** mixed
**molto** very
**nero** black
**nocciola** hazelnut
**noccioline** peanut
**noce** walnut
**noce di cocco** coconut
**non** not
**non fumatori** non-smoking
**o** or
**olio** oil
**olive** olives
**omelette** omelet
**ostriche** oysters

pallina   scoop
pancetta   thick bacon
pane   bread
panforte   fruitcake
panino   roll, sandwich
panna   cream, whipped cream
parmigiano   parmesan cheese
pasticcini   pastry
pastina   noodles
patate   potatoes
patate fritte   French fries
penne   tube-shaped noodles
pepe   pepper
peperoni   bell peppers
pera   pear
percorino   sheep cheese
pesca   peach
pesce   fish
pezzo   piece
piatto   plate
picante   spicy hot
piccolo   small
piselli   peas
pistacchio   pistachio
polenta   moist cornmeal
pollame   poultry
pollo   chicken
pomodori   tomatoes
pompelmo   grapefruit
pranzo   lunch
prima colazione   breakfast
primo piatto   first course
prosciutto   cured ham

prugna   prune
quattro   four
ribollita   hearty cabbage soup
rigatone   tube-shaped noodles
ripieno   stuffed
riso   rice
risotto   saffron-flavored rice
ristorante   restaurant
rosato   rosé
rosso   red
rosticceria   deli
rotelline   wheel-shaped pasta
salame   pork sausage
salamino piccante   pepperoni
sale   salt
salmone   salmon
salsiccia   sausage
saporito   mild
sarde   sardines
scaloppine   thin-sliced veal
scampi   prawns
secco   dry
secondo piatto   second course
senape   mustard
senza   without
servizio   service charge
servizio incluso   service included
servizio non incluso   service not
   included
sogliola   sole
sorbetto   sherbet
specialità   speciality
spinaci   spinach

**spremuta** freshly-squeezed juice
**spuntino** snack
**stagioni** seasons (& pizza toppings)
**stracchino** spreadable cheese
**stracciatella** chocolate chips with vanilla
**strapazzate** scrambled
**stufato** stew
**succo** juice
**sugo** sauce, usually tomato
**susina** plum
**tacchino** turkey
**tagliatelle** flat noodles
**tartina** tart
**tartufo** super-chocolate ice cream
**tavola calda** fast food
**tavolo** table
**tazza** cup
**tè** tea
**tonno** tuna

**torta** cake
**torte** pie
**tortellini** stuffed noodles
**tovagliolo** napkin
**tramezzini** crustless sandwiches
**trippa** tripe
**trota** trout
**uova** eggs
**uva** grapes
**vegetariano** vegetarian
**veloce** fast
**verde** green
**verdure** vegetables
**verza** cabbage
**vino** wine
**vitello** veal
**vongole** clams
**yogurt** yoghurt
**zucchero** sugar
**zuppa** soup

# Sightseeing

| Where is...? | Dov'è...? | doh-**veh** |
|---|---|---|
| ...the best view | ...la vista più bella | lah **vee**-stah pew **behl**-lah |
| ...the main square | ...la piazza principale | lah peeaht-sah preen-chee-**pah**-lay |
| ...the old town center | ...il centro storico | eel **chehn**-troh **stoh**-ree-koh |
| ...the museum | ...il museo | eel moo-**zay**-oh |
| ...the castle | ...il castello | eel kah-**stehl**-loh |
| ...the palace | ...il palazzo | eel pah-**laht**-soh |
| ...the ruins | ...le rovine | lay roh-**vee**-nay |
| ...a festival | ...un festival | oon **fehs**-tee-vahl |
| ...tourist information | ...informazioni per turisti | een-for-maht-seeoh-nee pehr too-ree-stee |
| Do you have...? | Avete...? | ah-**vay**-tay |
| ...a map | ...una cartina | **oo**-nah kar-**tee**-nah |
| ...information | ...informazioni | een-for-maht-seeoh-nee |
| ...a guidebook | ...una guida | **oo**-nah **gwee**-dah |
| ...a tour | ...una gita | **oo**-nah **jee**-tah |
| ...in English | ...in inglese | een een-**glay**-zay |
| When is the next tour? | Quando è la prossima gita? | **kwahn**-doh eh lah **pros**-see-mah **jee**-tah |
| Is it free? | È gratis? | eh **grah**-tees |
| How much is it? | Quanto costa? | **kwahn**-toh **kos**-tah |
| Any discount for...? | Fate sconti per...? | **fah**-tay **skohn**-tee pehr |
| ...youth | ...giovani | joh-**vah**-nee |
| ...students | ...studenti | stoo-**dehn**-tee |
| ...seniors | ...anziani | ahnt-seeah-nee |

# Shopping

## Names of Italian shops:

| | | |
|---|---|---|
| antiques | **antiquario** | ahn-tee-**kwah**-reeoh |
| bakery | **panificio** | pah-nee-**fee**-choh |
| barber shop | **barbiere** | bar-beeay-ray |
| beauty salon | **parrucchiere** | pah-roo-keeay-ray |
| book shop | **libreria** | lee-bray-**ree**-ah |
| camera shop | **foto-ottica** | foh-toh-**ot**-tee-kah |
| department store | **grande magazzino** | **grahn**-day mah-gahd-**zee**-noh |
| flea market | **mercato delle pulci** | mehr-**kah**-toh **day**-lay **pool**-chee |
| flower market | **fiorista** | fee-oh-**ree**-stah |
| grocery store | **alimentari** | ah-lee-mayn-**tah**-ree |
| jewelry shop | **gioielliere** | joh-yay-leeay-ray |
| laundromat | **lavanderia** | lah-vahn-day-**ree**-ah |
| newsstand | **giornalaio** | jor-nah-**lah**-yoh |
| open air market | **mercato** | mehr-**kah**-toh |
| optician | **ottico** | **ot**-tee-koh |
| pharmacy | **farmacia** | far-mah-**chee**-ah |
| supermarket | **supermercato** | soo-pehr-mehr-**kah**-toh |
| toy store | **negozio di giocattoli** | nay-**goht**-seeoh dee joh-**kah**-toh-lee |
| travel agency | **agenzia di viaggi** | ah-jehnt-**see**-ah dee veeah-jee |

## Shop till you drop:

| | | |
|---|---|---|
| sale | **saldo** | **sahl**-doh |
| How much is it? | **Quanto costa?** | **kwahn**-toh **kos**-tah |
| I'm / We're... | **Sto / Stiamo...** | stoh / steeah-moh |
| ...just browsing. | **...solo guardando.** | **soh**-loh gwar-**dahn**-doh |
| I'd like... | **Vorrei...** | vor-**rehee** |
| Do you have...? | **Avete...?** | ah-**vay**-tay |
| ...something cheaper | **...qualcosa di meno caro** | kwahl-**koh**-zah dee **may**-noh kah-roh |
| Can I see more? | **Posso vederne ancora?** | **pos**-soh vay-**dehr**-nay ahn-**koh**-rah |
| Can I try it on? | **Lo posso provare?** | loh **pos**-soh proh-**vah**-ray |
| A mirror? | **Ha uno specchio?** | ah **oo**-noh **spay**-keeoh |
| Too... | **Troppo...** | **trop**-poh |
| ...big. | **...grande.** | **grahn**-day |
| ...small. | **...piccolo.** | **pee**-koh-loh |
| ...expensive. | **...caro.** | **kah**-roh |
| I'll think about it. | **Ci penserò.** | chee pehn-say-**roh** |
| Is that your final price? | **È questo il prezzo finale?** | eh **kway**-stoh eel **preht**-soh fee-**nah**-lay |
| My last offer. | **La mia ultima offerta.** | lah **mee**-ah **ool**-tee-mah oh-**fehr**-tah |
| I'm nearly broke. | **Sono quasi al verde.** | **soh**-noh **kwah**-zee ahl **vehr**-day |

Most businesses close daily from 13:00 until 15:00 or 16:00.

# Entertainment

| | | |
|---|---|---|
| What's happening tonight? | **Che cosa succede stasera?** | kay **koh**-zah soo-**chay**-day stah-**zay**-rah |
| What do you recommend? | **Che cosa raccomanda?** | kay **koh**-zah rah-koh-**mahn**-dah |
| Is it free? | **È gratis?** | eh **grah**-tees |
| Where can I buy a ticket? | **Dove si comprano i biglietti?** | **doh**-vay see kohm-**prah**-noh ee beel-**yay**-tee |
| When does it start? | **A che ora comincia?** | ah kay **oh**-rah koh-**meen**-chah |
| When does it end? | **A che ora finisce?** | ah kay **oh**-rah fee-**nee**-shay |

## What's happening:

| | | |
|---|---|---|
| movie... | **cinema...** | **chee**-nay-mah |
| ...original version | **...versione originale** | vehr-seeoh-nay oh-ree-jee-**nah**-lay |
| ...in English | **...in inglese** | een een-**glay**-zay |
| ...with subtitles | **...con sottotitoli** | kohn soh-toh-**tee**-toh-lee |
| music... | **musica...** | **moo**-zee-kah |
| ...live | **...dal vivo** | dahl **vee**-voh |
| ...classical | **...classica** | **klah**-see-kah |
| ...folk | **...folk** | fohlk |
| old rock | **rock vecchio stile** | rok **vehk**-eeoh **stee**-lay |
| jazz / blues | **jazz / blues** | jahzz / "blues" |
| concert | **concerto** | kohn-**chehr**-toh |
| dancing | **ballare** | bah-**lah**-ray |
| no cover charge | **ingresso libero** | een-**gray**-soh **lee**-bay-roh |

# Phoning

| | | |
|---|---|---|
| Where is the nearest phone? | **Dov'è il telefono più vicino?** | doh-**veh** eel tay-**lay**-foh-noh pew vee-**chee**-noh |
| I'd like to telephone... | **Vorrei fare una telefonata...** | vor-**rehee** fah-ray **oo**-nah tay-lay-foh-**nah**-tah |
| ...the United States. | **...negli Stati Uniti.** | **nayl**-yee **stah**-tee oo-**nee**-tee |
| How much per minute? | **Quanto costa al minuto?** | **kwahn**-toh **kos**-tah ahl mee-**noo**-toh |
| I'd like to make a... call. | **Vorrei fare una telefonata...** | vor-**rehee** fah-ray **oo**-nah tay-lay-foh-**nah**-tah |
| ...local | **...urbana.** | oor-**bah**-nah |
| ...collect | **...a carico dell'utente.** | ah **kah**-ree-koh day-loo-**tehn**-tay |
| ...credit card | **...con la carta di credito.** | kohn lah **kar**-tah dee **kray**-dee-toh |
| ...long distance (within Italy) | **...interurbana.** | een-tay-roor-**bah**-nah |
| ...international | **...internazionale.** | een-tehr-naht-seeoh-**nah**-lay |
| It doesn't work. | **Non funziona.** | nohn foont-seeoh-nah |
| May I use your phone? | **Posso usare il telefono?** | **pos**-soh oo-**zah**-ray eel tay-**lay**-foh-noh |
| Can you dial for me? | **Può fare il numero per me?** | pwoh fah-ray eel **noo**-may-roh pehr may |
| Can you talk for me? | **Può parlare per me?** | pwoh par-**lah**-ray pehr may |
| It's busy. | **È occupato.** | eh oh-koo-**pah**-toh |
| Will you try again? | **Può riprovare?** | pwoh ree-proh-**vah**-ray |

| Hello. (on phone) | **Pronto.** | **pron**-toh |
| My name is... | **Mi chiamo...** | mee keeah-moh |
| My number is... | **Il mio numero è...** | eel mee-oh noo-may-roh eh |
| Speak slowly. | **Parli lentamente.** | **par**-lee layn-tah-**mayn**-tay |
| Wait a moment. | **Un momento.** | oon moh-**mayn**-toh |
| Don't hang up. | **Non agganci.** | nohn ah-**gahn**-chee |

## Key telephone words:

| telephone | **telefono** | tay-**lay**-foh-noh |
| telephone card | **carta telefonica** | **kar**-tah tay-lay-**foh**-nee-kah |
| operator | **centralinista** | chayn-trah-lee-**nee**-stah |
| international assistance | **assistenza per chiamate internazionali** | ah-see-**stehnt**-sah pehr keeah-**mah**-tay een-tehr-naht-seeoh-**nah**-lee |
| country code | **prefisso per il paese** | pray-**fee**-soh pehr eel pah-**ay**-zay |
| area code | **prefisso** | pray-**fee**-soh |
| telephone book | **elenco telefonico** | ay-**lehn**-koh tay-lay-**foh**-nee-koh |
| out of service | **guasto** | gooah-stoh |

Instead of using coins to make your calls, try a handy *carta telefonica* (telephone card), available at post offices, train stations, *tabaccheria* (tobacco shops), and machines near phone booths. For more tips, see "Let's Talk Telephones" later in this book.

# Mailing

| Where is the post office? | **Dov'è la Posta?** | doh-**veh** lah **poh**-stah |
| Which window for...? | **Qual'è lo sportello per...?** | kwah-**leh** loh spor-**tehl**-loh pehr |
| ...stamps | **...francobolli** | frahn-koh-**boh**-lee |
| ...packages | **...pacchi** | **pah**-kee |
| To the United States... | **Per Stati Uniti...** | pehr **stah**-tee oo-**nee**-tee |
| ...by air mail. | **...per via aerea.** | pehr **vee**-ah ah-**ay**-ray-ah |
| ...slow and cheap. | **...lento e economico.** | **lehn**-toh ay ay-koh-**noh**-mee-koh |

## Licking the postal code:

| post office | **ufficio postale** | oo-**fee**-choh poh-**stah**-lay |
| stamp | **francobollo** | frahn-koh-**boh**-loh |
| postcard | **cartolina** | kar-toh-**lee**-nah |
| letter | **lettera** | **leht**-tay-rah |
| envelope | **busta** | **boo**-stah |
| package | **pacco** | **pah**-koh |
| box | **scatola** | **skah**-toh-lah |
| string | **filo** | **fee**-loh |
| tape | **cassetta** | kah-**say**-tah |
| mailbox | **cassetta postale** | kah-**say**-tah poh-**stah**-lay |
| air mail | **via aerea** | **vee**-ah ah-**ay**-ray-ah |
| book rate | **prezzo di listino** | **preht**-soh dee lee-**stee**-noh |

# Help!

| | | |
|---|---|---|
| Help! | **Aiuto!** | ah-**yoo**-toh |
| Help me! | **Aiutatemi!** | ah-yoo-**tah**-tay-mee |
| Call a doctor! | **Chiamate un dottore!** | keeah-**mah**-tay oon doh-**toh**-ray |
| ambulance | **ambulanza** | ahm-boo-**lahnt**-sah |
| accident | **incidente** | een-chee-**dehn**-tay |
| injured | **ferito** | fay-**ree**-toh |
| emergency | **emergenza** | ay-mehr-**jehnt**-sah |
| fire | **fuoco** | **fwoh**-koh |
| police | **polizia** | poh-leet-**see**-ah |
| thief | **ladro** | **lah**-droh |
| pick-pocket | **borsaiolo** | bor-sah-**yoh**-loh |
| I've been ripped off. | **Sono stato[a] imbrogliato[a].** | **soh**-noh **stah**-toh eem-brohl-**yah**-toh |
| I've lost my... | **Ho perso il mio...** | oh **pehr**-soh eel **mee**-oh |
| ...passport. | **...passaporto.** | pah-sah-**por**-toh |
| ...ticket. | **...biglietto.** | beel-**yay**-toh |
| ...baggage. | **...bagaglio.** | bah-**gahl**-yoh |
| ...wallet. | **...portafoglio.** | por-tah-**fohl**-yoh |
| I've lost... | **Ho perso...** | oh **pehr**-soh |
| ...my purse. | **...la mia borsa.** | la **mee**-ah **bor**-sah |
| ...my faith in humankind. | **...la fiducia nel prossimo.** | lah fee-**doo**-chah nayl **pros**-see-moh |
| I'm lost. | **Mi sono perso[a].** | mee **soh**-noh **pehr**-soh |

## Help for women:

| Leave me alone. | Mi lasci in pace. | mee **lah**-shee een **pah**-chay |
| *I vant to be alone.* | Voglio stare sola. | **vohl**-yoh **stah**-ray **soh**-lah |
| I'm not interested. | **Non sono interessata.** | nohn **soh**-noh een-tay-ray-**sah**-tah |
| I'm married. | **Sono sposata.** | **soh**-noh spoh-**zah**-tah |
| I'm a lesbian. | **Sono lesbica.** | **soh**-noh **lehz**-bee-kah |
| I have a contagious disease. | **Ho una malattia contagiosa.** | oh **oo**-nah mah-lah-**tee**-ah kohn-tah-**joh**-zah |
| Don't touch me. | **Non mi tocchi.** | nohn mee **toh**-kee |
| You're disgusting. | **Tu sei disgustoso.** | too **seh**ee dees-goo-**stoh**-zoh |
| Stop following me. | **La smetta di seguirmi.** | lah **zmay**-tah dee **say**-gweer-mee |
| This man is bothering me. | **Questo uomo mi importuna.** | **kway**-stoh **woh**-moh mee eem-por-**too**-nah |
| Enough! | **Basta!** | **bah**-stah |
| Get lost! | **Sparisca!** | spah-**ree**-skah |
| Drop dead! | **Crepi!** | **kray**-pee |
| I'll call the police. | **Chiamo la polizia.** | **kee**ah-moh lah poh-leet-**see**-ah |

Whenever macho males threaten to make leering a contact sport, local women stroll arm-in-arm or holding hands. Wearing conservative clothes and avoiding smiley eye contact also convey a "don't hustle me" message.

# Health

| I feel sick. | Mi sento male. | mee **sehn**-toh **mah**-lay |
| I need a doctor... | Ho bisogno di un dottore... | oh bee-**zohn**-yoh dee oon doh-**toh**-ray |
| ...who speaks English. | ...che parli inglese. | kay **par**-lee een-**glay**-zay |
| It hurts here. | Fa male qui. | fah **mah**-lay kwee |
| I'm allergic to... | Sono allergico[a]... | **soh**-noh ah-**lehr**-jee-koh |
| ...penicillin. | ...alla penicillina. | **ah**-lah pay-nee-chee-**lee**-nah |
| I am diabetic. | Ho il diabete. | oh eel deeah-**bay**-tay |
| I've missed a period. | Ha saltato il ciclo mestruale. | ah sahl-**tah**-toh eel **chee**-kloh may-stroo-**ah**-lay |
| I have... | Ho... | oh |
| ...a burn. | ...un bruciatura. | oon broo-chah-**too**-rah |
| ...chest pains. | ...dolore al petto. | doh-**loh**-ray ahl **peht**-toh |
| ...a cold. | ...un raffreddore. | oon rah-fray-**doh**-ray |
| ...constipation. | ...stitichezza. | stee-tee-**kayt**-sah |
| ...a cough. | ...la tosse. | lah **tos**-say |
| ...diarrhea. | ...diarrea. | dee-ah-**ray**-ah |
| ...a fever. | ...la febbre. | lah **fehb**-bray |
| ...the flu. | ...l'influenza. | leen-floo-**ehnt**-sah |
| ...the giggles. | ...la ridarella. | lah ree-dah-**ray**-lah |
| ...a headache. | ...il mal di testa. | eel mahl dee **tehs**-tah |
| ...hemorrhoids. | ...le emorroidi. | lay ay-moh-rohee-dee |
| ...indigestion. | ...indigestione. | een-dee-jay-steeoh-nay |
| ...an infection. | ...una infezione. | **oo**-nah een-fay-tseeoh-nay |

| ...nausea. | ...nausea. | **now**-zee-ah |
| ...a rash. | ...infiammazione. | een-feeah-maht-see**oh**-nay |
| ...a sore throat. | ...gola infiammata. | **goh**-lah een-feeah-**mah**-tah |
| ...a stomach ache. | ...il mal di stomaco. | eel mahl dee **stom**-ah-koh |
| ...swelling. | ...un gonfiore. | oon gohn-fee**oh**-ray |
| ...a toothache. | ...mal di denti. | mahl dee **dehn**-tee |
| ...worms. | ...vermi. | **vehr**-mee |
| I have body odor. | Io puzzo. | ee**oh** **poot**-soh |
| Is it serious? | È grave? | eh **grah**-vay |

## Handy health words:

| doctor | dottore | doh-**toh**-ray |
| dentist | dentista | dayn-**tee**-stah |
| health insurance | assicurazione medica | ah-see-koo-raht-see**oh**-nay **mehd**-ee-kah |
| hospital | ospedale | oh-spay-**dah**-lay |
| pharmacy | farmacia | far-mah-**chee**-ah |
| bandage | cerotti | chay-**rot**-tee |
| aspirin | aspirina | ah-spee-**ree**-nah |
| non-aspirin substitute | Saridon | **sah**-ree-dohn |
| cough drops | sciroppo per la tosse | skee-**roh**-poh pehr lah **tos**-say |
| medicine... | medicina... | may-dee-**chee**-nah |
| ...for a cold | ...per il raffreddore | pehr eel rah-fray-**doh**-ray |
| ...for pain | ...per il dolore | pehr eel doh-**loh**-ray |
| antibiotic | antibiotici | ahn-tee-bee**oh**-tee-chee |
| prescription | prescrizione | pray-skreet-see**oh**-nay |

HEALTH

# Chatting

| | | |
|---|---|---|
| My name is... | **Mi chiamo...** | mee keeah-moh |
| What's your name? | **Come si chiama?** | koh-may see keeah-mah |
| Where are you from? | **Di dove è?** | dee doh-vay eh |
| I'm... | **Sono...** | soh-noh |
| ...American. | **...Americano[a].** | ah-may-ree-kah-noh |
| ...Canadian. | **...Canadese.** | kah-nah-day-zay |
| I'm... years old. | **Ho... anni.** | oh... ahn-nee |
| How old are you? | **Quanti anni ha?** | kwahn-tee ahn-nee ah |
| I'm rich and single. | **Sono ricco[a]** | soh-noh ree-koh |
| | **e singolo[a].** | ay seeng-goh-loh |
| I'm married. | **Sono sposato[a].** | soh-noh spoh-zah-toh |
| Are you married? | **È sposata?** | eh spoh-zah-tah |
| (asked of a woman) | | |
| Are you married? | **È sposato?** | eh spoh-zah-toh |
| (asked of a man) | | |
| Do you have children? | **Ha bambini?** | ah bahm-bee-nee |

## The right thing to say:

| | | |
|---|---|---|
| Beautiful child! | **Bel bambino!** | behl bahm-bee-noh |
| Beautiful children! | **Bei bambini!** | behee bahm-bee-nee |
| Great! | **Ottimo!** | ot-tee-moh |
| Well done! | **Bravo[a]!** | brah-voh |
| Congratulations! | **Congratulazioni!** | kohn-grah-too-laht-seeoh-nee |
| You're welcome. | **Prego.** | pray-goh |
| Bless you! (sneeze) | **Salute!** | sah-loo-tay |
| Excuse me. | **Mi scusi.** | mee skoo-zee |

## Travel talk:

| | | |
|---|---|---|
| I am / Are you...? | Sono / È...? | **soh**-noh / eh |
| ...on vacation | ...in vacanza | een vah-**kahnt**-sah |
| ...on business | ...qui per lavoro | kwee pehr lah-**voh**-roh |
| How long have you been traveling? | Da quanto tempo è in viaggio? | dah **kwahn**-toh **tehm**-poh eh een veeah-joh |
| day / week | giorno / settimana | **jor**-noh / say-tee-**mah**-nah |
| month / year | mese / anno | **may**-zay / **ahn**-noh |
| Where are you going? | Dove va? | **doh**-vay vah |
| Where have you traveled? | Dove è stato[a]? | **doh**-vay eh **stah**-toh |
| Where would you like to go? | Dove vorrebbe andare? | **doh**-vay voh-**ray**-bay ahn-**dah**-ray |
| When are you going home? | Quando ritorna a casa? | **kwahn**-doh ree-**tor**-nah ah **kah**-zah |
| I've traveled to... | Sono stato[a] a... | **soh**-noh **stah**-toh ah |
| Next I'll go to... | Poi andrò a... | pohee ahn-**droh** ah |
| This is my first time in... | Questa è la mia prima volta in... | **kway**-stah eh lah **mee**-ah **pree**-mah **vohl**-tah een |
| I'm happy here. | Sono felice qui. | **soh**-noh fay-**lee**-chay kwee |
| The Italians are friendly. | Gli italiani sono amichevoli. | leeyee ee-tah-leeah-nee **soh**-noh ah-mee-kay-**voh**-lee |
| Italy is fantastic. | L'Italia è fantastica. | lee-**tahl**-yah eh fahn-**tah**-stee-koh |
| Have a good trip! | Buon viaggio! | bwohn veeah-joh |

## Profanity & other animal noises:
What the more colorful locals are saying...

| | | |
|---|---|---|
| Damn it. | **Dannazione.** | dah-naht-see**oh**-nay |
| Screw it. | **Vai a fa'n culo.** | **vah**ee ah fahn **koo**-loh |
| Stick it between your teeth. | **Ficcatelo tra i denti.** | fee-kah-**tay**-loh trah ee **dayn**-tee |
| Go to hell. | **Vai al diavolo.** | **vah**ee ahl deeah-voh-loh |
| bastard / bitch | **bastardo / cagna** | bah-**star**-doh / **kahn**-yah |
| breasts (colloq.) | **seno** | **say**-noh |
| penis (colloq.) | **cazzo** | **kaht**-soh |
| butthole | **stronzo** | **stront**-soh |
| shit | **merda** | **mehr**-dah |
| idiot | **idiota** | ee-dee**oh**-tah |
| jerk | **imbecille** | eem-bay-**chee**-lay |
| Did someone...? | **Ma qualcuno ha fatto...?** | mah kwahl-**koo**-noh ah **fah**-toh |
| ...burp | **...un rutto** | oon **roo**-toh |
| ...fart | **...una scoreggia** | **oo**-nah skoh-**ray**-jah |

## *Conversing with Italian animals:*

| | | |
|---|---|---|
| rooster / cock-a-doodle-doo | **gallo / chicchirichì** | **gah**-loh / kee-kee-ree-**kee** |
| bird / tweet tweet | **uccello / cip cip** | oo-**chehl**-loh / cheep cheep |
| cat / meow | **gatto / miao** | **gah**-toh / **mee**-ow |
| dog / bark bark | **cane / bau bau** | **kah**-nay / bow bow |
| duck / quack quack | **oca / quac quac** | **oh**-kah / kwahk kwahk |
| cow / moo | **mucca / muu** | **moo**-kah / moo |
| pig / oink oink | **maiale / oinc oinc** | mah-**yah**-lay / oynk oynk |

# GERMAN

A map of Germany showing cities and surrounding countries. Inset map shows location within Europe. Scale: 0 KM 100 200, 0 MI 100.

Countries and regions labeled: DENMARK, COPE., BALTIC SEA, KIEL, LÜBECK, ROSTOCK, NORTH SEA, HAMBURG, NETH., BREMEN, ELBE R., POLAND, AMSTERDAM, HANNOVER, POTSDAM, BERLIN, RHINE, GERMANY, DUSSELDORF, KÖLN, BONN, MARBURG, LEIPZIG, DRESDEN, AACHEN, WEIMAR, BELG., KOBLENZ, FRANKFURT, LUX., MOSEL, RHINE, WÜRZBURG, BAYREUTH, PRAGUE, MAINZ, HEIDEL-BERG, NÜRNBERG, CZECH REP., TRIER, FRANCE, BADEN-BADEN, ROTHENBURG, STRASBOURG, STUTTGART, PASSAU, COLMAR, BLACK FOREST, BAVARIA, MUNICH, DANUBE R., FREI-BURG, LINDAU, FÜSSEN, SALZBURG, AUST., BASEL, LAKE CONSTANCE, REHTE, BERCHTES-GADEN, SWITZ., INNSBRUCK

DCH

# Getting Started

## Versatile, entertaining German

...is spoken throughout Germany, Austria, and most of Switzerland. In addition, German rivals English as the handiest second language in Scandinavia, the Netherlands, Eastern Europe, and Turkey.

German is kind of a "lego language." Be on the lookout for fun combination words. A *Fingerhut* (finger hat) is a thimble, a *Halbinsel* (half island) is a peninsula, a *Stinktier* (stinky animal) is a skunk, and a *Dummkopf* (dumb head) is . . . um . . . uh . . .

German has some key twists to its pronunciation:

*CH* sounds like the guttural CH in Scottish loch.
*J* sounds like Y in yes.
*S* can sound like S in sun or Z in zoo.
   But *S* followed by *CH* sounds like SH in shine.
*V* sounds like F in fun.
*W* sounds like V in volt.
*Z* sounds like TS in hits.
*EI* sounds like I in light.
*EU* sounds like OY in joy.
*IE* sounds like EE in seed.

German has a few unusual signs and sounds. The letter *ß* is not a letter B at all—it's the sound of "ss." Some of the German vowels are double-dotted with an "umlaut." The *ü* has a sound uncommon in English. To make the *ü* sound, round your lips to say "o," but say "ee." The German *ch* has a clearing-your-throat sound. Say *Achtung!*

Here's a guide to the phonetics we've used in the German section of this book:

| | |
|---|---|
| ah | like A in father. |
| ay | like AY in play. |
| e, eh | like E in let. |
| ee | like EE in seed. |
| ehr | sounds like "air." |
| ew | pucker your lips and say "ee." |
| g | like G in go. |
| i | like I in bit. |
| ī | like I in light. |
| kh | like the guttural CH in Scottish loch. |
| o | like O in cost. |
| oh | like O in note. |
| oo | like OO in too. |
| ow | like OW in cow. |
| oy | like OY in joy. |
| ts | like TS in hits. It's a small explosive sound. |
| u | like U in put. |
| ur | like UR in purr. |

Each German-speaking country has a distinct dialect. The multilingual Swiss greet you with a cheery *"Gruetzi,"* use *"Merci"* for thank you, and say goodbye with a *"Ciao."* Austrians and Bavarians greet one another with *"Grüss Gott"* (May God greet you).

# German Basics

## Meeting and greeting Germans:

| | | |
|---|---|---|
| Good day. | **Guten Tag.** | **goo**-ten tahg |
| Good morning. | **Guten Morgen.** | **goo**-ten **mor**-gen |
| Good evening. | **Guten Abend.** | **goo**-ten **ah**-bent |
| Good night. | **Gute Nacht.** | **goo**-teh nahkht |
| Hi. (informal) | **Hallo.** | **hah**-loh |
| Welcome! | **Willkommen!** | vil-**kom**-men |
| Mr. / Mrs. / Miss | **Herr / Frau / Fräulein** | hehr / frow / **froy**-līn |
| How are you? | **Wie geht's?** | vee gayts |
| Very well, thanks. | **Sehr gut, danke.** | zehr goot **dahng**-keh |
| And you? | **Und Ihnen?** | oont **ee**-nen |
| My name is... | **Ich heiße...** | ikh **hī**-seh |
| What's your name? | **Wie heißen Sie?** | vee **hī**-sen zee |
| Pleased to meet you. | **Sehr erfreut.** | zehr ehr-**froyt** |
| Where are you from? | **Woher kommen Sie?** | **voh**-hehr **kom**-men zee |
| I am / Are you...? | **Ich bin / Sind Sie...?** | ikh bin / zint zee |
| ...on vacation | **...auf Urlaub** | owf **oor**-lowp |
| Are you working today? | **Arbeiten Sie heute?** | ar-**bīt**-en zee **hoy**-teh |
| See you later! | **Bis später!** | bis **shpay**-ter |
| So long! (informal) | **Tschüss!** | chewss |
| Goodbye. | **Auf Wiedersehen.** | owf **vee**-der-zayn |
| Good luck! | **Viel Glück!** | feel glewk |
| Have a good trip! | **Gute Reise!** | **goo**-teh **rī**-zeh |

## Survival Phrases

Patton made it all the way to Berlin by using only these phrases. They're repeated on your tear-out "cheat sheet" near the end of this book.

## The essentials:

| | | |
|---|---|---|
| Good day. | **Guten Tag.** | **goo**-ten tahg |
| Do you speak English? | **Sprechen Sie Englisch?** | **shprekh**-en zee **eng**-lish |
| Yes. / No. | **Ja. / Nein.** | yah / nīn |
| I don't speak German. | **Ich spreche kein Deutsch.** | ikh **shprekh**-eh kīn doych |
| I'm sorry. | **Entschuldigung.** | ent-**shool**-dee-goong |
| Please. | **Bitte.** | **bit**-teh |
| Thank you. | **Danke.** | **dahng**-keh |
| No problem. | **Kein Problem.** | kīn proh-**blaym** |
| Very good. | **Sehr gut.** | zehr goot |
| You are very kind. | **Sie sind sehr freundlich.** | zee zint zehr **froynd**-likh |
| Goodbye. | **Auf Wiedersehen.** | owf **vee**-der-zayn |

Please is a magic word in any language. If you want something and you don't know the word for it, just point and say, *"Bitte"* (Please). If you know the word for what you want, such as the bill, simply say, *"Rechnung, bitte"* (Bill, please).

## Where?

| Where is...? | Wo ist...? | voh ist |
|---|---|---|
| ...a hotel | ...ein Hotel | īn hoh-**tel** |
| ...a youth hostel | ...eine Jugend-herberge | ī-neh **yoo**-gend-hehr-behr-geh |
| ...a restaurant | ...ein Restaurant | īn res-tow-**rahnt** |
| ...a supermarket | ...ein Supermarkt | īn **zoo**-per-markt |
| ...a pharmacy | ...eine Apotheke | ī-neh ah-poh-**tay**-keh |
| ...a bank | ...eine Bank | ī-neh bahnk |
| ...the train station | ...der Bahnhof | dehr **bahn**-hohf |
| ...the tourist information office | ...das Touristen-informationsbüro | dahs **too**-ris-ten-in-for-maht-see-**ohns**-bew-roh |
| ...the toilet | ...die Toilette | dee toh-**leh**-teh |
| men / women | Herren / Damen | **hehr**-ren / **dah**-men |

## How much?

| How much is it? | Wieviel kostet das? | vee-**feel kos**-tet dahs |
|---|---|---|
| Write it? | Schreiben? | **shrī**-ben |
| Cheap / Cheaper / Cheapest. | Billig / Billiger / Am Billigsten. | **bil**-lig / **bil**-lig-er / ahm **bil**-lig-sten |
| Is it free? | Ist es umsonst? | ist es oom-**zohnst** |
| Included? | Eingeschlossen? | **īn**-geh-shlos-sen |
| Do you have...? | Haben Sie...? | **hah**-ben zee |
| I would like... | Ich hätte gern... | ikh **het**-teh gehrn |

| We would like... | **Wir hätten gern...** | veer **het**-ten gehrn |
| ...this. | **...dies.** | deez |
| ...just a little. | **...nur ein bißchen.** | noor īn **bis**-yen |
| ...more. | **...mehr.** | mehr |
| ...a ticket. | **...ein Karte.** | īn **kar**-teh |
| ...a room. | **...ein Zimmer.** | īn **tsim**-mer |
| ...the bill. | **...die Rechnung.** | dee **rekh**-noong |

## How many?

| one | **eins** | īns |
| two | **zwei** | tsvī |
| three | **drei** | drī |
| four | **vier** | feer |
| five | **fünf** | fewnf |
| six | **sechs** | zex |
| seven | **sieben** | **zee**-ben |
| eight | **acht** | ahkht |
| nine | **neun** | noyn |
| ten | **zehn** | tsayn |

## When?

| At what time? | **Um wieviel Uhr?** | oom vee-**feel** oor |
| Just a moment. | **Moment.** | moh-**ment** |
| now / soon / later | **jetzt / bald / später** | yetzt / bahld / **shpay**-ter |
| today / tomorrow | **heute / morgen** | **hoy**-teh / **mor**-gen |

Have fun! Mix and match these survival phrases to say:
"Two, please," or "No, thank you," or "I'd like a cheap
hotel," or "Cheaper, please?"

## Struggling with German:

| | | |
|---|---|---|
| Do you speak English? | **Sprechen Sie Englisch?** | shprekh-en zee eng-lish |
| A teeny weeny bit? | **Ein ganz klein bißchen?** | īn gahnts klīn bis-yen |
| Please speak English. | **Bitte sprechen Sie Englisch.** | bit-teh shprekh-en zee eng-lish |
| You speak English well. | **Ihr Englisch ist sehr gut.** | eer eng-lish ist zehr goot |
| I don't speak German. | **Ich spreche kein Deutsch.** | ikh shprekh-eh kīn doych |
| I speak a little German. | **Ich spreche ein bißchen Deutsch.** | ikh shprekh-eh īn bis-yen doych |
| What is this in German? | **Wie heißt das auf Deutsch?** | vee hīst dahs owf doych |
| Repeat? | **Noch einmal?** | nokh īn-mahl |
| Slowly. | **Langsam.** | lahng-zahm |
| Do you understand? | **Verstehen Sie?** | fehr-shtay-hen zee |
| I understand. | **Ich verstehe.** | ikh fehr-shtay-heh |
| I don't understand. | **Ich verstehe nicht.** | ikh fehr-shtay-heh nikht |
| Write it? | **Schreiben?** | shrī-ben |
| Who speaks English? | **Wer kann Englisch?** | vehr kahn eng-lish |

To prompt a simple answer, ask, *"Ja oder nein?"* (Yes or no?). To turn a word or sentence into a question, ask it in a questioning tone. An easy way to ask, "Where is the toilet?" is to say, *"Toilette?"*

## Handy questions:

| | | |
|---|---|---|
| How much? | **Wieviel?** | vee-**feel** |
| How long...? | **Wie lang...?** | vee lahng |
| ...is the trip | **...dauert die Reise** | **dow**-ert dee rī-zeh |
| How far? | **Wie weit?** | vee vīt |
| How? | **Wie?** | vee |
| Is it possible? | **Ist es möglich?** | ist es **mur**-glikh |
| Is it necessary? | **Ist das nötig?** | ist dahs **nur**-tig |
| Can you help me? | **Können Sie mir helfen?** | **kurn**-nen zee meer **hehl**-fen |
| What? | **Was?** | vahs |
| What is that? | **Was ist das?** | vahs ist dahs |
| When? | **Wann?** | vahn |
| What time is it? | **Wie spät ist es?** | vee shpayt ist es |
| At what time? | **Um wieviel Uhr?** | oom vee-**feel** oor |
| When does this...? | **Um wieviel Uhr ist hier...?** | oom vee-**feel** oor ist heer |
| ...open | **...geöffnet** | geh-**urf**-net |
| ...close | **...geschlossen** | geh-**shlos**-sen |
| Where is / are...? | **Wo ist / sind...?** | voh ist / zint |
| Do you have...? | **Haben Sie...?** | **hah**-ben zee |
| Who? | **Wer?** | vehr |
| Why? | **Warum?** | vah-**room** |
| Why not? | **Warum nicht?** | vah-**room** nikht |
| Yes or no? | **Ja oder nein?** | yah **oh**-der nīn |

## Das yin und yang:

| cheap / expensive | billig / teuer | bil-lig / toy-er |
| big / small | groß / klein | grohs / klīn |
| hot / cold | heiß / kalt | hīs / kahlt |
| open / closed | geöffnet / geschlossen | geh-urf-net / geh-shlos-sen |
| entrance / exit | Eingang / Ausgang | īn-gahng / ows-gahng |
| arrive / depart | ankommen / abfahren | ahn-kom-men / ahp-fah-ren |
| early / late | früh / spät | frew / shpayt |
| soon / later | bald / später | bahld / shpay-ter |
| fast / slow | schnell / langsam | shnel / lahng-zahm |
| here / there | hier / dort | heer / dort |
| near / far | nah / fern | nah / fehrn |
| good / bad | gut / schlecht | goot / shlekht |
| a little / lots | wenig / viel | vay-nig / feel |
| more / less | mehr / weniger | mehr / vay-nig-er |
| easy / difficult | leicht / schwierig | līkht / shvee-rig |
| left / right | links / rechts | links / rekhts |
| young / old | jung / alt | yoong / ahlt |
| new / old | neu / alt | noy / ahlt |
| heavy / light | schwer / leicht | shvehr / līkht |
| beautiful / ugly | schön / häßlich | shurn / hes-likh |
| smart / stupid | klug / dumm | kloog / dum |
| vacant / occupied | frei / besetzt | frī / beh-zetst |
| with / without | mit / ohne | mit / oh-neh |

## Common German expressions:

| | | |
|---|---|---|
| **Stimmt.** | shtimt | Correct. |
| **Ach so.** | ahkh zoh | I see. |
| **Genau.** | geh-**now** | Exactly. |
| **Gemütlich.** | geh-**mewt**-likh | Cozy. |
| **Bitte.** | **bit**-teh | Please. / Can I help you? / You're welcome. |

## Big little words:

| | | |
|---|---|---|
| I | **ich** | ikh |
| you (formal) | **Sie** | zee |
| you (informal) | **du** | doo |
| we / they | **wir / sie** | veer / zee |
| he / she | **er / sie** | ehr / zee |
| and | **und** | oont |
| at | **bei** | bī |
| because | **weil** | vīl |
| but | **aber** | **ah**-ber |
| by (via) | **mit** | mit |
| for | **für** | fewr |
| from | **von** | fon |
| here | **hier** | heer |
| in | **in** | in |
| not | **nicht** | nikht |
| now | **jetzt** | yetst |
| only | **nur** | noor |
| or | **oder** | **oh**-der |
| this / that | **dies / das** | deez / dahs |
| to | **nach** | nahkh |
| very | **sehr** | zehr |

# Numbers

| | | |
|---|---|---|
| 1 | **eins** | īns |
| 2 | **zwei** | tsvī |
| 3 | **drei** | drī |
| 4 | **vier** | feer |
| 5 | **fünf** | fewnf |
| 6 | **sechs** | zex |
| 7 | **sieben** | **zee**-ben |
| 8 | **acht** | ahkht |
| 9 | **neun** | noyn |
| 10 | **zehn** | tsayn |
| 11 | **elf** | elf |
| 12 | **zwölf** | tsvurlf |
| 13 | **dreizehn** | **drī**-tsayn |
| 14 | **vierzehn** | **feer**-tsayn |
| 15 | **fünfzehn** | **fewnf**-tsayn |
| 16 | **sechzehn** | **zekh**-tsayn |
| 17 | **siebzehn** | **zeeb**-tsayn |
| 18 | **achtzehn** | **ahkht**-tsayn |
| 19 | **neunzehn** | **noyn**-tsayn |
| 20 | **zwanzig** | **tsvahn**-tsig |
| 21 | **einundzwanzig** | **īn**-oont-tsvahn-tsig |
| 22 | **zweiundzwanzig** | **tsvī**-oont-tsvahn-tsig |
| 23 | **dreiundzwanzig** | **drī**-oont-tsvahn-tsig |
| 30 | **dreißig** | **drī**-sig |
| 31 | **einunddreißig** | **īn**-oont-drī-sig |
| 40 | **vierzig** | **feer**-tsig |

| 41 | **einundvierzig** | **īn**-oont-feer-tsig |
| 50 | **fünfzig** | **fewnf**-tsig |
| 60 | **sechzig** | **zekh**-tsig |
| 70 | **siebzig** | **zeeb**-tsig |
| 80 | **achtzig** | **ahkht**-tsig |
| 90 | **neunzig** | **noyn**-tsig |
| 100 | **hundert** | **hoon**-dert |
| 101 | **hunderteins** | hoon-dert-**īns** |
| 102 | **hundertzwei** | hoon-dert-**tsvī** |
| 200 | **zweihundert** | **tsvī**-hoon-dert |
| 1000 | **tausend** | **tow**-zend |
| 1996 | **neunzehnhundert-sechsundneunzig** | **noyn**-tsayn-hoon-dert-zex-oont-**noyn**-tsig |
| 2000 | **zweitausend** | **tsvī**-tow-zend |
| 10,000 | **zehntausend** | **tsayn**-tow-zend |
| million | **Million** | mil-**yohn** |
| billion | **Milliarde** | mil-**yar**-deh |
| first | **erste** | **ehr**-steh |
| second | **zweite** | **tsvī**-teh |
| third | **dritte** | **drit**-teh |
| half | **halb** | hahlp |
| 100% | **hundert Prozent** | **hoon**-dert proh-**tsent** |
| number one | **Nummer eins** | **num**-mer īns |

The number *zwei* (two) is sometimes pronounced "zwoh" in restaurants, hotels, and phone conversations to help distinguish between the similar sounds of *eins* (one) and *zwei* (two).

# Money

| Can you change dollars? | **Können Sie Dollar wechseln?** | **kurn**-nen zee **dol**-lar **vekh**-seln |
| What is your exchange rate for dollars...? | **Was ist ihr Wechselkurs für Dollars...?** | vahs ist eer **vekh**-sel-koors fewr **dol**-lars |
| ...in traveler's checks | **...in Reiseschecks** | in **rī**-zeh-sheks |
| What is the commission? | **Wieviel ist die Kommission?** | vee-**feel** ist dee kom-mis-see-**ohn** |
| Any extra fee? | **Extra Gebühren?** | **ex**-trah geh-**bew**-ren |

## Key money words:

| bank | **Bank** | bahnk |
| change money | **Geld wechseln** | gelt **vekh**-seln |
| money | **Geld** | gelt |
| large bills | **große Banknoten** | **groh**-seh **bahnk**-noh-ten |
| small bills | **kleine Banknoten** | **klī**-neh **bahnk**-noh-ten |
| coins | **Münzen** | **mewn**-tsen |
| cashier | **Kassierer** | kah-**seer**-er |
| credit card | **Kreditkarte** | kreh-**deet**-kar-teh |
| cash advance | **Vorschuß in Bargeld** | **for**-shoos in **bar**-gelt |
| cash machine | **Geldautomat** | gelt-ow-toh-**maht** |
| receipt | **Beleg** | bay-**leg** |

# Time

| What time is it? | **Wie spät ist es?** | vee shpayt ist es |
|---|---|---|
| It's... | **Es ist...** | es ist |
| ...8:00. | **...acht Uhr.** | ahkht oor |
| ...16:00. | **...sechzehn Uhr.** | **zekh**-tsayn oor |
| ...4:00 in the afternoon. | **...vier Uhr nachmittags.** | feer oor **nahkh**-mit-tahgs |
| ...10:30 (half eleven) in the evening. | **...halb elf Uhr abends.** | hahlp elf oor **ah**-bents |
| ...a quarter past nine. | **...viertel nach neun.** | **feer**-tel nahkh noyn |
| ...a quarter to eleven. | **...viertel vor elf.** | **feer**-tel for elf |
| ...noon. | **...Mittag.** | **mit**-tahg |
| ...midnight | **...Mitternacht.** | **mit**-ter-nahkht |
| ...sunrise. | **...Sonnenaufgang.** | **zoh**-nen-owf-gahng |
| ...sunset. | **...Sonnenuntergang.** | **zoh**-nen-oon-ter-gahng |
| ...early / late. | **...früh / spät.** | frew / shpayt |
| ...on time | **...pünktlich.** | **pewnkt**-likh |

In Germany, the 24-hour clock (or military time) is used by hotels, for the opening and closing hours of museums, and for train, bus, and boat schedules. Informally, the Germans use the same "12-hour clock" we use. People say *"Guten Morgen"* (Good morning) until noon, and *"Guten Tag"* (Good day) switches to *"Guten Abend"* (Good evening) around 6 p.m.

## Timely words:

| | | |
|---|---|---|
| minute | **Minute** | mee-**noo**-teh |
| hour | **Stunde** | **shtoon**-deh |
| morning | **Morgen** | **mor**-gen |
| afternoon | **Nachmittag** | **nahkh**-mit-tahg |
| evening | **Abend** | **ah**-bent |
| night | **Nacht** | nahkht |
| day | **Tag** | tahg |
| today | **heute** | **hoy**-teh |
| yesterday | **gestern** | **geh**-stern |
| tomorrow | **morgen** | **mor**-gen |
| tomorow morning | **morgen früh** | **mor**-gen frew |
| anytime | **jederzeit** | yay-der-**tsīt** |
| immediately | **jetzt** | yetst |
| in one hour | **in einer Stunde** | in ī-ner **shtoon**-deh |
| every hour | **jede Stunde** | **yay**-deh **shtoon**-deh |
| every day | **jeden Tag** | **yay**-den tahg |
| last | **letzte** | **lehts**-teh |
| this | **diese** | **dee**-zeh |
| next | **nächste** | **nekh**-steh |
| May 15 | **fünfzehnten Mai** | **fewnf**-tsayn-ten mī |

For dates of the month, take any number, add the sound "ten" to the end, then say the month. June 19 is *neunzehnten Juni*. Germany's national holiday is Oct. 3, Austria's is Oct. 26, and Switzerland's is Aug. 1.

| week | Woche | vokh-eh |
| Monday | Montag | mohn-tahg |
| Tuesday | Dienstag | deen-stahg |
| Wednesday | Mittwoch | mit-vokh |
| Thursday | Donnerstag | don-ner-stahg |
| Friday | Freitag | frī-tahg |
| Saturday | Samstag, | zahm-stahg, |
| | Sonnabend | zon-ah-bent |
| Sunday | Sonntag | zon-tahg |
| | | |
| month | Monat | moh-naht |
| January | Januar | yah-noo-ar |
| February | Februar | fay-broo-ar |
| March | März | mehrts |
| April | April | ah-pril |
| May | Mai | mī |
| June | Juni | yoo-nee |
| July | Juli | yoo-lee |
| August | August | ow-gust |
| September | September | sep-tem-ber |
| October | Oktober | ok-toh-ber |
| November | November | noh-vem-ber |
| December | Dezember | day-tsem-ber |
| | | |
| year | Jahr | yar |
| spring | Frühling | frew-ling |
| summer | Sommer | zom-mer |
| fall | Herbst | hehrpst |
| winter | Winter | vin-ter |

# Transportation

### Trains:

| | | |
|---|---|---|
| Is this the line for...? | **Ist das die Schlange für...?** | ist dahs dee **shlahn**-geh fewr |
| ...tickets | **...Fahrkarten** | **far**-kar-ten |
| ...reservations | **...Reservierungen** | reh-zehr-**vee**-roong-en |
| How much is a ticket to...? | **Wieviel kostet eine Fahrkarte nach...?** | vee-**feel kos**-tet ī-neh **far**-kar-teh nahkh |
| A ticket to ___. | **Eine Fahrkarte nach ___.** | ī-neh **far**-kar-teh nahkh |
| When is the next train? | **Wann ist der nächste Zug?** | vahn ist dehr **nekh**-steh tsoog |
| I'd like to leave... | **Ich möchte... abfahren.** | ikh **murkh**-teh... **ahp**-fah-ren |
| I'd like to arrive... | **Ich möchte... ankommen.** | ikh **murkh**-teh... **ahn**-kom-men |
| ...by ___. | **...vor ___** | for |
| ...in the morning. | **...am Morgen** | ahm **mor**-gen |
| ...in the afternoon. | **...am Nachmittag** | ahm **nahkh**-mit-tahg |
| ...in the evening. | **...am Abend** | ahm **ah**-bent |
| Is there a...? | **Gibt es einen...?** | gipt es ī-nen |
| ...earlier train | **...früherer Zug** | **frew**-hehr-er tsoog |
| ...later train | **...späterer Zug** | **shpay**-ter-er tsoog |
| ...overnight train | **...Nachtzug** | **nahkht**-tsoog |
| ...supplement | **..Zuschlag** | **tsoo**-shlahg |

| Is there a discount for...? | Gibt es Ermäßigung für...? | gipt es ehr-**may**-see-goong fewr |
|---|---|---|
| ...youths | ...Jugendliche | yoo-gend-**likh**-eh |
| ...seniors | ...Senioren | zen-**yor**-en |
| Is a reservation required? | Brauche ich eine Platzkarte? | **browkh**-eh ikh **ī**-neh **plahts**-kar-teh |
| I'd like to reserve a... | Ich möchte einen... reservieren. | ikh **murkh**-teh **ī**-nen... reh-zer-**vee**-ren |
| ...seat. | ...Sitzplatz | **zits**-plahts |
| ...berth. | ...Liegewagenplatz | **lee**-geh-vah-gen-plahts |
| ...sleeper. | ...Schlafwagenplatz | **shlahf**-vah-gen-plahts |
| Where does (the train) leave from? | Von wo geht er ab? | fon voh gayt ehr ahp |
| What track? | Welchem Gleis? | **velkh**-em glīs |
| On time? Late? | Pünktlich? Spät? | **pewnkt**-likh / shpayt |
| When will it arrive? | Wann kommt er an? | vahn komt ehr ahn |
| Is it direct? | Direktverbindung? | dee-**rekt**-fehr-bin-doong |
| Must I transfer? | Muß ich umsteigen? | mus ikh **oom**-shtī-gen |
| When? Where? | Wann? Wo? | vahn / voh |
| Is this seat free? | Ist dieser Platz frei? | ist **dee**-zer plahts frī |
| That's my seat. | Das ist mein Platz. | dahs ist mīn plahts |
| Save my place? | Halten Sie meinen Platz frei? | **halh**-ten zee **mī**-nen plahts frī |
| Where are you going? | Wohin fahren Sie? | **voh**-hin **far**-en zee |
| I'm going to... | Ich fahre nach... | ikh **far**-reh nahkh |
| Can you tell me when to get off? | Können Sie mir Bescheid sagen? | **kurn**-nen zee meer beh-**shīt** zah-gen |

## *Ticket talk:*

| | | |
|---|---|---|
| ticket | **Fahrkarte** | **far**-kar-teh |
| one-way ticket | **Hinfahrkarte** | **hin**-far-kar-teh |
| roundtrip ticket | **Rückfahrkarte** | **rewk**-far-kar-teh |
| first class | **erster Klasse** | **ehr**-ster **klah**-seh |
| second class | **zweiter Klasse** | **tsvī**-ter **klah**-seh |
| reduced fare | **verbilligte Karte** | fehr-**bil**-lig-teh **kar**-teh |
| validate | **abstempeln** | **ahp**-shtem-peln |
| schedule | **Fahrplan** | **far**-plahn |
| departure | **Abfahrtszeit** | **ahp**-farts-tsīt |
| direct | **Direkt** | dee-**rekt** |
| connection | **Anschluß** | **ahn**-shlus |
| reservation | **Platzkarte** | **plahts**-kar-teh |
| non-smoking | **Nichtraucher** | **nikht**-rowkh-er |
| seat | **Platz** | plahts |
| window seat | **Fensterplatz** | **fen**-ster-plahts |
| aisle seat | **Platz am Gang** | plahts ahm gahng |
| berth... | **Liege...** | **lee**-geh |
| ...upper | **...obere** | **oh**-ber-eh |
| ...middle | **...mittlere** | mit-**leh**-reh |
| ...lower | **...untere** | **oon**-ter-eh |
| refund | **Rückvergütung** | **rewk**-fehr-gew-toong |

## *At the train station:*

| | | |
|---|---|---|
| German State Railways | Deutsche Bundes-bahn (DB) | doy-cheh boon-des-bahn (day bay) |
| train station | Bahnhof | bahn-hohf |
| central train station | Hauptbahnhof | howpt-bahn-hohf |
| train information | Zugauskunft | tsoog-ows-koonft |
| train | Zug, Eisenbahn | tsoog, Ī-zen-bahn |
| high speed train | Intercity, Schnellzug | "inter-city," shnel-tsoog |
| arrival | Ankunft | ahn-koonft |
| departure | Abfahrt | ahp-fart |
| delay | Verspätung | fehr-shpay-toong |
| waiting room | Wartesaal | var-teh-zahl |
| lockers | Schließfächer | shlees-fekh-er |
| baggage check room | Gepäckaufgabe | geh-pek-owf-gah-beh |
| lost and found office | Fundbüro | foond-bew-roh |
| tourist information | Touristen-information | too-ris-ten-in-for-maht-see-ohn |
| to the trains | zu den Zugen | tsoo dayn tsoo-gen |
| platform | Bahnsteig | bahn-shtīg |
| track | Gleis | glīs |
| train car | Wagen | vah-gen |
| dining car | Speisewagen | shpī-zeh-vah-gen |
| sleeper car | Liegewagen | lee-geh-vah-gen |
| conductor | Schaffner | shahf-ner |

## *Reading train schedules:*

| | |
|---|---|
| **Abfahrt** | departure |
| **Ankunft** | arrival |
| **außer** | except |
| **bis** | until |
| **Feiertag** | holiday |
| **jeden** | every |
| **nach** | to |
| **nur** | only |
| **Richtung** | direction |
| **Samstag** | Saturday |
| **Sonntag** | Sunday |
| **täglich (tgl.)** | daily |
| **tagsüber** | days |
| **über** | via |
| **verspätet** | late |
| **von** | from |
| **werktags** | Monday-Saturday (workdays) |
| **wochentags** | weekdays |
| **1-5** | Monday-Friday |
| **6, 7** | Saturday, Sunday |

German schedules use the 24-hour clock. It's like American time until noon. After that, subtract twelve and add p.m. So 13:00 is 1 p.m., 20:00 is 8 p.m., and 24:00 is midnight. One minute after midnight is 00:01.

## Buses and subways:

| English | German | Pronunciation |
|---|---|---|
| How do I get to...? | **Wie komme ich zu...?** | vee **kom**-meh ikh tsoo |
| Which bus to...? | **Welcher Bus nach...?** | **velkh**-er boos nahkh |
| Does it stop at...? | **Hält er in...?** | helt er in |
| Which stop for...? | **Welche Haltestelle für...?** | **velkh**-eh **hahl**-teh-shtel-leh fewr |
| Must I transfer? | **Muß ich umsteigen?** | mus ikh **oom**-shtī-gen |
| How much is a ticket? | **Wieviel kostet eine Fahrkarte?** | vee-**feel** kos-tet ī-neh **far**-kar-teh |
| Where can I buy a ticket? | **Wo kaufe ich eine Fahrkarte?** | voh **kow**-feh ikh ī-neh **far**-kar-teh |
| Is there a...? | **Gibt es eine...?** | gipt es ī-neh |
| ...one-day pass | **...Tagesnetzkarte** | **tahg**-es-nets-kar-teh |
| ...discount for buying more tickets | **...Preisnachlaß, wenn ich mehrere Fahrkarten kaufe?** | prīs-**nahkh**-lahs ven ikh **meh**-reh-reh far-kar-ten **kow**-feh |
| When is the...? | **Wann fährt der... ab?** | vahn fart dehr... ahp |
| ...first | **...erste** | **ehr**-steh |
| ...next | **...nächste** | **nekh**-steh |
| ...last | **...letzte** | **lets**-teh |
| ...bus / subway | **...Bus / U-Bahn** | boos / **oo**-bahn |
| What's the frequency per hour / day? | **Wie oft pro Stunde / Tag?** | vee oft proh **shtoon**-deh / tahg |
| I'm going to... | **Ich fahre nach...** | ikh **far**-eh nahkh |
| Can you tell me when to get off? | **Können Sie mir Bescheid sagen?** | **kurn**-nen zee meer beh-**shīt** zah-gen |

## Key bus and subway words:

| | | |
|---|---|---|
| ticket | **Fahrkarte** | **far**-kar-teh |
| bus | **Bus** | boos |
| bus stop | **Bushaltestelle** | **boos**-hahl-teh-**shtel**-leh |
| bus station | **Busbahnhof** | **boos**-bahn-hof |
| subway | **U-Bahn** | **oo**-bahn |
| subway map | **U-Bahnkarte** | **oo**-bahn-kar-teh |
| subway entrance | **U-Bahnstation** | **oo**-bahn-shtaht-see-ohn |
| subway stop | **U-Bahnhaltestelle** | **oo**-bahn-hahl-teh-**shtel**-leh |
| subway exit | **U-Bahnausgang** | **oo**-bahn-ows-gahng |
| direct | **Direkt** | dee-**rekt** |
| direction | **Richtung** | **rikh**-toong |
| connection | **Anschluß** | **ahn**-shlus |

Most big German cities offer deals on public transportation, such as one-day tickets, cheaper fares for youths and seniors, or a discount for buying a batch of tickets (which you can share with friends). Major cities like Munich and Berlin have a *U-Bahn* (subway) and *S-Bahn* (urban rail system). If your Eurailpass is valid on the day you're traveling, you can use the *S-Bahn* for free.

## Taxis:

| | | |
|---|---|---|
| Taxi! | **Taxi!** | **tahk**-see |
| Can you call a taxi? | **Können Sie mir ein Taxi rufen?** | **kurn**-nen zee meer īn **tahk**-see **roo**-fen |
| Where is a taxi stand? | **Wo ist ein Taxistand?** | voh ist īn **tahk**-see-shtahnt |
| Are you free? | **Sind Sie frei?** | zint zee frī |
| Occupied. | **Besetzt.** | beh-**zetst** |
| How much will it cost to...? | **Wieviel kostet die Fahrt...?** | vee-**feel kos**-tet dee fart |
| Too much. | **Zu viel.** | tsoo feel |
| Can you take ___ people? | **Können Sie ___ Personen mitnehman?** | **kurn**-nen zee ___ pehr-**zoh**-nen mit-**nay**-mahn |
| Any extra fee? | **Extra Gebühren?** | **ex**-trah geh-**bew**-ren |
| The meter, please. | **Den Zähler, bitte.** | dayn **tsay**-ler **bit**-teh |
| The most direct route. | **Auf direktem Weg.** | owf dee-**rek**-tem vayg |
| Slow down. | **Fahren Sie langsamer.** | **far**-en zee **lahng**-zah-mer |
| If you don't slow down, I'll throw up. | **Wenn Sie nicht langsamer fahren, wird mir schlecht.** | ven zee nikht **lahng**-zah-mer **far**-en virt meer shlekht |
| Stop here. | **Halten Sie hier.** | **hahl**-ten zee heer |
| Can you wait? | **Können Sie warten?** | **kurn**-nen zee **var**-ten |
| My change, please. | **Mein Wechselgeld, bitte.** | mīn **vek**-sel-gelt **bit**-teh |
| Keep the change. | **Stimmt so.** | shtimt zoh |

## Rental wheels:

| | | |
|---|---|---|
| I'd like to rent a... | **Ich möchte ein...** **mieten.** | ikh **murkh**-teh īn... **mee**-ten |
| ...car. | **...Auto** | **ow**-toh |
| ...station wagon. | **...Kombi** | **kohm**-bee |
| ...van. | **...Kleinbus** | **klīn**-boos |
| ...motorcycle. | **...Motorrad** | **moh**-tor-raht |
| ...motor scooter. | **...Moped** | **moh**-ped |
| ...bicycle. | **...Fahrrad** | **far**-raht |
| ...tank. | **...Pahnzer** | **pahn**-tser |
| How much per...? | **Wieviel pro...?** | vee-**feel** proh |
| ...hour | **...Stunde** | **shtoon**-deh |
| ...day | **...Tag** | tahg |
| ...week | **...Woche** | **vokh**-eh |
| Unlimited mileage? | **Unbegrenzte kilometer?** | oon-beh-**grents**-teh kee-loh-**may**-ter |
| I brake for bakeries. | **Ich bremse für Bäckereien.** | ikh **brem**-zeh fewr bek-eh-**rī**-en |
| Is there a...? | **Gibt es eine...?** | gipt es **ī**-neh |
| ...helmet | **...Helm** | helm |
| ...discount | **...Ermäßigung** | ehr-**may**-see-goong |
| ...deposit | **...Kaution** | **kowt**-see-ohn |
| ...insurance | **...Versicherung** | fehr-**zikh**-eh-roong |
| When do I bring it back? | **Wann bringe ich es zurück?** | vahn **bring**-geh ikh es tsoo-**rewk** |

## Driving:

| | | |
|---|---|---|
| gas station | **Tankstelle** | **tahnk**-shtel-leh |
| The nearest gas station? | **Die nächste Tankstelle?** | dee **nekh**-steh **tahnk**-shtel-leh |
| Self-service? | **Selbstbedienung?** | **zehlpst**-beh-dee-noong |
| Fill the tank. | **Volltanken.** | **fol**-tahnk-en |
| I need... | **Ich brauche...** | ikh **browkh**-eh |
| ...gas. | **...Benzin.** | ben-**tseen** |
| ...unleaded. | **...Bleifrei.** | blī-frī |
| ...regular. | **...Normal.** | nor-**mahl** |
| ...super. | **...Super.** | **zoo**-per |
| ...diesel. | **...Diesel.** | **dee**-zel |
| Check the... | **Sehen Sie nach...** | **zay**-hen zee nahkh |
| ...oil. | **...Öl.** | url |
| ...air in the tires. | **...Luftdruck in Reifen.** | **luft**-druk in rī-fen |
| ...radiator. | **...Kühler.** | **kew**-ler |
| ...battery. | **...Batterie.** | baht-teh-**ree** |
| ...fuses. | **...Sicherungen.** | **zikh**-eh-roong-en |
| ...fanbelt. | **...Keilriemen.** | **kīl**-ree-men |
| ...brakes. | **...Bremsen.** | **brem**-zen |
| ...my pulse. | **...Puls.** | pools |

Getting gas is a piece of *Strudel*. Regular is *normal* and super is *super,* and marks and liters replace dollars and gallons. If a mark is 2/3 of a dollar and there are about 4 liters in a gallon, gas costing 1.50 DM a liter = $4 a gallon.

## *Car trouble:*

| accident | **Unfall** | **oon**-fahl |
| breakdown | **Panne** | **pah**-neh |
| electrical problem | **elektrische Schwierigkeiten** | eh-**lek**-trish-eh **shvee**-rig-kī-ten |
| funny noise | **komisches Geräusch** | koh-mish-es geh-**roysh** |
| My car won't start. | **Mein Auto springt nicht an.** | mīn **ow**-toh shpringt nikht ahn |
| It's overheating. | **Es überhitzt.** | es **ew**-behr-hitst |
| This doesn't work. | **Das geht nicht.** | dahs gayt nikht |
| My car is broken. | **Mein Auto ist kaputt.** | mīn **ow**-toh ist kah-**put** |
| I need a... | **Ich brauche einen...** | ikh **browkh**-eh ī-nen |
| ...tow truck. | **...Abschleppwagen.** | **ahp**-shlep-vah-gen |
| ...mechanic. | **...Mechaniker.** | mekh-**ahn**-i-ker |
| ...stiff drink. | **...Schnaps.** | shnahps |

## *Parking:*

| parking garage | **Garage** | gah-**rah**-zheh |
| Where can I park? | **Wo kann ich parken?** | voh kahn ikh **par**-ken |
| Can I park here? | **Darf ich hier parken?** | darf ikh heer **par**-ken |
| How long can I park here? | **Wie lange darf ich hier parken?** | vee **lahng**-eh darf ikh heer **par**-ken |
| Must I pay to park here? | **Kostet Parken hier etwas?** | **kos**-tet **par**-ken heer et-vahs |
| Is this a safe place to park? | **Ist dies ein sicherer Parkplatz?** | ist deez īn **zikh**-her-er **park**-plahts |

## Finding your way:

| | | |
|---|---|---|
| I'm going to... (if you're on foot) | **Ich gehe nach...** | ikh **gay**-heh nahkh |
| I'm going to... (if you're using wheels) | **Ich fahre nach...** | ikh **fah**-reh nahkh |
| How do I get to...? | **Wie komme ich nach...?** | vee **kom**-meh ikh nahkh |
| Do you have a...? | **Haben Sie eine...?** | **hah**-ben zee **ī**-neh |
| ...city map | **...Stadtplan** | **shtaht**-plahn |
| ...road map | **...Straßenkarte** | **shtrah**-sen-kar-teh |
| How many minutes / hours...? | **Wieviele Minuten / Stunden...?** | vee-**fee**-leh mee-**noo**-ten / **shtoon**-den |
| ...by foot | **...zu Fuß** | tsoo foos |
| ...by bicycle | **...mit dem Rad** | mit daym raht |
| ...by car | **...mit dem Auto** | mit daym **ow**-toh |
| How many kilometers to...? | **Wieviele Kilometer sind es nach...?** | vee-**fee**-leh kee-loh-**may**-ter zint es nahkh |
| What's the... | **Was ist der...** | vahs ist dehr... |
| route to Berlin? | **Weg nach Berlin?** | vayg nahkh behr-**lin** |
| ...best | **...beste** | **bes**-teh |
| ...fastest | **...schnellste** | **shnel**-steh |
| ...most interesting | **...interessanteste** | in-tehr-es-**sahn**-tes-teh |
| Point it out? | **Zeigen Sie es mir?** | **tsī**-gen zee es meer |
| I'm lost. | **Ich habe mich verlaufen.** | ikh **hah**-beh mikh fehr-**lowf**-en |
| Where am I? | **Wo bin ich?** | voh bin ikh |
| Who am I? | **Wie heiße ich?** | vee **hī**-seh ikh |

| Where is...? | **Wo ist...?** | voh ist |
| The nearest...? | **Der nächste...?** | dehr **nekh**-steh |
| Where is this address? | **Wo ist diese Adresse?** | voh ist **dee**-zeh ah-**dres**-seh |

## *Key route-finding words:*

| city map | **Stadtplan** | **shtaht**-plahn |
| road map | **Straßenkarte** | **shtrah**-sen-kar-teh |
| straight ahead | **geradeaus** | geh-**rah**-deh-**ows** |
| left / right | **links / rechts** | links / rekhts |
| first / next | **erste / nächste** | **ehr**-steh / **nekh**-steh |
| intersection | **Kreuzung** | **kroy**-tsoong |
| stoplight | **Ampel** | **ahm**-pel |
| (main) square | **(Markt)platz** | (markt)-plahts |
| street | **Straße** | **shtrah**-seh |
| bridge | **Brücke** | **brew**-keh |
| tunnel | **Tunnel** | **too**-nel |
| highway | **Landstraße** | **lahnd**-shtrah-seh |
| freeway | **Autobahn** | **ow**-toh-bahn |
| north / south | **Norden / Süden** | **nor**-den / **zew**-den |
| east / west | **Osten / Westen** | **os**-ten / **ves**-ten |

The German word for journey or trip is *Fahrt*. Many tourists enjoy collecting Fahrts. In Germany you'll see signs for *Einfahrt* (entrance), *Rundfahrt* (round trip), *Rückfahrt* (return trip), *Himmelfahrt* (ascend to heaven day, August 15th), *Panoramafahrt* (scenic journey), *Zugfahrt* (train trip), *Ausfahrt* (trip out), and throughout your trip, people will smile and wish you a *"Gute Fahrt."*

# Sleeping

## Places to stay:

| hotel | **Hotel** | **hoh**-tel |
| small hotel | **Pension** | pen-see-**ohn** |
| room in private home or bed & breakfast | **Gästezimmer, Fremdenzimmer** | **ges**-teh-tsim-mer, **frem**-den-tsim-mer |
| youth hostel | **Jugendherberge** | **yoo**-gend-hehr-behr-geh |
| vacancy | **Zimmer frei** | **tsim**-mer frī |
| no vacancy | **belegt** | beh-**legt** |

## Reserving a room by phone:

As you're traveling, a good time to reserve a room is the morning of the day you plan to arrive. To reserve by fax from the U.S.A., use the handy form in the appendix.

| Hello. | **Gutentag.** | **goo**-ten tahg |
| My name is... | **Ich heiße...** | ikh **hī**-seh |
| Do you speak English? | **Sprechen Sie Englisch?** | **shprekh**-en zee **eng**-lish |
| Do you have a room...? | **Haben Sie ein Zimmer...?** | **hah**-ben zee īn **tsim**-mer |
| ...for one person | **...für eine Person** | fewr ī-neh pehr-**zohn** |
| ...for two people | **...für zwei Personen** | fewr tsvī pehr-**zoh**-nen |
| ...for tonight | **...für heute abend** | fewr **hoy**-teh ah-bent |
| ...for two nights | **...für zwei Nächte** | fewr tsvī **naykh**-teh |
| ...for Friday | **...für Freitag** | fewr **frī**-tahg |

| English | German | Pronunciation |
|---|---|---|
| ...for June 21 | ...für einundzwanzigsten Juni | fewr īn-oont-tsvahn-tsig-ten **yoo**-nee |
| Yes or no? | Ja oder nein? | yah **oh**-der nīn |
| I'd like... | Ich möchte... | ikh **murkh**-teh |
| ...a private bathroom. | ...eigenes Bad. | **ī**-geh-nes baht |
| ...your cheapest room. | ...ihr billigstes Zimmer. | eer **bil**-lig-stes **tsim**-mer |
| ...___ bed(s) for ___ people in ___ room(s). | ...___ Bett(en) für ___ Personen in ___ Zimmer(n). | ___ bet-(ten) fewr ___ pehr-**zoh**-nen in ___ **tsim**-mer(n) |
| How much is it? | Wieviel kostet das? | vee-**feel** kos-tet dahs |
| Anything cheaper? | Etwas billigeres? | et-vahs **bil**-lig-er-es |
| I'll take it. | Ich nehme es. | ikh **nay**-meh es |
| I'll stay for... | Ich bleibe für... | ikh **blī**-beh fewr |
| We'll stay for... | Wir bleiben für... | veer **blī**-ben fewr |
| ...one night. | ...eine nacht. | **ī**-neh nahkht |
| ...___ nights. | ...___ nächte. | ___ **naykh**-teh |
| I'll come... | Ich komme... | ikh **kom**-meh |
| We'll come... | Wir kommen... | veer **kom**-men |
| ...in one hour. | ...in einer Stunde. | in **ī**-ner **shtoon**-deh |
| ...before 16:00. | ...vor sechzehn Uhr. | for **zekh**-tsayn oor |
| ...Friday before 6 p.m. | ...Freitag vor sechs Uhr abends. | **frī**-tahg for zex oor **ah**-bents |
| Thank you. | Danke. | **dahng**-keh |

## Getting specific:

| | | |
|---|---|---|
| I'd like a room... | **Ich möchte ein Zimmer...** | ikh **murkh**-teh īn **tsim**-mer |
| ...with / without / and | **...mit / ohne / und** | mit / **oh**-neh / oont |
| ...toilet | **...Toilette** | toh-**leh**-teh |
| ...shower | **...Dusche** | **doo**-sheh |
| ...shower down the hall | **...Dusche im Gang** | **doo**-sheh im gahng |
| ...bathtub | **...Badewanne** | **bah**-deh-vah-neh |
| ...double bed | **...Doppelbett** | **dop**-pel-bet |
| ...twin beds | **...zwei Einzelbetten** | tsvī **īn**-tsel-bet-ten |
| ...balcony | **...Balkon** | **bahl**-kohn |
| ...view | **...Ausblick** | **ows**-blick |
| ...with only a sink | **...nur mit Waschbecken** | noor mit **vahsh**-bek-en |
| ...on the ground floor | **...im Erdgeschoß** | im **ehrd**-geh-shos |
| Is there an elevator? | **Gibt es einen Fahrstuhl?** | gipt es **ī**-nen **far**-shtool |
| We arrive Monday, depart Wednesday. | **Wir kommen am Montag, und reisen am Mittwoch ab.** | veer **kom**-men ahm **mohn**-tahg oont rī-zen ahm **mit**-vokh ahp |
| I have a reservation. | **Ich habe eine Reservierung.** | ikh **hah**-beh **ī**-neh reh-zehr-**vee**-roong |
| Confirm my reservation? | **Meine Reservierung bestätigen?** | **mī**-neh reh-zehr-**vee**-roong beh-**shtet**-i-gen |

SLEEPING

## Nailing down the price:

| How much is...? | **Wieviel kostet...?** | vee-**feel** kos-tet |
| ...a room for ___ people | **...ein Zimmer für ___ Personen** | īn tsim-mer fewr ___ pehr-**zoh**-nen |
| ...your cheapest room | **...ihr billigstes Zimmer** | eer **bil**-lig-stes **tsim**-mer |
| Breakfast included? | **Frühstück eingeschlossen?** | frew-**shtewk** īn-geh-shlos-sen |
| How much without breakfast? | **Wieviel ohne Frühstück?** | vee-**feel oh**-neh frew-**shtewk** |
| Complete price? | **Vollpreis?** | fol-**prīs** |
| Is it cheaper if I stay ___ nights? | **Ist is billiger, wenn ich ___ Nächte bleibe?** | ist es **bil**-lig-er ven ikh ___ **naykh**-teh **blī**-beh |
| I'll stay ___ nights. | **Ich werde ___ Nächte bleiben.** | ikh **vehr**-deh ___ **naykh**-teh **blī**-ben |

## Choosing a room:

| Can I see the room? | **Kann ich das Zimmer sehen?** | kahn ikh dahs **tsim**-mer **zay**-hen |
| Do you have something...? | **Haben Sie etwas...?** | **hah**-ben zee **et**-vahs |
| ...larger / smaller | **...größeres / kleineres** | **grur**-ser-es / **klī**-ner-es |
| ...better / cheaper | **...besseres / billigeres** | **bes**-ser-es / **bil**-lig-er-es |
| ...brighter | **...heller** | **hel**-ler |
| ...quieter | **...ruhigeres** | **roo**-i-ger-es |
| Key, please. | **Schlüssel, bitte.** | **shlew**-sel **bit**-teh |

## Hotel help:

| I'd like... | Ich hätte gern... | ikh **het**-teh gehrn |
| ...a / another | ...ein / noch ein | īn / nokh īn |
| ...towel. | ...Handtuch. | **hahnd**-tookh |
| ...pillow. | ...Kissen. | **kis**-sen |
| ...clean sheets. | ...saubere Laken. | **zow**-ber-eh **lah**-ken |
| ...blanket. | ...Decke. | **dek**-eh |
| ...glass. | ...Glas. | glahs |
| ...soap. | ...Seife. | **zī**-feh |
| ...toilet paper. | ...Klopapier. | **kloh**-pah-peer |
| ...crib. | ...Kinderbett. | **kin**-der-bet |
| ...small extra bed. | ...kleines Extrabett. | **klī**-nes **ehk**-strah-bet |
| ...different room. | ...anderes Zimmer. | **ahn**-der-es **tsim**-mer |
| ...silence. | ...Ruhe. | **roo**-heh |
| Where can I wash / hang my laundry? | Wo kann ich meine Wäsche waschen / aufhängen? | voh kahn ikh **mī**-neh **vesh**-eh **vahsh**-en / **owf**-heng-en |
| I'd like to stay another night. | Ich möchte noch eine Nacht bleiben. | ikh **murkh**-teh nokh **ī**-neh nahkht **blī**-ben |
| Where can I park? | Wo soll ich parken? | voh zol ikh **par**-ken |
| What time do you lock up? | Um wieviel Uhr schließen Sie ab? | oom vee-**feel** oor **shlee**-sen zee ahp |
| What time is breakfast? | Um wieviel Uhr ist Frühstück? | oom vee-**feel** oor ist **frew**-shtewk |
| Please wake me at 7:00. | Wecken Sie mich um sieben Uhr, bitte. | **vek**-en zee mikh oom **zee**-ben oor **bit**-teh |

SLEEPING

## Hotel hassles:

| | | |
|---|---|---|
| Come with me. | **Kommen Sie mit.** | **kom**-men zee mit |
| I have a problem in my room. | **Es gibt ein Problem mit meinem Zimmer.** | es gipt īn proh-**blaym** mit mī-nem **tsim**-mer |
| Lamp... | **Lampe...** | **lahm**-peh |
| Lightbulb... | **Birne...** | **bir**-neh |
| Key... | **Schlüssel...** | **shlew**-sel |
| Lock... | **Schloß...** | shlos |
| Window... | **Fenster...** | **fen**-ster |
| Faucet... | **Wasserhahn...** | **vah**-ser-hahn |
| Sink... | **Waschbecken...** | **vahsh**-bek-en |
| Toilet... | **Klo...** | kloh |
| Shower... | **Dusche...** | **doo**-sheh |
| ...doesn't work. | **...ist kaputt.** | ist kah-**put** |
| There is no hot water. | **Es gibt kein warmes Wasser.** | es gipt kīn **var**-mes **vahs**-ser |
| When is the water hot? | **Wann wird das Wasser warm?** | vahn virt dahs **vahs**-ser varm |

## Checking out:

| | | |
|---|---|---|
| I'll leave... | **Ich fahre... ab.** | ikh **fah**-reh... ahp |
| We'll leave... | **Wir fahren... ab.** | veer **fah**-ren... ahp |
| ...today / tomorrow | **...heute / morgen** | **hoy**-teh / **mor**-gen |
| ...very early | **...sehr früh** | zehr frew |
| When is check-out time? | **Wann muß ich das Zimmer verlassen?** | vahn mus ikh dahs **tsim**-mer fehr-**lah**-sen |

| English | German | Pronunciation |
|---|---|---|
| Can I pay now? | **Kann ich zahlen?** | kahn ikh **tsah-**len |
| Bill, please. | **Rechnung, bitte.** | **rekh-**noong **bit-**teh |
| Credit card O.K.? | **Kreditkarte O.K.?** | kreh-**deet-**kar-teh "O.K." |
| I slept like a bear. | **Ich habe wie ein Bär geschlafen.** | ikh **hah-**beh vee īn bar geh-**shlahf-**en |
| Everything was great. | **Alles war gut.** | **ahl-**les var goot |
| Will you call my next hotel for me? | **Können Sie mein nächstes Hotel anrufen?** | **kurn-**nen zee mīn **nekh-**stes hoh-**tel ahn-**roo-fen |
| Can I...? | **Kann ich...?** | kahn ikh |
| Can we...? | **Können wir...?** | **kurn-**nen veer |
| ...leave luggage here until ___ | **...das Gepäck hierlassen bis ___** | dahs geh-**pek heer-**lah-sen bis |

**SLEEPING**

## Camping:

| English | German | Pronunciation |
|---|---|---|
| tent | **Zelt** | tselt |
| camping | **Camping** | **kahm-**ping |
| Where is a campground? | **Wo ist ein Campingplatz?** | voh ist īn **kahm-**ping-plahts |
| Can I...? | **Kann ich...?** | kahn ikh |
| Can we...? | **Können wir...?** | **kurn-**nen veer |
| ...camp here for one night | **...hier eine Nacht zelten** | heer ī-neh nahkht **tsehl-**ten |
| Are showers included? | **Duschen eingeschlossen?** | **doo-**shen **īn-**geh-shlos-sen |

# Eating

## Finding a restaurant:

| Where's a good... | Wo ist hier ein | voh ist heer īn |
| restaurant nearby? | gutes... Restaurant? | **goo**-tes... res-tow-**rahnt** |
| ...cheap | ...billiges | **bil**-lig-es |
| ...local-style | ...typisches | **tew**-pish-es |
| ...untouristy | ...nicht für Touristen | nikht fewr too-**ris**-ten |
| | gedachtes | geh-**dahkh**-tes |
| ...Chinese | ...chinesisches | khee-**nayz**-ish-es |
| ...Italian | ...italienisches | i-**tahl**-yehn-ish-es |
| ...Turkish | ...türkisches | **tewrk**-ish-es |
| ...fast food | ...Schnellimbiß | shnel-**im**-bis |
| ...self-service buffet | ...Selbstbedienungs- | **zelpst**-beh-dee-noongs- |
| | buffett | boo-fay |
| with a salad bar | mit Salatbar | mit zah-**laht**-bar |

## Getting a table and menu:

| Waiter. | Kellner. | **kel**-ner |
| Waitress. | Kellnerin. | **kel**-ner-in |
| I'd like... | Ich hätte gern... | ikh **het**-teh gehrn |
| ...a table for | ...einen Tisch für | **ī**-nen tish fewr |
| one / two. | ein / zwei. | īn / tsvī |
| ...non-smoking. | ...Nichtraucher. | **nikht**-rowkh-er |
| ...just a drink. | ...nur etwas zu | noor **et**-vahs tsoo |
| | trinken. | **trink**-en |
| ...a snack. | ...eine Kleinigkeit. | **ī**-neh **klī**-nig-kīt |

| Can I...? | Kann ich...? | kahn ikh |
|---|---|---|
| ...see the menu | ...die Karte sehen | dee kar-teh zay-hen |
| ...order | ...bestellen | beh-shtel-len |
| ...pay | ...zahlen | tsahl-en |
| ...throw up | ...mich übergeben | mikh ew-ber-gay-ben |
| What do you recommend? | Was schlagen Sie vor? | vahs shlah-gen zee for |
| What's your favorite? | Was ist ihr Lieblingsessen? | vahs ist eer leeb-lings-es-sen |
| Is it...? | Ist es...? | ist es |
| ...good | ...gut | goot |
| ..expensive | ...teuer | toy-er |
| ...light | ...leicht | līkht |
| ...filling | ...sättigend | set-tee-gend |
| What's cheap and filling? | Was ist billig und sättigend? | vahs ist bil-lig oont set-tee-gend |
| What is fast? | Was geht schnell? | vahs gayt shnel |
| What is local? | Was ist typisch? | vahs ist tew-pish |
| What is that? | Was ist das? | vahs ist dahs |
| Do you have...? | Haben Sie...? | hah-ben zee |
| ...an English menu | ...eine Speisekarte auf englisch | ī-neh shpī-zeh-kar-teh owf eng-lish |
| ...a children's portion | ...einen Kinderteller | ī-nen kin-der-tel-ler |

German restaurants close one day a week. It's called *Ruhetag* (quiet day). Before tracking down a recommended restaurant, call to make sure it's open.

## The menu:

| menu | Karte, Speisekarte | kar-teh, shpī-zeh-kar-teh |
| menu of the day | Tageskarte | tah-ges-kar-teh |
| tourist menu | Touristenmenü | too-ris-ten-meh-new |
| specialty of the house | Spezialität des Hauses | shpayt-see-ahl-ee-tayt des how-zes |
| drink menu | Getränkekarte | geh-trenk-eh-kar-teh |
| breakfast | Frühstück | frew-shtewk |
| lunch | Mittagessen | mit-tahg-es-sen |
| dinner | Abendessen | ah-bent-es-sen |
| appetizers | Vorspeise | for-shpī-zeh |
| bread | Brot | broht |
| salad | Salat | zah-laht |
| soup | Suppe | zup-peh |
| first course | erster Gang | ehr-ster gahng |
| main course | Hauptspeise | howpt-shpī-zeh |
| meat | Fleisch | flīsh |
| poultry | Geflügel | geh-flew-gel |
| seafood | Meeresfrüchte | meh-res-frewkh-teh |
| side dishes | Beilagen | bī-lah-gen |
| vegetables | Gemüse | geh-mew-zeh |
| cheese | Käse | kay-zeh |
| dessert | Nachspeise | nahkh-shpī-zeh |
| beverages | Getränke | geh-trenk-eh |
| beer | Bier | beer |

EATING

| wine | **Wein** | vīn |
| cover charge | **Eintritt** | **īn**-trit |
| service included | **mit Bedienung** | mit beh-**dee**-noong |
| service not included | **ohne Bedienung** | **oh**-neh beh-**dee**-noong |
| with / without | **mit / ohne** | mit / **oh**-neh |
| and / or | **und / oder** | oont / **oh**-der |

## Dietary restrictions:

| I'm allergic to... | **Ich bin allergisch gegen...** | ikh bin ah-**lehr**-gish **gay**-gen |
| I cannot eat... | **Ich darf kein... essen.** | ikh darf kīn... **es**-sen |
| ...dairy products. | **...Milchprodukte** | milkh-proh-**dook**-teh |
| ...meat. | **...Fleisch** | flīsh |
| ...pork. | **...Schweinefleisch** | **shvī**-neh-flīsh |
| ...salt / sugar. | **...Salz / Zucker** | zahlts / **tsoo**-ker |
| I'm a diabetic. | **Ich bin Diabetiker.** | ikh bin dee-ah-**bet**-i-ker |
| Low cholesterol? | **Niedriger Cholesterin?** | **nee**-dri-ger koh-**les**-ter-in |
| No caffeine. | **Koffeinfrei.** | koh-fay-**in**-frī |
| No alcohol. | **Kein alkohol.** | kīn **ahl**-koh-hohl |
| I'm a... | **Ich bin...** | ikh bin |
| ...vegetarian. | **...Vegetarier.** | veh-geh-**tar**-ee-er |
| ...strict vegetarian. | **...strenger Vegetarier.** | **shtreng**-er veh-geh-**tar**-ee-er |
| ...carnivore. | **...Fleischfresser.** | **flīsh**-fres-ser |

## Tableware and condiments:

| plate | **Teller** | **tel**-ler |
|-------|-----------|-------------|
| napkin | **Serviette** | zehr-vee-**et**-teh |
| knife | **Messer** | **mes**-ser |
| fork | **Gabel** | **gah**-bel |
| spoon | **Löffel** | **lurf**-fel |
| cup | **Tasse** | **tah**-seh |
| glass | **Glas** | glahs |
| carafe | **Karaffe** | kah-**rah**-fah |
| water | **Wasser** | **vah**-ser |
| bread | **Brot** | broht |
| large pretzels | **Bretzeln** | **bret**-seln |
| butter | **Butter** | **but**-ter |
| margarine | **Margarine** | mar-gah-**ree**-neh |
| salt / pepper | **Salz / Pfeffer** | zahlts / **fef**-fer |
| sugar | **Zucker** | **tsoo**-ker |
| artificial sweetener | **Süßstoff** | **sews**-shtohf |
| honey | **Honig** | **hoh**-nig |
| mustard... | **Senf...** | zenf |
| ...mild / sharp / sweet | **...mild / scharf /süß** | milled / sharf / zews |
| mayonnaise | **Mayonnaise** | mah-yoh-**nay**-zeh |
| ketchup | **Ketchup** | "ketchup" |

In many bars and restaurants you'll see tables with little signs that say *Stammtisch* ("this table reserved for our regulars"). Don't sit there unless you're invited by a local.

**EATING**

## Restaurant requests and regrets:

| A little. | Ein bißchen. | īn **bis**-yen |
| More. / Another. | Mehr. / Noch ein. | mehr / nokh īn |
| The same. | Das gleiche. | dahs **glīkh**-eh |
| I did not order this. | Dies habe ich nicht bestellt. | deez **hah**-beh ikh nikht beh-**shtelt** |
| Is it included with the meal? | Ist das im Essen eingeschlossen? | ist dahs im **es**-sen īn-geh-**shlos**-sen |
| I'm in a hurry. | Ich habe wenig Zeit. | ikh **hah**-beh **vay**-nig tsīt |
| I must leave at ___. | Ich muß um ___ gehen. | ikh mus oom ___ **gay**-hen |
| When will the food be ready? | Wann ist das Essen fertig? | vahn ist dahs **es**-sen **fehr**-tig |
| I've changed my mind. | Ich möchte das doch nicht. | ikh **murkh**-teh dahs dokh nikht |
| Can I get it "to go"? | Zum Mitnehmen? | tsoom **mit**-nay-men |
| This is... | Dies ist... | deez ist |
| .dirty. | ...schmutzig. | **shmut**-tsig |
| ..too greasy. | ...zu fettig. | tsoo **fet**-tig |
| ...too salty. | ...zu salzig. | tsoo **zahl**-tsig |
| ...undercooked. | ...zu wenig gekocht. | tsoo **vay**-nig geh-**kokht** |
| ...overcooked. | ...zu lang gekocht. | tsoo lahng geh-**kokht** |
| ...inedible. | ...nicht eßbar. | nikht **es**-bar |
| ...cold. | ...kalt. | kahlt |
| Heat this up? | Dies aufwärmen? | deez **owf**-vehr-men |
| Enjoy your meal! | Guten Appetit! | **goo**-ten ah-peh-**teet** |

| Enough. | **Genug.** | geh-**noog** |
| Finished. | **Fertig.** | **fehr**-tig |
| Do any of your customers return? | **Kommen ihre Kunden je zurück?** | **kom**-men **eer**-eh **koon**-den yay tsoo-**rewk** |
| Yuck! | **Igitt!** | ee-**git** |
| Delicious! | **Lecker!** | **lek**-er |
| It tastes very good! | **Schmeckt sehr gut!** | shmekht zehr goot |
| Excellent! | **Ausgezeichnet!** | ows-get-**sīkh**-net |

**EATING**

## Paying for your meal:

| Waiter / Waitress. | **Kellner / Kellnerin.** | **kel**-ner / **kel**-ner-in |
| Bill, please. | **Rechnung, bitte.** | **rekh**-noong **bit**-teh |
| Separate checks. | **Getrennte Rechnung.** | geh-**tren**-teh **rekh**-noong |
| Together. | **Zusammen.** | tsoo-**zah**-men |
| Credit card O.K.? | **Kreditkarte O.K.?** | kreh-**deet**-kar-teh "O.K." |
| Is there a cover charge? | **Kostet es Eintritt?** | **kos**-tet es **īn**-trit |
| This is not correct. | **Dies stimmt nicht.** | deez shtimt nikht |
| Please explain. | **Erklären Sie, bitte.** | ehr-**klehr**-en zee **bit**-teh |
| What if I wash the dishes? | **Und wenn ich die Teller abwasche?** | oont ven ikh dee **tel**-ler **ahp**-vah-sheh |
| Keep the change. | **Stimmt so.** | shtimt zoh |
| This is for you. | **Dies ist für Sie.** | deez ist fewr zee |

To get the bill, ask for the *"Rechnung"* (reckoning). The service charge is always included. Tipping is not expected, although it's good style to round up the bill.

## Breakfast:

| | | |
|---|---|---|
| breakfast | **Frühstück** | **frew**-shtewk |
| bread | **Brot** | broht |
| roll (Germany, Austria) | **Brötchen, Semmel** | **brurt**-khen, **zem**-mel |
| toast | **Toast** | tohst |
| butter | **Butter** | **but**-ter |
| jelly | **Gelee** | jeh-**lee** |
| pastry | **Kuchen** | **kookh**-en |
| croissant | **Butterhörnchen** | **but**-ter-hurn-khen |
| omelet | **Omelett** | **om**-let |
| eggs | **Eier** | **ī**-er |
| fried eggs | **Spiegeleier** | **shpee**-gel-ī-er |
| scrambled eggs | **Rühreier** | **rew**-rī-er |
| soft boiled / | **weichgekocht /** | **vīkh**-geh-kokht / |
| hard boiled | **hartgekocht** | **hart**-geh-kokht |
| bacon | **Speck** | shpek |
| ham / cheese | **Schinken / Käse** | **shink**-en / **kay**-zeh |
| yogurt | **Joghurt** | **yoh**-gurt |
| cereal | **Cornflakes** | "cornflakes" |
| granola cereal | **Müsli** | **mews**-lee |
| milk | **Milch** | milkh |
| hot chocolate | **Heißer Schokolade** | **hī**-ser shoh-koh-**lah**-deh |
| fruit juice | **Fruchtsaft** | **frookht**-zahft |
| orange juice (fresh) | **Orangensaft (frischgepreßt)** | oh-**rahn**-jen-zahft (frish-geh-**prest**) |
| coffee / tea | **Kaffee / Tee** | kah-**fay** / tee |
| Is breakfast included? | **Ist Frühstück eingeschlossen?** | ist **frew**-shtewk **īn**-geh-shlos-sen |

## Snacks and easy lunches:

| | | |
|---|---|---|
| toast with ham and cheese | **Toast mit Schinken und Käse** | tohst mit **shink**-en oont **kay**-zeh |
| bread with cheese | **Käsebrot** | **kay**-zeh-broht |
| sausage with... | **Wurst mit...** | vurst mit |
| ...sauerkraut | **...Kraut** | krowt |
| ...bread and mustard | **...Brot und Senf** | broht oont zenf |
| sandwich | **Sandwich** | **sahnd**-vich |
| vegetable platter | **Gemüseplatte** | geh-**mew**-zeh-plah-teh |

## Soups and salads:

| | | |
|---|---|---|
| soup | **Suppe** | **zup**-peh |
| soup of the day | **Suppe des Tages** | **zup**-peh des **tahg**-es |
| chicken broth... | **Hühnerbrühe...** | **hew**-ner-brew-heh |
| beef broth... | **Rinderbrühe...** | **rin**-der-brew-heh |
| ...with noodles | **...mit Nudeln** | mit **noo**-deln |
| ...with rice | **...mit Reis** | mit rīs |
| vegetable soup | **Gemüsesuppe** | geh-**mew**-zeh-zup-peh |
| goulash soup | **Gulaschsuppe** | **goo**-lahsh-zup-peh |
| liver dumpling soup | **Leberknödelsuppe** | **lay**-ber-kuh-nur-del-zup-peh |
| green salad | **grüner Salat** | **grew**-ner zah-**laht** |
| mixed salad | **gemischter Salat** | geh-**mish**-ter zah-**laht** |
| potato salad | **Kartoffelsalat** | kar-**tof**-fel-zah-laht |
| Greek salad | **Griechischer Salat** | **greekh**-ish-er zah-**laht** |

| chef's salad... | gemischter Salat des Hauses... | geh-**mish**-ter zah-**laht** des **how**-zes |
| ...with ham, egg, and cheese | ...mit Schinken, Ei, und Käse | mit **shink**-en, ī, oont **kay**-zeh |
| lettuce | Salat | zah-**laht** |
| tomatoes | Tomaten | toh-**mah**-ten |
| cucumber | Gurken | **gur**-ken |
| oil / vinegar | Öl / Essig | url / **es**-sig |
| salad dressing | Salatsoße | zah-**laht**-zoh-seh |
| dressing on the side | Salatsoße extra | zah-**laht**-zoh-seh **ehk**-strah |
| What is in this salad? | Was ist in diesem Salat? | vahs ist in **dee**-zem zah-**laht** |

## Seafood:

| seafood | Meeresfrüchte | **meh**-res-frewkh-teh |
| assorted seafood | gemischte Meeresfrüchte | geh-**mish**-teh **meh**-res-frewkh-teh |
| fish | Fisch | fish |
| tuna | Thunfisch | **tun**-fish |
| herring | Hering | **hehr**-ing |
| clams | Muscheln | **moo**-sheln |
| cod | Dorsch | dorsh |
| trout | Forelle | foh-**rel**-leh |
| Where did this live? | Wo hat dieses Tier gelebt? | voh haht **dee**-zes teer geh-**laypt** |
| Just the head, please. | Nur den Kopf, bitte. | noor dayn kopf **bit**-teh |

## Poultry and meat:

| | | |
|---|---|---|
| poultry | **Geflügel** | geh-**flew**-gel |
| chicken | **Hähnchen** | **haynkh**-en |
| roast chicken | **Brathänchen** | **braht**-hayn-khen |
| turkey | **Pute** | **poo**-teh |
| duck | **Ente** | **en**-teh |
| meat | **Fleisch** | flīsh |
| mixed grill | **Grillteller** | **gril**-tel-ler |
| beef | **Rindfleisch** | rint-**flīsh** |
| roast beef | **Rinderbraten** | **rin**-der-brah-ten |
| beef steak | **Beefsteak** | **beef**-shtayk |
| veal | **Kalbfleisch** | **kahlp**-flīsh |
| cutlet | **Kotelett** | **kot**-let |
| pork | **Schweinefleisch** | **shvī**-neh-flīsh |
| ham | **Schinken** | **shink**-en |
| sausage | **Wurst** | vurst |
| bacon | **Speck** | shpek |
| lamb | **Lamm** | lahm |
| bunny | **Kaninchen** | kah-**neen**-khen |
| organs | **Innereien** | in-neh-**rī**-en |
| brains | **Brägen** | **breh**-gen |
| liver | **Leber** | **lay**-ber |
| tripe | **Kutteln** | **kut**-teln |
| How long has this been dead? | **Wie lange ist dieses Tier schon tot?** | vee **lahng**-eh ist **dee**-zes teer shohn toht |

## How it's prepared:

| | | |
|---|---|---|
| hot / cold | **heiß / kalt** | hīs / kahlt |
| raw / cooked | **roh / gekocht** | roh / geh-**kokht** |
| assorted | **gemischte** | geh-**mish**-teh |
| baked | **gebacken** | geh-**bah**-ken |
| boiled | **gekocht** | geh-**kokht** |
| deep-fried | **frittiert** | **frit**-ti-ert |
| fillet | **Filet** | fi-**lay** |
| fresh | **frisch** | frish |
| fried | **gebraten** | geh-**brah**-ten |
| grilled | **gegrillt** | geh-**grilt** |
| homemade | **hausgemachte** | hows-geh-**mahkh**-teh |
| in cream sauce | **in Rahmsauce** | in **rahm**-zohs |
| microwave | **Mikrowelle** | **mee**-kroh-vel-leh |
| mild | **mild** | milled |
| mixed | **gemischte** | geh-**mish**-teh |
| poached | **pochieren** | pohkh-**ee**-ren |
| roast | **Braten** | **brah**-ten |
| roasted | **geröstet** | geh-**rurs**-tet |
| smoked | **geräuchert** | geh-**roykh**-ert |
| spicy hot | **scharf** | sharf |
| steamed | **gedünstet** | geh-**dewn**-stet |
| stuffed | **gefüllt** | geh-**fewlt** |

## Avoiding mis-steaks:

| | | |
|---|---|---|
| raw | **roh** | roh |
| rare | **halbgar** | **hahlp**-gar |
| medium | **mittel** | **mit**-tel |
| well-done | **durchgebraten** | **durkh**-geh-brah-ten |
| almost burnt | **fast verkohlt** | fahst fehr-**kohlt** |

## German specialties:

| | |
|---|---|
| **Brotzeit-Teller** | plate of assorted meats and cheeses |
| **Fleischfondue** | meat cubes cooked in a pot of boiling oil and dipped in sauces |
| **Fondue (Switz.)** | bread cubes dipped in a mixture of melted cheese and white wine |
| **Handkäse** | curd cheese |
| **Knödel** | dense dumpling |
| **Leberkäse** | high quality Spam |
| **Maultaschen** | meat- or cheese-filled ravioli (grilled or in soup) |
| **Raclette (Switz.)** | melted cheese, ham, boiled potatoes, and pickle |
| **Rösti (Switz.)** | hashbrowns |
| **Sauerbraten** | braised beef, marinated in vinegar |
| **Schlachtplatte** | assorted cold meats (schlachten = slaughter, Schlacht = battle) |
| **Schnitzel** | thin slice of pork or veal, usually breaded |
| **Schwarzwälder Schinken** | smoked, cured ham |

## The best of the wurst:

| | |
|---|---|
| **Blutwurst** | made from (gulp!) blood |
| **Bratwurst** | pork sausage, 2 inches in diameter, grilled or fried |
| **Nürnberger** | spicy pork sausage, grilled or fried, smaller than a hot dog |
| **Schweinewurst** | pork sausage |

EATING

**Weisswurst**                     white boiled veal that falls apart
                                   when you cut it. Don't eat the skin!

**mit Brot**                       with bread

**mit Kraut**                      with sauerkraut

## Side dishes:

| | | |
|---|---|---|
| vegetables | **Gemüse** | geh-**mew**-zeh |
| rice | **Reis** | rīs |
| spaghetti | **Spaghetti** | shpah-**geh**-tee |
| noodles | **Nudeln** | **noo**-deln |
| boiled German-style noodles | **Spätzle** | **shpets**-leh |
| liver / bread... | **Leber / Semmel...** | **lay**-ber / **zem**-mel |
| ...dumplings | **...knödel** | kuh-**nur**-del |
| sauerkraut | **Sauerkraut** | "sauerkraut" |
| sliced pancakes | **Frittaten** | fri-**tah**-ten |
| potatoes | **Kartoffeln** | kar-**tof**-feln |
| French fries | **Pommes frites** | pom frits |
| potato salad | **Kartoffelsalat** | kar-**tof**-fel-zah-laht |
| green salad | **grüner Salat** | **grew**-ner zah-**laht** |
| mixed salad | **gemischter Salat** | geh-**mish**-ter zah-**laht** |

## Veggies and beans:

| | | |
|---|---|---|
| vegetables | **Gemüse** | geh-**mew**-zeh |
| mixed vegetables | **gemischtes Gemüse** | geh-**mish**-tes geh-**mew**-zeh |
| artichoke | **Artischocke** | art-i-**shoh**-keh |
| asparagus | **Spargel** | **shpar**-gel |
| beans | **Bohnen** | **boh**-nen |
| beets | **Rote Beete** | **roh**-teh **bee**-teh |
| broccoli | **Brokkoli** | **brok**-koh-lee |
| cabbage | **Kohl** | kohl |
| carrots | **Karotten** | kah-**rot**-ten |
| cauliflower | **Blumenkohl** | **bloo**-men-kohl |
| corn | **Mais** | mīs |
| cucumber | **Gurken** | **gur**-ken |
| eggplant | **Aubergine** | oh-behr-**zhee**-neh |
| French fries | **Pommes frites** | pom frits |
| garlic | **Knoblauch** | kuh-**noh**-blowkh |
| green beans | **grüne Bohnen** | **grew**-neh **boh**-nen |
| lentils | **Linsen** | **lin**-zen |
| mushrooms | **Champignons** | **shahm**-pin-yohn |
| olives | **Oliven** | oh-**leev**-en |
| onions | **Zwiebeln** | **tsvee**-beln |
| peas | **Erbsen** | **ehrb**-zen |
| pepper... | **Paprika...** | **pah**-pree-kah |
| ...green / red | **...grün / rot** | grewn / roht |
| pickles | **Essiggurken** | **es**-sig-goor-ken |
| potatoes | **Kartoffeln** | kar-**tof**-feln |

| radishes | **Radieschen** | rah-**dee**-shen |
| spinach | **Spinat** | **shpee**-naht |
| tomatoes | **Tomaten** | toh-**mah**-ten |
| zucchini | **Zuccini** | **tsoo**-kee-nee |

## If you knead bread:

| bread | **Brot** | broht |
| dark bread | **Vollkornbrot** | **fol**-korn-broht |
| three-grain bread | **Dreikornbrot** | **drī**-korn-broht |
| rye bread | **Roggenmischbrot** | **roh**-gen-mish-broht |
| dark rye bread | **Schwarzbrot** | **shvartz**-broht |
| whole wheat bread | **Graubrot** | **grow**-broht |
| light bread | **Weißbrot** | **vīs**-broht |
| wimpy white bread | **Toast** | tohst |
| French bread | **Baguette** | bah-**get** |
| roll (Germany, Austria) | **Brötchen, Semmel** | **brurt**-khen, **zem**-mel |

## Say cheese:

| cheese | **Käse** | **kay**-zeh |
| mild / sharp | **mild / scharf** | milled / sharf |
| cheese platter | **Käseplatte** | **kay**-zeh-**plah**-teh |
| gorgonzola | **Gorgonzola** | **gor**-gon-tsoh-lah |
| bleu cheese | **Blaukäse** | **blow**-kay-zeh |
| cream cheese | **Frischkäse** | **frish**-kay-zeh |
| Swiss cheese | **Emmentaler** | **em**-men-tah-ler |
| a strong cheese | **Bergkäse** | **berg**-kay-zeh |
| Can I taste it? | **Kann ich probieren?** | kahn ikh **proh**-beer-en |

## Fruits and nuts:

| | | |
|---|---|---|
| almond | **Mandel** | **mahn**-del |
| apple | **Apfel** | **ahp**-fel |
| apricot | **Aprikose** | ahp-ri-**koh**-zeh |
| banana | **Banane** | bah-**nah**-neh |
| canteloupe | **Melone** | meh-**loh**-neh |
| cherry | **Kirsche** | **keer**-sheh |
| chestnut | **Kastanie** | **kahs**-tah-nee |
| coconut | **Kokosnuß** | **koh**-kohs-noos |
| date | **Dattel** | **daht**-tel |
| fig | **Feige** | **fī**-geh |
| fruit | **Obst** | ohpst |
| grapefruit | **Pampelmuse** | **pahm**-pel-moo-zeh |
| grapes | **Trauben** | **trow**-ben |
| hazelnut | **Haselnuß** | **hah**-zel-noos |
| lemon | **Zitrone** | tsee-**troh**-neh |
| orange | **Apfelsine** | ahp-fel-**zee**-neh |
| peach | **Pfirsich** | **feer**-zikh |
| peanut | **Erdnuß** | **ehrd**-noos |
| pear | **Birne** | **beer**-neh |
| pineapple | **Ananas** | **ahn**-ahn-ahs |
| plum | **Pflaume** | **flow**-meh |
| prune | **Backpflaume** | **bahk**-flow-meh |
| raspberry | **Himbeere** | **him**-behr-eh |
| strawberry | **Erdbeere** | **ehrt**-behr-eh |
| tangerine | **Mandarine** | mahn-dah-**ree**-neh |
| walnut | **Wallnuß** | **vahl**-noos |
| watermelon | **Wassermelone** | **vah**-ser-meh-loh-neh |

**EATING**

## Teutonic treats:

| | | |
|---|---|---|
| dessert | **Nachspeise** | nahkh-shpī-zeh |
| strudel | **Strudel** | shtroo-del |
| cake | **Torte** | tor-teh |
| sherbet | **Sorbet** | zor-**bet** |
| ice cream... | **Eis...** | īs |
| ...scoop | **...Kugel** | koog-el |
| ...cone | **...Waffel** | vah-fel |
| ...small bowl | **...Becher** | bekh-er |
| fruit cup | **Früchtebecher** | frewkh-teh-bekh-er |
| tart | **Törtchen** | turt-khen |
| pie | **Kuchen** | kookh-en |
| cream | **Schlag** | shlahg |
| whipped cream | **Schlagsahne** | shlahg-zah-neh |
| chocolate mousse | **Mousse** | moos |
| pudding | **Pudding** | "pudding" |
| pastry | **Gebäck** | geh-**bek** |
| cookies | **Kekse** | kayk-zeh |
| candy | **Bonbons** | bon-bonz |
| low calorie | **kalorienarm** | kah-loh-**ree**-en-arm |
| homemade | **hausgemacht** | **hows**-geh-mahkht |
| Delicious! | **Köstlich! Lecker!** | **kurst**-likh / **lek**-er |
| Heavenly. | **Himmlisch.** | him-lish |
| I'm in seventh heaven. | **Ich bin im siebten Himmel.** | ikh bin im **zeeb**-ten **him**-mel |

# Drinking

## Water, milk, and juice:

| | | |
|---|---|---|
| mineral water... | **Mineralwasser...** | min-eh-**rahl**-vah-ser |
| ...with / without carbonation | **...mit / ohne Kohlensäure** | mit / **oh**-neh **koh**-len-zoy-reh |
| whole milk | **Vollmilch** | **fol**-milkh |
| skim milk | **Magermilch** | **mah**-ger-milkh |
| fresh milk | **frische Milch** | **frish**-eh milkh |
| hot chocolate | **Heiße Schokolade** | **hī**-seh shoh-koh-**lah**-deh |
| milkshake | **Milchshake** | **milkh**-shayk |
| Fanta & Coke mix | **Mezzo Mix, Spezi** | **met**-soh mix, **shpet**-see |
| fruit juice | **Fruchtsaft** | **frookht**-zahft |
| apple juice | **Apfelsaft** | **ahp**-fel-zahft |
| orange juice (fresh) | **Orangensaft (frischgepreßt)** | oh-**rahn**-jen-zahft (frish-geh-**prest**) |
| with / without... | **mit / ohne...** | mit / **oh**-neh |
| ...ice / sugar | **...Eis / Zucker** | **īs** / **tsoo**-ker |
| glass / cup | **Glas / Tasse** | glahs / **tah**-seh |
| small / large bottle | **kleine / große Flasche** | **klī**-neh / **groh**-seh **flah**-sheh |
| Is the water safe to drink? | **Ist das Trinkwasser?** | ist dahs **trink**-vahs-ser |

**EATING**

## Coffee and tea:

| | | |
|---|---|---|
| coffee | **Kaffee** | kah-**fay** |
| espresso | **Espresso** | es-**pres**-soh |
| cappucino | **Cappucino** | kah-poo-**chee**-noh |
| iced coffee | **Eiskaffee** | īs-kah-fay |
| instant | **Pulverkaffee, Nescafe** | pool-ver-kah-**fay**, "nescafe" |
| decaffeinated | **koffeinfrei, Hag** | koh-fay-**in**-frī, hahg |
| black | **schwarz** | shvarts |
| with cream / milk | **mit Sahne / Milch** | mit **zah**-neh / milkh |
| with sugar | **mit Zucker** | mit **tsoo**-ker |
| hot water | **heißes Wasser** | **hī**-ses **vah**-ser |
| tea / lemon | **Tee / Zitrone** | tee / tsee-**troh**-neh |
| tea bag | **Teebeutel** | **tee**-boy-tel |
| iced tea | **Eistee** | **īs**-tee |
| herbal tea | **Kräutertee** | **kroy**-ter-tee |
| little pot | **Kännchen** | **kaynkh**-en |
| small / big | **klein / groß** | klīn / grohs |
| Another cup. | **Noch eine Tasse.** | nokh **ī**-neh **tah**-seh |

In Austria, coffee has a language of its own. Ask for a *Brauner* to get coffee with cream, a *Melange* for coffee with lots of milk, a *Mokka* for black espresso, and *Obers* for cream.

## Wine:

| | | |
|---|---|---|
| I would like... | **Ich hätte gern...** | ikh **het**-teh gehrn |
| We would like... | **Wir hätten gern...** | veer **het**-ten gehrn |
| ...an eighth liter | **...ein Achtel** | īn **ahkh**-tel |
| ...a quarter liter | **...ein Viertel** | īn **feer**-tel |
| ...a carafe | **...eine Karaffe** | ī-neh kah-**rah**-feh |
| ...a half bottle | **...eine halbe Flasche** | ī-neh **hahl**-beh **flah**-sheh |
| ...a bottle | **...eine Flasche** | ī-neh **flah**-sheh |
| ...of red wine | **...Rotwein** | **roht**-vīn |
| ...of white wine | **...Weißwein** | **vīs**-vīn |
| ...the wine list | **...die Weinkarte** | dee **vīn**-kar-teh |

### *Wine words:*

| | | |
|---|---|---|
| wine | **Wein** | vīn |
| table wine | **Tafelwein** | **tah**-fel-vīn |
| house wine | **Hausmarke** | **hows**-mar-keh |
| local | **einheimisch** | **īn**-hī-mish |
| red wine | **Rotwein** | **roht**-vīn |
| white wine | **Weißwein** | **vīs**-vīn |
| rosé | **rosé** | roh-**zay** |
| sparkling | **sprudelnd** | **shproo**-delnd |
| sweet | **süß** | zews |
| medium | **halbtrocken** | **hahlp**-trok-en |
| (very) dry | **(sehr) trocken** | (zehr) **trok**-en |
| wine spritzer | **Wein gespritzt** | vīn geh-**shpritzt** |
| cork | **Korken** | **kor**-ken |

**EATING**

## Beer:

| beer | **Bier** | beer |
|------|----------|------|
| from the tap | **vom Faß** | fom fahs |
| bottle | **Flasche** | **flah**-sheh |
| light (Germ., Aust.) | **helles, Märzen** | **hel**-les, **mehr**-tzen |
| dark | **dunkles** | **doonk**-les |
| local / imported | **einheimisch / importiert** | **īn**-hī-mish / im-por-tee-**ert** |
| small / large | **kleines / großes** | **klī**-nes / **groh**-ses |
| half-liter | **Halbes** | **hahl**-bes |
| liter | **Mass** | mahs |
| alcohol-free | **alkoholfrei** | ahl-koh-hohl-**frī** |
| low calorie | **Light** | "light" |
| cold / colder | **kalt / kälter** | kahlt / **kel**-ter |

## Bar talk:

| What would you like? | **Was darf ich bringen?** | vahs darf ikh **bring**-en |
|------|----------|------|
| What is the local specialty? | **Was ist die Spezialität hier?** | vahs ist dee **shpayt**-see-ahl-ee-**tayt** heer |
| Straight. | **Pur.** | poor |
| With / Without... | **Mit / Ohne...** | mit / **oh**-neh |
| ...alcohol. | **...Alkohol.** | **ahl**-koh-hohl |
| ...ice. | **...Eis.** | īs |
| One more. | **Noch eins.** | nokh īns |
| Cheers! | **Prost!** | prohst |
| To you! | **Zum Wohl!** | tsoom vohl |

# Picnicking

## At the grocery:

| | | |
|---|---|---|
| Self-service? | **Selbstbedienung?** | **zelpst**-beh-dee-noong |
| Ripe for today? | **Jetzt reif?** | yetst rīf |
| Does this need to be cooked? | **Muß man das kochen?** | mus mahn dahs **kokh**-en |
| Can I taste it? | **Kann ich probieren?** | kahn ikh proh-**beer**-en |
| Fifty grams. | **Fünfzig Gramm.** | **fewnf**-tsig grahm |
| One hundred grams. | **Hundert Gramm.** | **hoon**-dert grahm |
| More. / Less. | **Mehr. / Weniger.** | mehr / **vay**-nig-er |
| A piece. | **Ein Stück.** | īn shtewk |
| A slice. | **Eine Scheibe.** | **ī**-neh **shī**-beh |
| Sliced. | **In Scheiben.** | in **shī**-ben |
| Can you make me a sandwich? | **Können Sie mir ein belegtes Brot machen?** | **kurn**-nen zee meer īn beh-**leg**-tes broht **mahkh**-en |
| To take out. | **Zum Mitnehmen.** | tsoom **mit**-nay-men |
| Is there a park nearby? | **Gibt es einen Park in der Nähe?** | gipt es **ī**-nen park in dehr **nay**-heh |
| Okay to picnic here? | **Darf man hier picknicken?** | darf mahn heer **pik**-nik-en |
| Enjoy your meal! | **Guten Appetit!** | **goo**-ten ah-peh-**teet** |

You can assemble your picnic at a *Markt* (open air market) or *Supermarkt* (supermarket). Buy meat and cheese by the gram. One hundred grams is about a quarter pound,

enough for two sandwiches. To get real juice, look for
"100%" or "kein Zucker" (no sugar) on the label.

## Tasty picnic words:

| | | |
|---|---|---|
| open air market | **Markt** | markt |
| grocery store | **Lebensmittelgeschäft** | lay-bens-mit-tel-geh-**sheft** |
| supermarket | **Supermarkt** | **zoo**-per-markt |
| picnic | **Picknick** | **pik**-nik |
| sandwich | **belegtes Brot** | beh-**leg**-tes broht |
| bread | **Brot** | broht |
| roll (Germany, Austria) | **Brötchen, Semmel** | **brurt**-khen, **zem**-mel |
| sausage | **Wurst** | vurst |
| ham | **Schinken** | **shink**-en |
| cheese | **Käse** | **kay**-zeh |
| mild / sharp / sweet | **mild / scharf / süß** | milled / sharf / zews |
| mustard... | **Senf...** | zenf |
| mayonnaise... | **Mayonnaise...** | mah-yoh-**nay**-zeh |
| ...in a tube | **...in Tube** | in **too**-beh |
| yogurt | **Joghurt** | **yoh**-gurt |
| fruit | **Obst** | ohpst |
| box of juice | **Karton Saft** | **kar**-ton zaft |
| cold drinks | **kalte Getränke** | **kahl**-teh geh-**trenk**-eh |
| plastic... | **Plastik...** | **plahs**-tik |
| ...spoon / fork | **...löffel / gabel** | **lurf**-fel / **gah**-bel |
| paper... | **Papier...** | pah-**peer** |
| ...plate / cup | **...teller / becher** | **tel**-ler / **bekh**-er |

# German-English Menu Decoder

This handy decoder won't list every word on the menu, but it'll get you *Bratwurst* (pork sausage) instead of *Blutwurst* (blood sausage).

**Abendessen** dinner
**Achtel** eighth liter
**Ananas** pineapple
**Apfel** apple
**Apfelsaft** apple juice
**Apfelsine** orange
**Aprikose** apricot
**Artischocke** artichoke
**Aubergine** eggplant
**Backpflaume** prune
**Banane** banana
**Bauern** with potatoes
**Becher** small bowl
**Bedienung** service
**Beeren** berries
**Beilagen** side dishes
**Bier** beer
**Birne** pear
**Blumenkohl** cauliflower
**Blutwurst** blood sausage
**Bohnen** beans
**braten** roast
**Brathähnchen** roast chicken

**Bratwurst** pork sausage
**Bretzeln** pretzels
**Brokkoli** broccoli
**Brot** bread
**Brötchen** roll
**Brotzeit** snack
**Butterhörnchen** croissant
**Champignons** mushrooms
**chinesisches** Chinese
**Dattel** date
**Dorsch** cod
**dunkles** dark
**Ei** egg
**Eier** eggs
**eingeschlossen** included
**einheimisch** local
**Eintritt** cover charge
**Eis** ice cream
**Eiskaffee** iced coffee
**Eistee** iced tea
**Ente** duck
**Erbsen** peas
**Erdbeere** strawberry

Erdnuß  peanut
erster Gang  first course
Essen  food
Essig  vinegar
Essiggurken  pickles
Feige  fig
Fett  fat
Fisch  fish
Flasche  bottle
Fleisch  meat
Forelle  trout
Französisch  French
frisch  fresh
frischgepreßt  freshly squeezed
Frittaten  sliced pancakes
frittiert  deep-fried
Früchtebecher  fruit cup
Fruchtsaft  fruit juice
Frühstück  breakfast
Gang  course
Gebäck  pastry
gebraten  fried
gedünstet  steamed
Geflügel  poultry
gefüllt  stuffed
gegrillt  grilled
gekocht  cooked
Gelee  jelly
gemischte  mixed

Gemüse  vegetables
Gemüseplatte  vegetable platter
geräuchert  smoked
geröstet  roasted
gespritzt  with mineral water
Getränke  beverages
Getränkekarte  drink menu
Glas  glass
Graubrot  whole wheat bread
Grillteller  mixed grill
groß  big
grüner  green
Gurken  cucumber
Hähnchen  chicken
halb  half
hartgekocht  hard-boiled
Haselnuß  hazelnut
Hauptspeise  main course
Haus  house
hausgemachte  homemade
heiß  hot
helles  light (beer)
Hering  herring
Himbeere  raspberry
Honig  honey
Hühnerbrühe  chicken broth
importiert  imported
Innereien  organs
Italienisch  Italian

**Jäger** with mushrooms and gravy
**Joghurt** yogurt
**Johannisbeeren** red currant
**Kaffee** coffee
**Kakao** cocoa
**Kalbfleisch** veal
**kalt** cold
**Kaninchen** bunny
**Kännchen** small pot of tea
**Karaffe** carafe
**Karotten** carrots
**Karte** menu
**Kartoffeln** potatoes
**Käse** cheese
**Käseplatte** cheese platter
**Kastanie** chestnut
**Kekse** cookies
**Kinderteller** children's portion
**Kirsche** cherry
**klein** small
**Kleinigkeit** snack
**Knoblauch** garlic
**Knödel** dumpling
**Kohl** cabbage
**Kohlensäure** carbonation
**Kokosnuß** coconut
**köstlich** delicious
**Kotelett** cutlet
**Kraut** sauerkraut

**Kräutertee** herbal tea
**Kugel** scoop
**Kutteln** tripe
**Lamm** lamb
**Leber** liver
**leicht** light
**Linsen** lentils
**Mais** corn
**Malaga** rum-raisin flavor
**Mandarine** tangerine
**Mandel** almond
**Mass** liter of beer
**Maultaschen** ravioli
**Meeresfrüchte** seafood
**Melone** canteloupe
**Miesmuscheln** mussels
**Mikrowelle** microwave
**Milch** milk
**mild** mild
**Mineralwasser** mineral water
**mit** with
**Mittagessen** lunch
**Muscheln** clams
**Müsli** granola cereal
**Nachspeise** dessert
**Nudeln** noodles
**Obst** fruit
**oder** or
**ohne** without

**MENU DECODER**

**Öl** oil
**Oliven** olives
**Omelett** omelet
**Orangensaft** orange juice
**Pampelmuse** grapefruit
**Paprika** bell pepper
**Pfeffer** pepper
**Pfirsich** peach
**Pflaume** plum
**Pistazien** pistachio
**pochieren** poached
**Pommes frites** French fries
**Pute** turkey
**Raclette** potatoes and cheese (Switz.)
**Radieschen** radishes
**Rahmsauce** cream sauce
**Rinderbraten** roast beef
**Rinderbrühe** beef broth
**Rindfleisch** beef
**Roggenmischbrot** rye bread
**roh** raw
**Rösti** hashbrowns (Switz.)
**Rote Beete** beets
**Rotwein** red wine
**Rühreier** scrambled eggs
**Salat** salad
**Salatsoße** salad dressing
**Salz** salt

**sättigend** filling
**Sauerbraten** braised beef
**Schalentiere** shellfish
**scharf** spicy
**Scheibe** slice
**Schinken** ham
**Schlachtplatte** assorted cold meats
**Schlag** cream
**Schlagsahne** whipped cream
**schnell** fast
**Schnellimbiss** fast food
**Schnitzel** thinly-sliced pork or veal
**Schokolade** chocolate
**Schwarzbrot** dark rye bread
**Schweinefleisch** pork
**sehr** very
**Semmel** roll
**Senf** mustard
**Sorbet** sherbet
**Spargel** asparagus
**Spätzle** German-style noodles
**Speck** bacon
**Spezialität** speciality
**Spiegeleier** fried eggs
**Spinat** spinach
**sprudelnd** sparkling
**Stück** piece
**Suppe** soup

**süß** sweet
**Tage** day
**Tageskarte** menu of the day
**Tasse** cup
**Tee** tea
**Teller** plate
**Thunfisch** tuna
**Tomaten** tomatoes
**Törtchen** tart
**Torte** cake
**Trauben** grapes
**trocken** dry
**typisch** local
**und** and
**Vanille** vanilla
**Vegetarier** vegetarian
**Viertel** quarter liter
**Vollkornbrot** dark bread
**Vorspeise** appetizers

**Waffel** cone
**Wallnuß** walnut
**Wasser** water
**Wassermelone** watermelon
**weichgekocht** soft-boiled
**Wein** wine
**Weinkarte** wine list
**Weißwein** white wine
**Wiener** breaded and fried
**Wiesswurst** boiled veal sausage
**Wurst** sausage
**Zitrone** lemon
**Zuccini** zucchini
**Zucker** sugar
**zum Mitnehman** "to go"
**Zwiebelbraten** pot roast with onions
**Zwiebeln** onions

# Sightseeing

| Where is...? | Wo ist...? | voh ist |
|---|---|---|
| ...the best view | ...der beste Ausblick | dehr **bes**-teh **ows**-blick |
| ...the main square | ...der Hauptplatz | dehr **howpt**-plahts |
| ...the old town center | ...die Altstadt | dee **ahlt**-shtaht |
| ...the museum | ...das Museum | dahs moo-**zay**-um |
| ...the castle / ruins | ...die Burg / Ruine | dee burg / roo-**ee**-neh |
| ...the palace | ...das Schloß | dahs shlos |
| ...a fair (rides, games) | ...ein Jahrmarkt | īn **yar**-markt |
| ...a festival (music) | ...ein Festival | īn fes-tee-**vahl** |
| ...the tourist information office | ...das Touristen- informationsbüro | dahs **too**-ris-ten-in-for- maht-see-**ohns**-bew-roh |
| Do you have...? | Haben Sie...? | **hah**-ben zee |
| ...a city map | ...einen Stadtplan | **ī**-nen **shtaht**-plahn |
| ...brochures | ...Broschüren | broh-**shewr**-en |
| ...guidebooks | ...Führer | **fewr**-er |
| ...tours | ...Führungen | **few**-roong-en |
| ...in English | ...auf englisch | owf **eng**-lish |
| When is the next tour? | Wann ist die nächste Führung? | vahn ist dee **nekh**-steh **few**-roong |
| Is it free? | Ist es umsonst? | ist es oom-**zonst** |
| How much is it? | Wieviel kostet das? | vee-**feel kos**-tet dahs |
| Is there a discount for...? | Gibt es Ermäßigung für...? | gipt es ehr-**may**-see-goong fewr |
| ...students | ...Studenten | shtoo-**den**-ten |
| ...youth / seniors | ...Kinder / Senioren | **kin**-der / zen-**yor**-en |

# Shopping

## Names of shops:

| | | |
|---|---|---|
| antiques | **Antiquitäten** | ahn-tee-kwee-**tay**-ten |
| bakery | **Bäckerei** | bek-eh-**rī** |
| barber shop | **Herrenfrisör** | hehr-ren-friz-**ur** |
| beauty salon | **Damenfrisör** | dah-men-friz-**ur** |
| book shop | **Buchladen** | **bookh**-lah-den |
| camera shop | **Photoladen** | **foh**-toh-lah-den |
| department store | **Kaufhaus** | **kowf**-hows |
| flea market | **Flohmarkt** | **floh**-markt |
| flower market | **Blumenmarkt** | **bloo**-men-markt |
| grocery store | **Lebensmittelgeschäft** | **lay**-bens-mit-tel-geh-**sheft** |
| jewelry shop | **Schmuckladen** | **shmuk**-lah-den |
| laundromat | **Waschsalon** | **vahsh**-zah-lon |
| newsstand | **Zeitungsstand** | **tsī**-toongs-shtahnt |
| office supplies | **Bürobedarf** | **bew**-roh-beh-darf |
| open air market | **Markt** | markt |
| optician | **Optiker** | **ohp**-ti-ker |
| pharmacy | **Apotheke** | ah-poh-**tay**-keh |
| shopping mall | **Shopping Center** | "shopping center" |
| souvenir shop | **Andenkenladen** | **ahr**-denk-en-**lah**-den |
| supermarket | **Supermarkt** | **zoo**-per-markt |
| toy store | **Spielzeugladen** | **shpeel**-tsoyg-lah-den |
| travel agency | **Reiseagentur** | **rī**-zeh-ah-gen-tur |

## Shop till you drop:

| | | |
|---|---|---|
| special | **Angebot** | **ahn**-geh-boht |
| How much is it? | **Wieviel kostet das?** | vee-**feel** kos-tet dahs |
| I'm just browsing. | **Ich sehe mich nur um.** | ikh **zay**-heh mikh noor oom |
| We're just browsing. | **Wir sehen uns nur um.** | veer **zay**-hen uns noor oom |
| I'd like... | **Ich möchte...** | ikh **murkh**-teh |
| Do you have...? | **Haben Sie...?** | **hah**-ben zee |
| ...more | **...mehr** | mehr |
| ...something cheaper | **...etwas billigeres** | et-vahs **bil**-lig-er-es |
| Can I try it on? | **Kann ich es anprobieren?** | kahn ikh es **ahn**-proh-beer-en |
| A mirror? | **Einen Spiegel?** | **Ī**-nen **shpee**-gel |
| Too... | **Zu...** | tsoo |
| ...big. | **...groß.** | grohs |
| ...small. | **...klein.** | klīn |
| ...expensive. | **...teuer.** | **toy**-er |
| I'll think about it. | **Ich denk drüber nach.** | ikh denk **drew**-ber nahkh |
| Is that your lowest price? | **Ist das der günstigste Preis?** | ist dahs dehr **gewn**-stig-steh prīs |
| My last offer. | **Mein letztes Angebot.** | mīn **lets**-tes **ahn**-geh-boht |
| I'm nearly broke. | **Ich bin fast pleite.** | ikh bin fahst **plī**-teh |

# Entertainment

| What's happening tonight? | **Was ist heute abend los?** | vahs ist **hoy**-teh **ah**-bent lohs |
| Can you recommend something? | **Können Sie etwas empfehlen?** | **kurn**-nen zee et-vahs emp-**fay**-len |
| Is it free? | **Ist es umsonst?** | ist es oom-**zohnst** |
| Where can I buy a ticket? | **Wo kann ich eine Karte kaufen?** | voh kahn ikh Ī-neh **kar**-teh **kowf**-en |
| When does it start? | **Wann fängt es an?** | vahn fengt es ahn |
| When does it end? | **Wann endet es?** | vahn **en**-det es |

## What's happening:

| movie... | **Film...** | film |
| ...original version | **...im Original** | im oh-rig-ee-**nahl** |
| ...in English | **...auf englisch** | owf **eng**-lish |
| ...with subtitles | **...mit Untertiteln** | mit **oon**-ter-tee-teln |
| music... | **Musik...** | moo-**zeek** |
| ...live | **...live** | "live" |
| ...classical | **...klassisch** | **klahs**-sish |
| folk music | **Volksmusik** | **fohlks**-moo-zeek |
| old rock | **Alter Rock** | **ahl**-ter rok |
| jazz / blues | **Jazz / Blues** | "jazz" / "blues" |
| concert | **Konzert** | kon-**tsert** |
| dancing | **Tanzen** | **tahn**-tsen |
| cover charge | **Eintritt** | **Ī**-trit |

# Phoning

| English | German | Pronunciation |
|---|---|---|
| Where is the nearest phone? | Wo ist das nächste Telefon? | voh ist dahs **nekh**-steh tel-eh-**fohn** |
| I'd like to telephone... | Ich möchte einen Anruf nach... machen. | ikh **murkh**-teh **ī**-nen **ahn**-roof nahkh... **mahkh**-en |
| ...the U.S.A. | ...U.S.A. | oo es ah |
| What is the cost per minute? | Wieviel kostet es pro Minute? | vee-**feel kos**-tet es proh mee-**noo**-teh |
| I'd like to make a... call. | Ich möchte ein... machen. | ikh **murkh**-teh **īn**... **mahkh**-en |
| ...local | ...Ortsgespräch | **orts**-geh-shpraykh |
| ...collect | ...Rückgespräch | **rewk**-geh-shpraykh |
| ...credit card | ...Kreditkartengespräch | kreh-**deet**-kar-ten-geh-shpraykh |
| ...long distance | ...Ferngespräch | **fehrn**-geh-shpraykh |
| It doesn't work. | Es außer Betrieb. | es **ow**-ser beh-**treep** |
| May I use your phone? | Darf ich mal Ihr Telefon benutzen? | darf ikh mahl eer tel-eh-**fohn** beh-**noo**-tsen |
| Can you dial for me? | Können Sie für mich wählen? | **kurn**-nen zee fewr mikh **vay**-len |
| Can you talk for me? | Können Sie für mich sprechen? | **kurn**-nen zee fewr mikh **shprekh**-en |
| It's busy. | Besetzt. | beh-**zetst** |
| Will you try again? | Noch einmal versuchen? | nokh **īn**-mahl fehr-**zookh**-en |
| Hello? (on phone) | Ja, bitte? | yah **bit**-teh |

| My name is... | **Ich heiße...** | ikh **hī**-seh |
| My number is.. | **Meine Telefon-nummer ist...** | **mī**-neh tel-eh-**fohn**-num-mer ist |
| Speak slowly. | **Sprechen Sie langsam.** | **shprekh**-en zee **lahng**-zahm |
| Wait a moment. | **Moment.** | moh-**ment** |
| Don't hang up. | **Nicht auflegen.** | nikht **owf**-lay-gen |

## Key telephone words:

| telephone | **Telefon** | tel-eh-**fohn** |
| telephone card | **Telefonkarte** | tel-eh-**fohn**-kar-teh |
| operator | **Vermittlung** | fehr-**mit**-loong |
| international assistance | **Internationale Auskunft** | in-tehr-naht-see-oh-**nah**-leh **ows**-koonft |
| country code | **Landesvorwahl** | **lahn**-des-for-vahl |
| area code | **Vorwahl** | **for**-vahl |
| telephone book | **Telefonbuch** | tel-eh-**fohn**-bookh |
| yellow pages | **Gelbe Seiten** | **gehlp**-eh **zī**-ten |
| toll-free | **gebührenfrei** | geh-**bew**-ren-frī |
| out of service | **Außer Betrieb** | **ow**-ser beh-**treep** |

In Germany, it's considered polite to identify yourself by name at the beginning of every phone conversation. A *Telefonkarte* (telephone card), available at post offices, is handier than using coins for your calls. Post offices also have easy-to-use metered phones. For more tips, see "Let's Talk Telephones" near the end of this book.

# Mailing

| | | |
|---|---|---|
| Where is the post office? | **Wo ist das Postamt?** | voh ist dahs **post**-ahmt |
| Which window for...? | **An welchem Schalter ist...?** | ahn **vehlkh**-em **shahl**-ter ist |
| ...stamps | **...Briefmarken** | **breef**-mar-ken |
| ...packages | **...Pakete** | pah-**kay**-teh |
| To America.... | **Nach Amerika...** | nahkh ah-**mehr**-ee-kah |
| ...by air mail. | **...mit Luftpost.** | mit **luft**-post |
| ...slow and cheap. | **...langsam und billig.** | **lahng**-zahm oont **bil**-lig |

## Licking the postal code:

| | | |
|---|---|---|
| post office | **Postamt** | **post**-ahmt |
| stamp | **Briefmarke** | **breef**-mar-keh |
| postcard | **Postkarte** | **post**-kar-teh |
| letter | **Brief** | breef |
| envelope | **Umschlag** | **oom**-shlahg |
| package | **Paket** | pah-**kayt** |
| box | **Karton** | kar-**ton** |
| string | **Schnur** | shnoor |
| tape | **Klebeband** | **klay**-beh-bahnd |
| mailbox | **Briefkasten** | **breef**-kahs-ten |
| air mail | **Luftpost** | **luft**-post |
| slow and cheap | **langsam und billig** | **lahng**-zahm oont **bil**-lig |
| book rate | **Büchersendung** | bewkh-er-**zayn**-doong |

# Help!

| | | |
|---|---|---|
| Help! | **Hilfe!** | **hil**-feh |
| Help me! | **Helfen Sie mir!** | **hel**-fen zee meer |
| Call a doctor! | **Rufen Sie einen Arzt!** | **roo**-fen zee ī-nen artst |
| ambulance | **Krankenwagen** | **krahn**-ken-vah-gen |
| accident | **Unfall** | **oon**-fahl |
| injured | **verletzt** | fehr-**letst** |
| emergency | **Notfall** | **noht**-fahl |
| police | **Polizei** | poh-leet-**sī** |
| thief | **Dieb** | deep |
| pick-pocket | **Taschendieb** | **tahsh**-en-deep |
| I've been ripped off. | **Ich bin bestohlen worden.** | ikh bin beh-**shtoh**-len **vor**-den |
| I've lost my... | **Ich habe meine... verloren.** | ikh **hah**-beh **mī**-neh... fehr-**lor**-en |
| ...passport. | **...Paß** | pahs |
| ...ticket. | **...Karte** | **kar**-teh |
| ...baggage. | **...Gepäck** | geh-**pek** |
| ...purse. | **...Handtasche** | **hahnd**-tash-eh |
| ...wallet. | **...Brieftasche** | **breef**-tash-eh |
| ...faith in humankind | **...Glauben an die Menschheit** | **glow**-ben ahn dee **mehnsh**-hīt |
| I'm lost. | **Ich habe mich verlaufen.** | ikh **hah**-beh mikh fehr-**lowf**-en |

**HELP!**

## Help for women:

| | | |
|---|---|---|
| Leave me alone. | **Lassen Sie mich in Ruhe.** | **lah**-sen zee mikh in **roo**-heh |
| I *vant* to be alone. | **Ich möchte alleine sein.** | ikh **murkh**-teh ah-**lī**-neh zīn |
| I'm not interested. | **Ich hab kein Interesse.** | ikh hahp kīn in-tehr-**es**-seh |
| I'm married. | **Ich bin verheiratet.** | ikh bin fehr-**hī**-rah-tet |
| I'm a lesbian. | **Ich bin Lesbierin.** | ikh bin les-**beer**-in |
| I have a contagious disease. | **Ich habe eine ansteckende Krankheit.** | ikh **hah**-beh ī-neh **ahn**-shtek-en-deh **krahnk**-hīt |
| Don't touch me. | **Fassen Sie mich nicht an.** | **fah**-sen zee mikh nikht ahn |
| You're disgusting. | **Sie sind eklig.** | zee zint **ek**-lig |
| Stop following me. | **Hör auf, mir nachzulaufen.** | hur owf meer **nahkh**-tsoo-**lowf**-en |
| This man is bothering me. | **Der Mann stört mich.** | dehr mahn shturt mikh |
| Enough! | **Das reicht!** | dahs rīkht |
| Get lost! | **Hau ab!** | how ahp |
| Drop dead! | **Verschwinde!** | fehr-**shvin**-deh |
| I'll call the police. | **Ich rufe die Polizei.** | ikh **roo**-feh dee poh-leet-**sī** |

# Health

| | | |
|---|---|---|
| I feel sick. | **Mir ist schlecht.** | meer ist shlekht |
| I need a doctor... | **Ich brauche einen Arzt...** | ikh **browkh**-eh ī-nen artst |
| ...who speaks English. | **...der Englisch spricht.** | dehr **eng**-lish shprikht |
| It hurts here. | **Hier tut es weh.** | heer toot es vay |
| I'm allergic to... | **Ich bin allergisch gegen...** | ikh bin ah-**lehr**-gish **gay**-gen |
| ...penicillin. | **...Penizillin.** | pen-ee-tsee-**leen** |
| I am diabetic. | **Ich bin Diabetiker.** | ikh bin dee-ah-**bet**-ee-ker |
| I've missed a period. | **Ich habe meine Tage nicht bekommen.** | ikh **hah**-beh mī-neh **tahg**-eh nikht beh-**kom**-men |
| I have... | **Ich habe...** | ikh **hah**-beh |
| ...a burn. | **...eine Verbrennung.** | ī-neh fehr-**bren**-noong |
| ...chest pains | **...Schmerzen in der Brust.** | **shmehrt**-sen in dehr brust |
| ...a cold. | **...eine Erkältung.** | ī-neh ehr-**kel**-toong |
| ...constipation | **...Verstopfung.** | fehr-**shtop**-foong |
| ...a cough. | **...einen Husten.** | ī-nen **hoo**-sten |
| ...diarrhea. | **...Durchfall.** | **durkh**-fahl |
| ...a fever. | **...Fieber.** | **fee**-ber |
| ...the flu. | **...die Grippe.** | dee **grip**-peh |
| ...giggles. | **...einen Lachanfall.** | ī-nen **lahkh**-ahn-fahl |
| ...a headache. | **...Kopfschmerzen.** | **kopf**-shmehrt-sen |
| ...hemorrhoids. | **...Hämorrholden.** | **hay**-mor-hohl-den |

| | | |
|---|---|---|
| ...indigestion. | ...Verdauungsstörung. | fehr-**dow**-oongs-shtur-oong |
| ...an infection. | ...eine Entzündung. | ī-neh ent-**sewn**-doong |
| ...nausea. | ...Übelkeit. | **ew**-bel-kīt |
| ...a rash. | ...einen Ausschlag. | ī-nen **ows**-shlahg |
| ...a sore throat. | ...Halsschmerzen. | **hahls**-shmehrt-sen |
| ...a stomach ache. | ...Magenschmerzen. | **mah**-gen-shmehrt-sen |
| ...a swelling. | ...eine Schwellung. | ī-neh **shvel**-loong |
| ...a toothache. | ...Zahnschmerzen. | **tsahn**-shmehrt-sen |
| ...worms. | ...Würmer. | **vewr**-mer |
| I have body odor. | Ich habe Körpergeruch. | ikh **hah**-beh **kur**-per-geh-rookh |
| Is it serious? | Ist es ernst? | ist es **ehrnst** |

## Handy health words:

| | | |
|---|---|---|
| doctor | Arzt | artst |
| dentist | Zahnarzt | **tsahn**-artst |
| health insurance | Krankenversicherung | **krahn**-ken-fehr-**zikh**-eh-roong |
| hospital | Krankenhaus | **krahn**-ken-hows |
| pharmacy | Apotheke | ah-poh-**tay**-keh |
| bandage | Verband | fehr-**bahnt** |
| medicine | Medikamente | med-ee-kah-**men**-teh |
| aspirin | Aspirin | ah-spir-**een** |
| non-aspirin substitute | Ben-u-ron | **behn**-oo-ron |
| cough drops | Hustenbonbons | **hoo**-sten-bohn-bohz |
| cold medicine | Grippemittel | **grip**-eh-mit-tel |
| antibiotic | Antibiotika | ahn-tee-bee-**oh**-tee-kah |
| pain killer | Schmerzmittel | **shmehrts**-mit-tel |
| prescription | Rezept | reh-**tsehpt** |

# Chatting

| My name is... | **Ich heiße...** | ikh **hī**-seh |
| What's your name? | **Wie heißen Sie?** | vee **hī**-sen zee |
| Where are you from? | **Woher kommen Sie?** | **voh**-hehr **kom**-men zee |
| I'm from... | **Ich bin aus...** | ikh bin ows |
| ...America. | **...Amerika.** | ah-**mehr**-i-kah |
| ...Canada. | **...Kanada.** | **kah**-nah-dah |
| I'm... years old. | **Ich bin... Jahre alt.** | ikh bin... **yah**-reh ahlt |
| How old are you? | **Wie alt sind Sie?** | vee ahlt zint zee |
| I'm rich and single. | **Ich bin reich und zu haben.** | ikh bin rīkh oont tsoo **hah**-ben |
| I'm married. | **Ich bin verheiratet.** | ikh bin fehr-**hī**-rah-tet |
| Are you married? | **Sind Sie verheiratet?** | zint zee fehr-**hī**-rah-tet |
| Do you have children? | **Haben Sie Kinder?** | **hah**-ben zee **kin**-der |

## The right thing to say:

| Beautiful child! | **Schönes Kind!** | **shur**-nes kint |
| Beautiful children! | **Schöne Kinder!** | **shur**-neh **kin**-der |
| Excellent! | **Ausgezeichnet!** | ows-get-**sīkh**-net |
| Well done! | **Gut gemacht!** | goot geh-**mahkht** |
| Congratulations! | **Herzlichen Glückwunsch!** | **hehrts**-likh-en **glewk**-vunsh |
| You're welcome. | **Bitte schön.** | **bit**-teh shurn |
| Bless you! (sneeze) | **Gesundheit!** | geh-**zoond**-hīt |
| Excuse me. | **Entschuldigung.** | ent-**shool**-dee-goong |

## Travel talk:

| English | German | Pronunciation |
|---|---|---|
| I am / Are you...? | Ich bin / Sind Sie...? | ikh bin / zint zee |
| ...on vacation | ...auf Urlaub | owf **oor**-lowp |
| How long have you been traveling? | Wie lange sind Sie schon im Urlaub? | vee **lahng**-eh zint zee shohn im **oor**-lowp |
| day / week / month / year | Tag / Woche / Monat / Jahr | tahg / **vokh**-eh / **moh**-naht / yar |
| Where are you going? | Wohin gehen Sie? | **voh**-hin **gay**-hen zee |
| Where have you traveled? | Wo sind Sie schon gewesen? | voh zint zee shohn geh-**vay**-zen |
| Where would you like to go? | Wohin möchten Sie? | **voh**-hin **murkh**-ten zee |
| When are you going home? | Wann fahren Sie zurück? | vahn **far**-en zee tsoo-**rewk** |
| I've traveled to... | Ich bin hier gewesen... | ikh bin heer geh-**vay**-zen |
| Next I'll go to... | Als nächstes gehe ich nach... | als **nekh**-stes **gay**-heh ikh nahkh |
| I'm happy here. | Ich bin glücklich hier. | ikh bin **glewk**-likh heer |
| The Germans / Austrians / Swiss... | Die Deutschen / Österreicher / Schweizer... | dee **doy**-chen / urs-teh-**rīkh**-er / **shvīt**-ser |
| ...are friendly. | ...sind freundlich. | zint **froynd**-likh |
| This is a wonderful country. | Dies ist ein wunderbares Land. | deez ist īn **voon**-dehr-bah-res lahnd |
| Have a good trip! | Gute Reise! | **goo**-teh **rī**-zeh |

## Austria

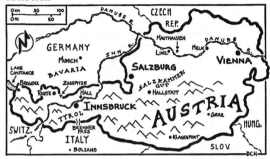

## Switzerland

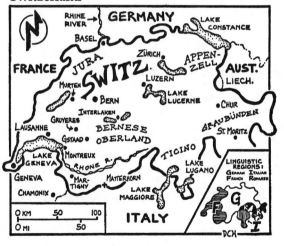

## Profanity and other animal noises:

So you'll know what the more colorful locals are saying...

| | | |
|---|---|---|
| Damn it. | **Verdammt.** | fehr-**dahmt** |
| Shit. | **Scheiße.** | shī-seh |
| Go to hell. | **Geh zur Hölle.** | gay tsur **hurl**-leh |
| Screw it. | **Scheiß drauf.** | shīs drowf |
| Sit on it. | **Am Arsch.** | ahm arsh |
| bastard (pig-dog) | **Schweinehund** | shvī-neh-hoont |
| bitch (goat) | **Ziege** | tsee-geh |
| breasts (colloq.) | **Titten** | tit-en |
| penis (colloq.) | **Schwanz** | shvahnts |
| butthole | **Arschloch** | arsh-lokh |
| stupid (dumb head) | **Dummkopf** | dum-kopf |
| Did someone...? | **Hat jemand...?** | haht yay-mahnd |
| ...burp | **...gerülpst** | geh-rewlpst |
| ...fart | **...gefurzt** | geh-furtst |

### Conversing with German animals:

| | | |
|---|---|---|
| rooster / cock-a-doodle-doo | **Hahn / kikeriki** | hahn / kee-keh-ree-**kee** |
| bird / tweet tweet | **Vogel / piep piep** | foh-gel / peep peep |
| cat / meow | **Katze / miau** | kaht-seh / mee-ow |
| dog / woof woof | **Hund / wuff wuff** | hoont / vuff vuff |
| duck / quack quack | **Ente / quak quak** | en-teh / kwahk kwahk |
| cow / moo | **Kuh / muh** | koo / moo |
| pig / oink oink | **Schwein / nöff nöff** | shvīn / nurf nurf |

# DICTIONARY

# Dictionary

| English | French | Italian | German |
|---------|--------|---------|--------|
| **A** | | **A** | |
| above | au dessus | sopra | über |
| accident | accident | incidente | Unfall |
| accountant | comptable | commercialista | Buchhalter |
| adaptor | adapteur | adattatore | Zwischenstecker |
| address | adresse | indirizzo | Adresse |
| adult | adulte | adulto | Erwachsener |
| afraid | peur | spaventato | ängstlich |
| after | après | dopo | nach |
| afternoon | après-midi | pomeriggio | Nachmittag |
| aftershave | après rasage | dopobarba | Rasierwasser |
| afterwards | après | più tardi | nachher |
| again | encore | ancora | noch einmal |
| age | âge | età | Alter |
| aggressive | aggressif | aggressivo | aggressiv |
| agree | d'accord | d'accordo | einverstanden |
| AIDS | SIDA | AIDS | AIDS |
| air | l'air | aria | Luft |
| air-conditioned | climatisé | aria condizionata | Klimaanlage |
| airline | ligne aérienne | aeroplano | Fluggesellschaft |
| air mail | par avion | via aerea | Luftpost |
| airport | aéroport | aeroporto | Flughafen |
| alarm clock | réveille-matin | sveglia | Wecker |
| alcohol | alcool | alcool | Alkohol |
| allergic | allergique | allergico | allergisch |
| allergies | allergies | allergie | Allergien |
| alone | seule | solo | allein |
| already | déjà | già | schon |

| English | French | Italian | German |
|---------|--------|---------|--------|
| always | toujours | sempre | immer |
| ancestor | ancêtre | antenato | Vorfahre |
| ancient | ancien | antico | altertümlich |
| and | et | e | und |
| angry | fâché | arrabbiato | wütend |
| ankle | cheville | caviglia | Fußknöchel |
| animal | animal | animale | Tier |
| another | encore | un altro | noch ein |
| answer | réponse | risposta | Antwort |
| antibiotic | antibiotique | antibiotico | Antibiotika |
| antiques | antiquités | antichità | Antiquitäten |
| apartment | appartement | appartamento | Wohnung |
| apology | excuse | scuse | Entschuldigung |
| appetizers | hors-d'oeuvre | antipasto | Vorspeise |
| apple | pomme | mela | Apfel |
| appointment | rendezvous | appuntamento | Verabredung |
| approximately | presque | più o meno | ungefähr |
| arm | bras | braccio | Arm |
| arrivals | arrivées | arrivi | Ankunften |
| arrive | arriver | arrivare | ankommen |
| art | l'art | arte | Kunst |
| artificial | artificial | artificiale | künstlich |
| artist | artiste | artista | Künstler |
| ashtray | cendrier | portacenere | Aschenbecher |
| ask | demander | domandare | fragen |
| aspirin | aspirine | aspirina | Aspirin |
| at | à | a | bei |
| attractive | attirant | bello | attraktiv |
| aunt | tante | zia | Tante |
| Austria | Autriche | Austria | Österreich |

| English | French | Italian | German |
|---------|--------|---------|--------|
| autumn | automne | autunno | Herbst |

## B                              ## B

| English | French | Italian | German |
|---------|--------|---------|--------|
| baby | bébé | bambino | Baby |
| babysitter | babysitter | bambinaia | Babysitter |
| backpack | sac à dos | zainetto | Rucksack |
| bad | mauvais | cattivo | schlecht |
| bag | sac | sachetto | Tüte |
| baggage | bagages | bagaglio | Gepäck |
| bakery | boulangerie | panificio | Bäckerei |
| balcony | balcon | balcone | Balkon |
| ball | balle | palla | Ball |
| banana | banane | banana | Banane |
| band-aid | bandage adhésif | cerotto | Pflaster |
| bank | banque | banca | Bank |
| barber | coiffeur | barbiere | Frisör |
| basement | sous-sol | seminterrato | Keller |
| basket | pannier | cestino | Korb |
| bath | bain | bagno | Bad |
| bathroom | salle de bains | bagno | Bad |
| bathtub | baignoire | vasca da bagno | Badewanne |
| battery | batterie | batteria | Batterie |
| beach | plage | spiaggia | Strand |
| beard | barbe | barba | Bart |
| beautiful | belle | bello | schön |
| because | parce que | perchè | weil |
| bed | lit | letto | Bett |
| bedroom | chambre | camera da letto | Zimmer |
| bedsheet | draps | lenzuolo | Laken |

| English | French | Italian | German |
|---|---|---|---|
| beef | boeuf | manzo | Rindfleisch |
| beer | bière | birra | Bier |
| before | avant | prima | vor |
| begin | commencer | cominciare | anfangen |
| behind | derrière | dietro | hinter |
| below | sous | sotto | unter |
| belt | ceinture | cintura | Gürtel |
| best | le meilleur | il migliore | am besten |
| better | meilleur | meglio | besser |
| bib | bavoir | bavaglino | Lätzchen |
| bicycle | vélo | bicicletta | Fahrrad |
| big | grand | grande | groß |
| bill (payment) | l'addition | conto | Rechnung |
| bird | oiseau | uccello | Vogel |
| birthday | anniversaire | compleanno | Geburtstag |
| black | noir | nero | schwarz |
| blanket | couverture | coperta | Decke |
| blond | blonde | biondo | blond |
| blood | sang | sangue | Blut |
| blouse | chemisier | camicetta | Bluse |
| blue | bleu | blu | blau |
| boat | bateau | barca | Schiff |
| body | corps | corpo | Körper |
| boiled | bouilli | bollito | gekocht |
| bomb | bombe | bomba | Bombe |
| book | livre | libro | Buch |
| book shop | librairie | libreria | Buchladen |
| boots | bottes | stivali | Stiefel |
| border | frontière | frontiera | Grenze |

| English | French | Italian | German |
|---------|--------|---------|--------|
| **borrow** | emprunter | prendere in prestito | leihen |
| **boss** | chef | capo | Boss |
| **bottle** | bouteille | bottiglia | Flasche |
| **bottom** | fond | fondo | Boden |
| **bowl** | bol | boccia | Schale |
| **box** | boîte | scatola | Karton |
| **boy** | garçon | ragazzo | Junge |
| **boyfriend** | petit ami | ragazzo | Freund |
| **bra** | soutien-gorge | reggiseno | B.H. |
| **bracelet** | bracelet | braccialetto | Armband |
| **bread** | pain | pane | Brot |
| **breakfast** | petit déjeuner | colazione | Frühstück |
| **bridge** | pont | ponte | Brücke |
| **briefs** | slip | mutandoni | Unterhosen |
| **Britain** | Grande-Bretagne | Britannia | England |
| **broken** | en panne | rotto | kaputt |
| **brother** | frère | fratello | Bruder |
| **brown** | brun | marrone | braun |
| **bucket** | seau | secchio | Eimer |
| **building** | bâtiment | edificio | Gebäude |
| **bulb** | ampoule | bulbo | Birne |
| **burn (n)** | brûlure | bruciatura | Verbrennung |
| **bus** | bus | autobus | Bus |
| **business** | affaires | affari | Geschäft |
| **but** | mais | ma | aber |
| **button** | bouton | bottone | Knopf |
| **buy** | acheter | comprare | kaufen |
| **by (via)** | en | in | mit |

| English | French | Italian | German |
|---|---|---|---|
| **C** | | **C** | |
| **calendar** | calendrier | calendario | Kalender |
| **calorie** | calorie | calorie | Kalorie |
| **camera** | appareil-photo | macchina fotografica | Photoapparat |
| **camping** | camping | campeggio | zelten |
| **can (n)** | boîte de conserve | lattina | Dose |
| **can (v)** | pouvoir | potere | können |
| **Canada** | Canada | Canada | Kanada |
| **can opener** | ouvre-boîte | apriscatola | Dosenöffner |
| **canal** | canal | canale | Kanal |
| **candle** | chandelle | candela | Kerze |
| **candy** | bonbon | caramella | Bonbons |
| **canoe** | canoë | canoa | Kanu |
| **cap** | casquette | berretto | Deckel |
| **captain** | capitaine | capitano | Kapitän |
| **car** | voiture | macchina | Auto |
| **carafe** | carafe | caraffa | Krug |
| **card** | carte | cartina | Karte |
| **cards (deck)** | jeu de cartes | carte | Karten |
| **careful** | prudent | prudente | vorsichtig |
| **carpet** | moquette | tappeto | Teppich |
| **carry** | porter | portare | tragen |
| **cashier** | caisse | cassiere | Kassierer |
| **cassette** | cassette | cassetta | Kassette |
| **castle** | château | castello | Burg |
| **cat** | chat | gatto | Katze |
| **catch (v)** | attraper | prendere | fangen |
| **cathedral** | cathédrale | cattedrale | Kathedrale |

| English | French | Italian | German |
|---|---|---|---|
| cave | grotte | grotta | Höhle |
| cellar | cave | cantina | Keller |
| center | centre | centro | Zentrum |
| century | siècle | secolo | Jahrhundert |
| chair | chaise | sedia | Stuhl |
| change (n) | change | cambio | Wechsel |
| change (v) | changer | cambiare | wechseln |
| charming | charmant | affascinante | bezaubernd |
| cheap | bon marché | economico | billig |
| check | chèque | assegno | Scheck |
| Cheers! | Santé! | Salute! | Prost! |
| cheese | fromage | formaggio | Käse |
| chicken | poulet | pollo | Hühnchen |
| children | enfants | bambini | Kinder |
| Chinese (adj) | chinois | cinese | chinesisches |
| chocolate | chocolat | cioccolato | Schokolade |
| Christmas | Noël | Natale | Weihnachten |
| church | église | chiesa | Kirche |
| cigarette | cigarette | sigarette | Zigarette |
| cinema | cinéma | cinema | Kino |
| city | ville | città | Stadt |
| class | classe | classe | Klasse |
| clean (adj) | propre | pulito | sauber |
| clear | clair | chiaro | klar |
| cliff | falaise | dirupo | Kliff |
| cloth | tissu | stoffa | Stoff |
| clothes | vêtements | vestiti | Kleider |
| closed | fermé | chiuso | geschlossen |
| clothesline | corde à linge | marca | Wäscheleine |
| clothes pins | pince à linge | spilla | Wäscheklammern |

| English | French | Italian | German |
|---|---|---|---|
| cloudy | nuageux | nuvoloso | bewölkt |
| coast | côte | costa | Küste |
| coat | manteau | cappotto | Mantel |
| coat hanger | cintre | appendiabiti | Kleiderbügel |
| coffee | café | caffè | Kaffee |
| coins | pièces | monete | Münzen |
| cold (adj) | froid | freddo | kalt |
| colors | couleurs | colori | Farben |
| comb (n) | peigne | pettine | Kamm |
| come | venir | venire | kommen |
| comfortable | confortable | confortevole | komfortabel |
| compact disc | disque compact | compact disc | C.D. |
| complain | se plaindre | protestare | sich beschweren |
| complicated | compliqué | complicato | kompliziert |
| computer | ordinateur | computer | Komputer |
| concert | concert | concerto | Konzert |
| condom | préservatif | preservativo | Präservativ |
| confirm | confirmer | confermare | konfirmieren |
| conductor | conducteur | conducente | Schaffner |
| congratulations | félicitations | congratulazioni | Glückwünsche |
| connection | correspondance | coincidenza | Verbindung |
| constipation | constipation | stitichezza | Verstopfung |
| cook (v) | cuisinier | cuocere | kochen |
| cool | frais | fresco | kühl |
| cork | bouchon | sughero | Korken |
| corkscrew | tire-bouchon | cavatappi | Korkenzieher |
| corner | coin | angolo | Ecke |
| corridor | couloir | corridoio | Flur |
| cost (v) | coûter | costare | kosten |
| cot | lit de camp | lettino | Liege |

| English | French | Italian | German |
|---|---|---|---|
| cotton | coton | cotone | Baumwolle |
| cough (v) | tousser | tossire | husten |
| cough drops | pastilles | pasticche | Hustenpastillen |
| country | pays | paese | Land |
| countryside | compagne | campagna | auf dem Land |
| cousin | cousin | cugino | Vetter |
| cow | vâche | mucca | Kuh |
| cozy | confortable | confortevole | gemütlich |
| crafts | arts | arte | Kunstgewerbe |
| cream | crème | panna | Sahne |
| credit card | carte de crédit | carta di credito | Kreditkarte |
| crowd (n) | foule | folla | Menge |
| cry (v) | pleurer | piangere | weinen |
| cup | tasse | tazza | Tasse |

### D　D

| | | | |
|---|---|---|---|
| dad | papa | papà | Papa |
| dance (v) | danser | ballare | tanzen |
| danger | danger | pericolo | Gefahr |
| dangerous | dangereux | pericoloso | gefährlich |
| dark | sombre | scuro | dunkel |
| daughter | fille | figlia | Tochter |
| day | jour | giorno | Tag |
| dead | mort | morto | tot |
| delay | retardement | ritardo | Verspätung |
| delicious | délicieux | delizioso | lecker |
| dental floss | fil dentaire | filo interdentale | Zahnseide |
| dentist | dentiste | dentista | Zahnarzt |
| deodorant | désodorisant | deodorante | Deodorant |

| English | French | Italian | German |
|---|---|---|---|
| **depart** | partir | partire | abfahren |
| **departures** | départs | partenze | Abfahrten |
| **deposit** | caution | deposito | Kaution |
| **dessert** | dessert | dolci | Nachtisch |
| **detour** | déviation | deviazione | Umleitung |
| **diabetic** | diabétique | diabetico | diabetisch |
| **diamond** | diamant | diamante | Diamant |
| **diaper** | couche | pannolino | Windel |
| **diarrhea** | diarrhée | diarrea | Durchfall |
| **dictionary** | dictionnaire | dizionario | Wörterbuch |
| **die** | mourir | morire | sterben |
| **difficult** | difficile | difficile | schwierig |
| **dinner** | dîner | cena | Abendessen |
| **direct** | direct | diretto | direkt |
| **direction** | direction | direzione | Richtung |
| **dirty** | sale | sporco | schmutzig |
| **discount** | réduction | sconto | Ermäßigung |
| **disease** | maladie | malattia | Krankheit |
| **disturb** | déranger | disturbare | stören |
| **divorced** | divorcé | divorziato | geschieden |
| **doctor** | docteur | dottore | Arzt |
| **dog** | chien | cane | Hund |
| **doll** | poupée | bambola | Puppe |
| **donkey** | âne | asino | Esel |
| **door** | porte | porta | Tür |
| **dormitory** | dortoire | camerata | Schlafsaal |
| **double** | double | doppio | doppel |
| **down** | en bas | giù | runter |
| **dream (n)** | rêve | sogno | Traum |
| **dream (v)** | rêver | sognare | träumen |

| English | French | Italian | German |
|---------|--------|---------|--------|
| **dress (n)** | robe | vestito | Kleid |
| **drink (n)** | boisson | bevanda | Getränk |
| **drive (v)** | conduire | guidare | fahren |
| **driver** | chauffeur | autista | Fahrer |
| **drunk** | ivre | ubriaco | betrunken |
| **dry** | sec | secco | trocken |

## E                          E

| English | French | Italian | German |
|---------|--------|---------|--------|
| **each** | chaque | ogni | jede |
| **ear** | oreille | orecchio | Ohr |
| **early** | tôt | presto | früh |
| **earplugs** | boules quiès | tappi per le orecchie | Ohrenschützer |
| **earrings** | boucle d'oreille | orecchini | Ohrringe |
| **earth** | terre | terra | Erde |
| **east** | est | est | Osten |
| **Easter** | Pâques | Pasqua | Ostern |
| **easy** | facile | facile | einfach |
| **eat** | manger | mangiare | essen |
| **elbow** | coude | gomito | Ellbogen |
| **elevator** | ascenseur | ascensore | Fahrstuhl |
| **embarrassing** | gênant | imbarazzante | peinlich |
| **embassy** | ambassade | ambasciata | Botschaft |
| **empty** | vide | vuoto | leer |
| **engineer** | ingénieur | ingeniere | Ingenieur |
| **English** | anglais | inglese | Englisch |
| **enjoy** | apprécier | divertirsi | genießen |
| **enough** | assez | abbastanza | genug |
| **entrance** | entrée | ingresso | Eingang |

| English | French | Italian | German |
|---------|--------|---------|--------|
| entry | entrée | entrata | Eingang |
| envelope | enveloppe | busta | Briefumschlag |
| eraser | gomme | gomma da cancellare | Radiergummi |
| especially | spécialement | specialmente | besonders |
| Europe | Europe | Europa | Europa |
| evening | soir | sera | Abend |
| every | chaque | ogni | jede |
| everything | tout | tutto | alles |
| exactly | exactement | esattamente | genau |
| example | exemple | esempio | Beispiel |
| excellent | excellent | eccellente | ausgezeichnet |
| except | sauf | eccetto | außer |
| exchange (n) | change | cambio | Wechsel |
| excuse me | pardon | mi scusi | Entschuldigung |
| exhausted | épuisé | esausto | erschöpft |
| exit | sortie | uscita | Ausgang |
| expensive | cher | caro | teuer |
| explain | expliquer | spiegare | erklären |
| eye | oeil | occhio | Auge |

## F

## F

| | | | |
|---------|--------|---------|--------|
| face | visage | faccia | Gesicht |
| factory | usine | fabbrica | Fabrik |
| fall (v) | tomber | cadere | fallen |
| false | faux | falso | falsch |
| family | famille | famiglia | Familie |
| famous | fameux | famoso | berühmt |
| fantastic | fantastique | fantastico | phantastisch |

| English | French | Italian | German |
|---------|--------|---------|--------|
| far | loin | lontano | weit |
| farm | ferme | fattoria | Bauernhof |
| farmer | fermier | contadino | Bauer |
| fashion | mode | moda | Mode |
| fat (adj) | gros | grasso | fett |
| father | père | padre | Vater |
| father-in-law | beau-père | suocero | Schwiegervater |
| faucet | robinet | rubinetto | Wasserhahn |
| fax | fax | fax | Fax |
| female | femelle | femmina | weiblich |
| ferry | bac | traghetto | Fähre |
| fever | fièvre | febbre | Fieber |
| few | peu | poco | wenig |
| field | champ | campo | Feld |
| fight (n) | lutte | lotta | Streit |
| fight (v) | combattre | combattere | streiten |
| fine (good) | bon | bene | gut |
| finger | doigt | dito | Finger |
| finish (v) | finir | finire | beenden |
| fireworks | feux d'artifices | fuochi d'artificio | Feuerwerk |
| first | premier | primo | erst |
| first aid | premiers secours | primo soccorso | erste Hilfe |
| first class | première classe | prima classe | erste Klasse |
| fish | poisson | pesce | Fisch |
| fish (v) | pêcher | pescare | fischen |
| fix (v) | réparer | aggiustare | reparieren |
| fizzy | pétillant | frizzante | sprudelnd |
| flag | drapeau | bandiera | Fahne |
| flashlight | lampe de poche | torcia | Taschenlampe |
| flavor | parfum | aroma | Geschmack |

| English | French | Italian | German |
|---|---|---|---|
| flea | puce | pulce | Floh |
| flight | vol | volo | Flug |
| flower | fleur | fiore | Blume |
| flu | grippe | influenza | Grippe |
| fly | voler | volare | fliegen |
| fog | brouillard | nebbia | Nebel |
| food | nourriture | cibo | Essen |
| foot | pied | piede | Fuß |
| football | football | calcio | Fußball |
| for | pour | per | für |
| forbidden | interdit | vietato | verboten |
| foreign | étranger | straniero | fremd |
| forget | oublier | dimenticare | vergessen |
| fork | fourchette | forchetta | Gabel |
| fountain | fontaine | fontana | Brunnen |
| France | France | Francia | Frankreich |
| free (no cost) | gratuit | gratis | umsonst |
| fresh | fraîche | fresco | frisch |
| Friday | vendredi | venerdì | Freitag |
| friend | ami | amico | Freund |
| friendship | amitié | amicizia | Freundschaft |
| frisbee | frisbee | frisbee | Frisbee |
| from | de | da | von |
| fruit | fruit | frutta | Obst |
| fun | amusement | divertimento | Spaß |
| funeral | enterrement | funerale | Beerdigung |
| funny | drôle | divertente | komisch |
| furniture | meubles | mobili | Möbel |
| future | avenir | futuro | Zukunft |

| English | French | Italian | German |
|---|---|---|---|

## G

**G**

| English | French | Italian | German |
|---|---|---|---|
| gallery | gallerie | galleria | Galerie |
| game | jeu | gioco | Spiel |
| garage | garage | garage | Garage |
| garden | jardin | giardino | Garten |
| gardening | jardinage | giardinaggio | Gärtnern |
| gas | essence | benzina | Benzin |
| gas station | station de service | benzinaio | Tankstelle |
| gay | homosexuel | omosessuale | schwul |
| gentleman | monsieur | signore | Herr |
| genuine | authentique | genuino | echt |
| Germany | Allemagne | Germania | Deutschland |
| gift | cadeau | regalo | Geschenk |
| girl | fille | ragazza | Mädchen |
| girlfriend | petite amie | ragazza | Freundin |
| give | donner | dare | geben |
| glass | verre | bicchiere | Glas |
| glasses (eye) | lunettes | occhiali | Brille |
| gloves | gants | guanti | Handschuhe |
| go | aller | andare | gehen |
| God | Dieu | Dio | Gott |
| gold | or | oro | Gold |
| golf | golf | golf | Golf |
| good | bien | buono | gut |
| goodbye | au revoir | arrivederci | auf Wiedersehen |
| good day | bonjour | buon giorno | guten Tag |
| go through | passer | attraversare | durchgehen |
| grammar | grammaire | grammatica | Grammatik |
| granddaughter | petite-fille | nipote | Enkelin |

| English | French | Italian | German |
|---|---|---|---|
| **grandfather** | grand-père | nonno | Großvater |
| **grandmother** | grand-mère | nonna | Großmutter |
| **grandson** | petit-fils | nipote | Enkel |
| **gray** | gris | grigio | grau |
| **greasy** | graisseux | grasso | fettig |
| **great** | super | ottimo | super |
| **Greece** | Grèce | Grecia | Griechenland |
| **green** | vert | verde | grün |
| **grocery store** | épicerie | alimentari | Lebensmittelladen |
| **guarantee** | guarantie | garantito | Garantie |
| **guest** | invité | ospite | Gast |
| **guide** | guide | guida | Führer |
| **guidebook** | guide | guida | Führer |
| **guitar** | guitare | chitarra | Gitarre |
| **gum** | chewing-gum | gomma da masticare | Kaugummi |
| **gun** | fusil | pistola | Gewehr |

## H

## H

| | | | |
|---|---|---|---|
| **hair** | cheveux | capelli | Haare |
| **hairbrush** | brosse | spazzola per capelli | Haarbürste |
| **haircut** | coupe de cheveux | taglio di capelli | Frisur |
| **hand** | main | mano | Hand |
| **handicapped** | handicapé | andicappato | behindert |
| **handicrafts** | produits artisanaux | artigianato | Handarbeiten |
| **handle (n)** | poignée | manico | Griff |
| **handsome** | beau | attraente | gutaussehend |
| **happy** | heureux | contento | glücklich |

| English | French | Italian | German |
|---|---|---|---|
| harbor | port | porto | Hafen |
| hard | dûr | duro | hart |
| hat | chapeau | cappello | Hut |
| hate (v) | détester | odiare | hassen |
| have | avoir | avere | haben |
| he | il | lui | er |
| head | tête | testa | Kopf |
| headache | mal de tête | mal di testa | Kopfschmerzen |
| healthy | bonne santé | sano | gesund |
| hear | entendre | udire | hören |
| heart | coeur | cuore | Herz |
| heat (n) | chauffage | calore | Hitze |
| heat (v) | chauffer | scaldare | aufwärmen |
| heaven | paradis | paradiso | Himmel |
| heavy | lourd | pesante | schwer |
| hello | bonjour | ciao | hallo |
| help (n) | secours | aiuto | Hilfe |
| help (v) | aider | aiutare | Hilfe |
| hemorrhoids | hémorroïdes | emorroidi | Hämorrholden |
| her | elle | lei | ihr |
| here | ici | qui | hier |
| hi | salut | ciao | hallo |
| high | haut | alto | hoch |
| highchair | chaise haute | seggiolone | Kinderstuhl |
| highway | route nationale | autostrada | Landstraße |
| hill | colline | collina | Hügel |
| history | histoire | storia | Geschichte |
| hitchhike | autostop | autostop | per Anhalter fahren |
| hobby | hobby | hobby | Hobby |
| hole | trou | buco | Loch |

| English | French | Italian | German |
|---------|--------|---------|--------|
| **holiday** | jour férié | giorno festivo | Feiertag |
| **homemade** | fait à la maison | fatto in casa | hausgemacht |
| **homesick** | nostalgique | nostalgico | Heimweh |
| **honest** | honnête | onesto | ehrlich |
| **honeymoon** | lune de miel | luna di miele | Hochzeitsreise |
| **horrible** | horrible | orribile | schrecklich |
| **horse** | cheval | cavallo | Pferd |
| **horse riding** | équitation | equitazione | reiten |
| **hospital** | hôpital | ospedale | Krankenhaus |
| **hot** | chaud | caldo | heiß |
| **hotel** | hôtel | hotel | Hotel |
| **hour** | heure | ora | Stunde |
| **house** | maison | casa | Haus |
| **how many** | combien | quanti | wieviele |
| **how much ($)** | combien | quanto costa | wieviel kostet |
| **how** | comment | come | wie |
| **hungry** | faim | affamato | hungrig |
| **hurry (v)** | se dépêcher | avere fretta | sich beeilen |
| **husband** | mari | marito | Ehemann |
| **hydrofoil** | hydroptère | aliscafo | Tragflächenboot |

## I

| | | I | |
|---------|--------|---------|--------|
| **I** | je | io | ich |
| **ice** | glaçons | ghiaccio | Eis |
| **ice cream** | glace | gelato | Eis |
| **ill** | malade | malato | krank |
| **immediately** | immédiatement | immediatamente | sofort |
| **important** | important | importante | wichtig |
| **imported** | importé | importato | importiert |

| English | French | Italian | German |
|---------|--------|---------|--------|
| **impossible** | impossible | impossibile | unmöglich |
| **in** | en, dans | in | in |
| **included** | inclus | incluso | eingeschlossen |
| **incredible** | incroyable | incredibile | unglaublich |
| **independent** | indépendant | indipendente | unabhängig |
| **indigestion** | indigestion | indigestione | Verdauungsstörung |
| **industry** | industrie | industria | Industrie |
| **infection** | infection | infezione | Entzündung |
| **information** | information | informazioni | Information |
| **injured** | blessé | infortunato | verletzt |
| **innocent** | innocent | innocente | unschuldig |
| **insect** | insecte | insetto | Insekt |
| **insect repellant** | bombe contre les insectes | lozione anti-zanzare | Mückenspray |
| **inside** | dedans | dentro | innen |
| **instant** | instant | istante | sofortig |
| **instead** | au lieu | invece | anstatt |
| **insurance** | assurance | assicurazione | Versicherung |
| **intelligent** | intelligent | intelligente | klug |
| **interesting** | intéressant | interessante | interessant |
| **invitation** | invitation | invito | Einladung |
| **iodine** | teinture d'iode | iodio | Jod |
| **is** | est | è | ist |
| **island** | île | isola | Insel |
| **Italy** | Italie | Italia | Italien |
| **itch (n)** | démangeaison | prurito | Jucken |

| English | French | Italian | German |
|---------|--------|---------|--------|

## J

## J

| **jacket** | veste | giubbotto | Jacke |
| **jaw** | machoire | mascella | Kiefer |
| **jeans** | jeans | jeans | Jeans |
| **jewelry** | bijoux | gioielleria | Schmuck |
| **job** | boulot | lavoro | Beruf |
| **jogging** | jogging | footing | Jogging |
| **joke (n)** | blague | scherzo | Witz |
| **journey** | voyage | viaggio | Reise |
| **juice** | jus | succo | Saft |
| **jump (v)** | sauter | saltare | springen |

## K

## K

| **keep** | garder | tenere | behalten |
| **kettle** | bouilloire | bollitore | Kessel |
| **key** | clé | chiave | Schlüssel |
| **kill** | tuer | uccidere | töten |
| **kind** | aimable | gentile | freundlich |
| **king** | roi | re | König |
| **kiss** | baiser | baciare | Küß |
| **kitchen** | cuisine | cucina | Küche |
| **knee** | genou | ginocchio | Knie |
| **knife** | couteau | coltello | Messer |
| **know** | savoir | sapere | wissen |

| English | French | Italian | German |
|---|---|---|---|

## L

## L

| | | | |
|---|---|---|---|
| **ladder** | échelle | scala | Leiter |
| **ladies** | mesdames | signore | Damen |
| **lake** | lac | lago | See |
| **lamb** | agneau | agnello | Lamm |
| **language** | langue | lingua | Sprache |
| **large** | grand | grande | groß |
| **last** | dernier | ultimo | letzte |
| **late** | tard | tardi | spät |
| **later** | plus tard | più tardi | später |
| **laugh (v)** | rire | ridere | lachen |
| **laundromat** | laverie | lavanderia | Waschsalon |
| **lawyer** | avocat | avvocato | Anwalt |
| **lazy** | paresseux | pigro | faul |
| **leather** | cuir | pelle | Leder |
| **left** | gauche | sinistra | links |
| **leg** | jambe | gamba | Bein |
| **lend** | prêter | prestare | leihen |
| **letter** | lettre | lettera | Brief |
| **library** | bibliothèque | biblioteca | Leihbücherei |
| **life** | vie | vita | Leben |
| **light (n)** | lumière | luce | Licht |
| **light bulb** | ampoule | lampadina | Glühbirne |
| **lighter (n)** | briquet | accendino | Feuerzeug |
| **lip** | lèvre | labbro | Lippe |
| **list** | liste | lista | Liste |
| **listen** | écouter | ascoltare | zuhören |
| **liter** | litre | litro | Liter |
| **little (adj)** | petit | piccolo | klein |

| English | French | Italian | German |
|---------|--------|---------|--------|
| **local** | régional | locale | örtlich |
| **lock (n)** | serrure | serratura | Schloß |
| **lock (v)** | fermer à clé | chiudere | abschließen |
| **lockers** | consigne automatique | armadietti | Schließfächer |
| **look** | regarder | guardare | gucken |
| **lost** | perdu | perso | verloren |
| **loud** | bruyant | forte | laut |
| **love (v)** | aimer | amare | lieben |
| **lover** | amant | amante | Liebhaber |
| **low** | bas | basso | niedrig |
| **lozenges** | pastilles | pastiglie | Halsbonbon |
| **luck** | chance | fortuna | Glück |
| **luggage** | bagage | bagaglio | Gepäck |
| **lukewarm** | tiède | tiepido | lau |
| **lungs** | poumons | polmoni | Lungen |

## M

## M

| English | French | Italian | German |
|---------|--------|---------|--------|
| **macho** | macho | macho | macho |
| **mad** | fâché | arrabbiato | wütend |
| **magazine** | magazine | rivista | Zeitschrift |
| **mail (n)** | courrier | posta | Post |
| **main** | principal | principale | Haupt |
| **make (v)** | faire | fare | machen |
| **male** | mâle | maschio | männlich |
| **man** | homme | uomo | Mann |
| **manager** | directeur | direttore | Geschäftsführer |
| **many** | beaucoup | molti | viele |
| **map** | carte | cartina | Karte |

| English | French | Italian | German |
|---------|--------|---------|--------|
| **market** | marché | mercato | Markt |
| **married** | marié | sposato | verheiratet |
| **matches** | allumettes | fiammiferi | Streichhölzer |
| **maximum** | maximum | massimo | Maximum |
| **maybe** | peut-être | forse | vielleicht |
| **meat** | viande | carne | Fleisch |
| **medicine** | médicaments | medicina | Medikamente |
| **medium** | moyen | medio | mittel |
| **men** | hommes | uomini | Herren |
| **menu** | carte | menu | Speisekarte |
| **message** | message | messaggio | Nachricht |
| **metal** | métal | metallo | Metall |
| **midnight** | minuit | mezzanotte | Mitternacht |
| **mineral water** | l'eau minérale | acqua minerale | Mineralwasser |
| **minimum** | minimum | minimo | Minimum |
| **minutes** | minutes | minuti | Minuten |
| **mirror** | miroir | specchio | Spiegel |
| **Miss** | Mademoiselle | Signorina | Fräulein |
| **mistake** | erreur | errore | Fehler |
| **misunder-standing** | malentendu | incomprensione | Mißverständnis |
| **mix (n)** | mélange | misto | Mischung |
| **modern** | moderne | moderno | modern |
| **moment** | moment | momento | Moment |
| **Monday** | lundi | lunedì | Montag |
| **money** | argent | soldi | Geld |
| **month** | mois | mese | Monat |
| **monument** | monument | monumento | Denkmal |
| **moon** | lune | luna | Mond |
| **more** | encore | ancora | mehr |

| English | French | Italian | German |
|---------|--------|---------|--------|
| **morning** | matin | mattina | Morgen |
| **mosquito** | moustique | zanzara | Mücke |
| **mother** | mère | madre | Mutter |
| **mother-in-law** | belle-mère | suocera | Schwiegermutter |
| **mountain** | montagne | montagna | Berg |
| **moustache** | moustache | baffi | Schnurrbart |
| **mouth** | bouche | bocca | Mund |
| **movie** | film | film | Film |
| **Mr.** | Monsieur | Signore | Herr |
| **Mrs.** | Madame | Signora | Frau |
| **much** | beaucoup | molto | viel |
| **muscle** | muscle | muscolo | Muskel |
| **museum** | musée | museo | Museum |
| **music** | musique | musica | Musik |
| **my** | mon | mio | mein |

## N

## N

| English | French | Italian | German |
|---------|--------|---------|--------|
| **nail clipper** | pince à ongles | tagliaunghie | Nagelschere |
| **naked** | nu | nudo | nackt |
| **name** | nom | nome | Name |
| **napkin** | serviette | salvietta | Serviette |
| **narrow** | étroit | stretto | schmal |
| **nationality** | nationalité | nazionalità | Nationalität |
| **natural** | naturel | naturale | natürlich |
| **nature** | nature | natura | Natur |
| **nausea** | nausée | nausea | Übelkeit |
| **near** | près | vicino | nahe |
| **necessary** | nécessaire | necessario | notwendig |
| **necklace** | collier | collana | Kette |

| English | French | Italian | German |
|---|---|---|---|
| need | avoir besoin de | avere bisogno di | brauchen |
| needle | aiguille | ago | Nadel |
| nephew | neveu | nipote | Neffe |
| nervous | nerveux | nervoso | nervös |
| never | jamais | mai | nie |
| new | nouveau | nuovo | neu |
| newspaper | journal | giornale | Zeitung |
| next | prochain | prossimo | nächste |
| nice | plaisant | bello | nett |
| nickname | sobriquet | soprannome | Spitzname |
| niece | nièce | nipote | Nichte |
| night | nuit | notte | Nacht |
| no | non | no | nein |
| noisy | bruillant | rumoroso | laut |
| non-smoking | non fumeur | vietato fumare | Nichtraucher |
| noon | midi | mezzogiorno | Mittag |
| normal | normale | normale | normal |
| north | nord | nord | Norden |
| nose | nez | naso | Nase |
| not | pas | non | nicht |
| notebook | calepin | blocco note | Notizbuch |
| nothing | rien | niente | nichts |
| no vacancy | complet | completo | belegt |
| now | maintenant | adesso | jetzt |
| nurse | garde-malade | infermiera | Krankenschwester |

| English | French | Italian | German |
|---------|--------|---------|--------|

## O

## O

| English | French | Italian | German |
|---------|--------|---------|--------|
| occupation | emploi | lavoro | Beruf |
| occupied | occupé | occupato | besetzt |
| ocean | océan | oceano | Meer |
| of | de | di | von |
| office | bureau | ufficio | Büro |
| O.K. | d'accord | d'accordo | O.K. |
| old | vieux | vecchio | alt |
| on | sur | su | auf |
| once | une fois | una volta | einmal |
| one way (street) | sens unique | senso unico | einfach |
| one way (ticket) | aller simple | andata | Hinfahrkarte |
| only | seulement | solo | nur |
| open (adj) | ouvert | aperto | offen |
| open (v) | ouvrir | aprire | öffnen |
| opera | opéra | opera | Oper |
| operator | standardiste | centralinista | Vermittlung |
| optician | opticien | ottico | Optiker |
| or | ou | o | oder |
| orange (color) | orange | arancione | orange |
| orange (fruit) | orange | arancia | Apfelsine |
| original | original | originale | Original |
| other | autre | altro | anderes |
| outdoors | en plein air | all'aria aperta | im Freien |
| oven | four | forno | Ofen |
| over (finished) | fini | finito | beendet |
| own | posséder | possedere | besitzen |
| owner | propriétaire | padrone | Besitzer |

| English | French | Italian | German |
|---------|--------|---------|--------|

## P

## P

| English | French | Italian | German |
|---------|--------|---------|--------|
| pacifier | tétine | succhiotto | Schnuller |
| package | colis | pacco | Paket |
| pail | seau | secchio | Eimer |
| pain | douleur | dolore | Schmerz |
| painting | tableau | quadro | Gemälde |
| palace | palais | palazzo | Schloß |
| panties | slip | mutande | Unterhosen |
| pants | pantalon | pantaloni | Hosen |
| paper | papier | carta | Papier |
| paper clip | trombone | graffetta | Büroklammer |
| parents | parents | genitori | Eltern |
| park (v) | garer | parcheggiare | parken |
| park (garden) | parc | parco | Park |
| party | soirée | festa | Party |
| passenger | passager | passeggero | Reisende |
| passport | passeport | passaporto | Paß |
| pay | payer | pagare | bezahlen |
| peace | paix | pace | Frieden |
| pedestrian | piéton | pedone | Fußgänger |
| pen | stylo | penna | Kugelschreiber |
| pencil | crayon | matita | Bleistift |
| people | gens | persone | Leute |
| percent | pourcentage | percentuale | Prozent |
| perfect | parfait | perfetto | perfekt |
| perfume | parfum | profumo | Parfum |
| period (time) | période | periodo | Zeitabschnitt |
| period (female) | règles | mestruazioni | Periode |
| person | personne | persona | Person |

| English | French | Italian | German |
|---|---|---|---|
| **pharmacy** | pharmacie | farmacia | Apotheke |
| **photo** | photo | foto | Photo |
| **pick-pocket** | pickpocket | borsaiolo | Taschendieb |
| **picnic** | pique-nique | picnic | Picknick |
| **piece** | morceau | pezzo | Stück |
| **pig** | cochon | maiale | Schwein |
| **pill** | pilule | pillola | Pille |
| **pillow** | oreiller | cuscino | Kissen |
| **pin** | épingle | spilla | Nadel |
| **pink** | rose | rosa | rosa |
| **pity, it's a** | quel dommage | che peccato | wie schade |
| **pizza** | pizza | pizza | Pizza |
| **plane** | avion | aereoplano | Flugzeug |
| **plain** | simple | semplice | einfach |
| **plant** | plante | pianta | Pflanze |
| **plastic** | plastique | plastica | Plastik |
| **plastic bag** | sac en plastique | sacchetto di plastica | Plastiktüte |
| **plate** | assiette | piatto | Teller |
| **platform (train)** | quai | binario | Bahnsteig |
| **play (v)** | jouer | giocare | spielen |
| **play** | théâtre | teatro | Theater |
| **please** | s'il vous plaît | per favore | bitte |
| **pliers** | pinces | pinzette | Zange |
| **pocket** | poche | tasca | Tasche |
| **point (v)** | indiquer | indicare | zeigen |
| **police** | police | polizia | Polizei |
| **poor** | pauvre | povero | arm |
| **pork** | porc | porco | Schweinefleisch |
| **possible** | possible | possibile | möglich |

| English | French | Italian | German |
|---------|--------|---------|--------|
| postcard | carte postale | cartolina | Postkarte |
| poster | affiche | poster | Poster |
| practical | pratique | pratico | praktisch |
| pregnant | enceinte | incinta | schwanger |
| prescription | ordonnance | prescrizione | Rezept |
| present (gift) | cadeau | regalo | Geschenk |
| pretty | jolie | carino | hübsch |
| price | prix | prezzo | Preis |
| priest | prêtre | prete | Priester |
| private | privé | privato | privat |
| problem | problème | problema | Problem |
| profession . | profession | professione | Beruf |
| prohibited | interdit | proibito | verboten |
| pronunciation | prononciation | pronuncia | Aussprache |
| public | publique | pubblico | öffentlich |
| pull | tirer | tirare | ziehen |
| purple | violet | viola | violett |
| purse | sac | borsa | Handtasche |
| push | pousser | spingere | drücken |

## Q

| English | French | Italian | German |
|---------|--------|---------|--------|
| quality | qualité | qualità | Qualität |
| quarter (1/4) | quart | quarto | Viertel |
| queen | reine | regina | Königin |
| question (n) | question | domanda | Frage |
| quiet | silence | tranquillo | ruhig |

| English | French | Italian | German |
|---------|--------|---------|--------|

## R

## R

| English | French | Italian | German |
|---------|--------|---------|--------|
| **R.V.** | camping-car | camper | Wohnwagen |
| **rabbit** | lapin | coniglio | Hase |
| **radio** | radio | radio | Radio |
| **raft** | radeau | gommone | Floß |
| **rain (n)** | pluie | pioggia | Regen |
| **rainbow** | arc-en-ciel | arcobaleno | Regenbogen |
| **raincoat** | imperméable | impermeabile | Regenmantel |
| **rape (n)** | viol | violenza carnale | Vergewaltigung |
| **raw** | cru | crudo | roh |
| **razor** | rasoir | rasoio | Rasierer |
| **ready** | pret | pronto | bereit |
| **receipt** | reçu | ricevuta | Beleg |
| **receive** | recevoir | ricevere | erhalten |
| **receptionist** | réceptioniste | centralinista | Empfangsperson |
| **recipe** | recette | ricetta | Rezept |
| **recommend** | suggérer | raccomandare | empfehlen |
| **red** | rouge | rosso | rot |
| **refill (v)** | remplir | riempire | nachschenken |
| **refund (n)** | remboursement | rimborso | Rückgabe |
| **relax (v)** | se reposer | riposare | sich erholen |
| **religion** | religion | religione | Religion |
| **remember** | se souvenir | ricordare | sich erinnern |
| **rent (v)** | louer | affittare | mieten |
| **repair (v)** | réparer | riparare | reparieren |
| **repeat** | répétez | ripeta | noch einmal |
| **reservation** | réservation | prenotazione | Reservierung |
| **reserve** | reserver | prenotare | reservieren |
| **rich** | riche | ricco | reich |

| English | French | Italian | German |
|---|---|---|---|
| **right** | droite | destra | rechts |
| **ring (n)** | bague | anello | Ring |
| **ripe** | mûr | maturo | reif |
| **river** | rivière | fiume | Fluß |
| **rock (n)** | rocher | pietra | Fels |
| **roller skates** | patins à roulettes | pattini a rotelle | Rollschuhe |
| **romantic** | romantique | romantico | romantisch |
| **roof** | toit | tetto | Dach |
| **room** | chambre | camera | Zimmer |
| **rope** | corde | corda | Seil |
| **rotten** | pourri | marcio | verdorben |
| **roundtrip** | aller-retour | ritorno | Rückfahrt |
| **rowboat** | canot | barca a remi | Ruderboot |
| **rucksack** | sac à dos | zaino | Rucksack |
| **rug** | tapis | tappeto | Teppich |
| **ruins** | ruines | rovine | Ruine |
| **run (v)** | courir | correre | laufen |

## S                          S

| English | French | Italian | German |
|---|---|---|---|
| **sad** | triste | triste | traurig |
| **safe** | en sécurité | sicuro | sicher |
| **safety pin** | épingle à nourrice | spilla da balia | Sicherheitsnadel |
| **sailing** | voile | vela | segeln |
| **sale** | solde | liquidazione | Ausverkauf |
| **same** | même | stesso | gleiche |
| **sandals** | sandales | sandali | Sandalen |
| **sandwich** | sandwich | panino | belegtes Brot |
| **sanitary napkins** | serviettes hygiéniques | assorbenti | Damenbinden |

| English | French | Italian | German |
|---|---|---|---|
| **Saturday** | samedi | sabato | Samstag |
| **scandalous** | scandaleux | scandaloso | sündig |
| **school** | école | scuola | Schule |
| **science** | science | scienza | Wissenschaft |
| **scientist** | homme / femme de sciences | scienziato | Wissenschaftler |
| **scissors** | ciseaux | forbici | Schere |
| **scotch tape** | du scotch | nastro adesivo | Tesafilm |
| **screwdriver** | tournevis | cacciaviti | Schraubenzieher |
| **sculptor** | sculpteur | scultore | Bildhauer |
| **sculpture** | sculpture | scultura | Skulptur |
| **sea** | mer | mare | Meer |
| **seafood** | fruits de mer | frutti di mare | Meeresfrüchte |
| **seat** | place | posto | Platz |
| **second** | deuxième | secondo | zweite |
| **second class** | deuxième classe | secondo classe | zweiter Klasse |
| **secret** | secret | segreto | Geheimnis |
| **see** | voir | vedere | sehen |
| **self-service** | libre service | self-service | Selbstbedienung |
| **sell** | vendre | vendere | verkaufen |
| **send** | envoyer | spedire | senden |
| **separate (adj)** | séparé | separato | getrennt |
| **serious** | sérieux | serio | ernst |
| **service** | service | servizio | Bedienung |
| **sex** | sexe | sesso | Sex |
| **sexy** | sexy | sexy | sexy |
| **shampoo** | shampooing | shampoo | Shampoo |
| **shaving cream** | crème à raser | crema da barba | Rasiercreme |
| **she** | elle | lei | sie |
| **sheet** | drap | lenzuolo | Laken |

| English | French | Italian | German |
|---|---|---|---|
| shell | coquille | conchiglia | Schale |
| ship (n) | navire | nave | Schiff |
| shirt | chemise | camicia | Hemd |
| shoes | chaussures | scarpe | Schuhe |
| shopping | shopping | fare spese | einkaufen |
| short | court | corto | kurz |
| shorts | short | pantaloncini | shorts |
| shoulder | épaule | spalle | Schulter |
| show (n) | spectacle | spettacolo | Vorführung |
| show (v) | montrer | mostrare | zeigen |
| shower | douche | doccia | Dusche |
| shy | timide | timido | ängstlich |
| sick | malade | malato | krank |
| sign | panneau | segno | Schild |
| signature | signature | firma | Unterschrift |
| silence | silence | silenzio | Ruhe |
| silk | soie | seta | Seide |
| silver | argent | argento | Silber |
| similar | semblable | simile | ähnlich |
| simple | simple | semplice | einfach |
| sing | chanter | cantare | singen |
| singer | chanteur | cantante | Sänger |
| single (unmarried) | célibataire | scapolo (male), nubile (female) | ledig |
| sink | lavabo | lavandino | Waschbecken |
| sir | monsieur | signor | mein Herr |
| sister | soeur | sorella | Schwester |
| size | taille | taglia | Größe |
| skating | patinage | pattinaggio | Rollschuhlaufen |
| ski (v) | faire du ski | sciare | skilaufen |

| English | French | Italian | German |
|---|---|---|---|
| **skin** | peau | pelle | Haut |
| **skinny** | maigre | magro | dünn |
| **skirt** | jupe | gonna | Rock |
| **sky** | ciel | cielo | Himmel |
| **sleep (v)** | dormir | dormire | schlafen |
| **sleepy** | avoir sommeil | assonnato | schläfrig |
| **slice** | tranche | fettina | Scheibe |
| **slide (photo)** | diapositive | diapositiva | Dia |
| **slippery** | glissant | scivoloso | glatt |
| **slow** | lent | lento | langsam |
| **small** | petit | piccolo | klein |
| **smell (n)** | odeur | odore | Geruch |
| **smile (n)** | sourire | sorriso | Lächeln |
| **smoking** | fumeur | fumare | Rauchen |
| **snack** | snack | merendina | Imbiß |
| **sneeze (v)** | éternuer | starnutire | niesen |
| **snore** | ronfler | russare | schnarchen |
| **snow** | neige | neve | Schnee |
| **soap** | savon | sapone | Seife |
| **soccer** | football | calcio | Fußball |
| **socks** | chaussettes | calzini | Socken |
| **something** | quelque chose | qualcosa | etwas |
| **son** | fils | figlio | Sohn |
| **song** | chanson | canzone | Lied |
| **soon** | bientôt | subito | bald |
| **sorry** | désolé | mi dispiace | Entschuldigung |
| **sour** | aigre | acerbo | sauer |
| **south** | sud | sud | Süden |
| **speak** | parler | parlare | sprechen |
| **specialty** | spécialité | specialità | Spezialität |

| English | French | Italian | German |
|---|---|---|---|
| **speed** | vitesse | velocità | Geschwindigkeit |
| **spend** | dépenser | spendere | ausgeben |
| **spicy** | piquant | piccante | scharf |
| **spider** | araignée | ragno | Spinne |
| **spoon** | cuillère | cucchiaio | Löffel |
| **sport** | sport | sport | Sport |
| **spring** | printemps | primavera | Frühling |
| **square (town)** | place | piazza | Platz |
| **stairs** | escalier | scale | Treppe |
| **stamp** | timbre | francobolli | Briefmarke |
| **stapler** | agraffeuse | pinzatrice | Klammeraffe |
| **star (in sky)** | étoile | stella | Stern |
| **state** | état | stato | Staat |
| **station** | station | stazione | Station |
| **stomach** | estomac | stomaco | Magen |
| **stop (n)** | stop, arrêt | stop, alt | Halt |
| **stop (v)** | arrêter | fermare | halten |
| **storm** | tempête | temporale | Sturm |
| **story (floor)** | étage | storia | Stock |
| **straight** | droit | dritto | geradeaus |
| **strange** | bizarre | strano | merkwürdig |
| **stream (n)** | ruisseau | corrente | Fluß |
| **street** | rue | strada | Straße |
| **string** | ficelle | filo | Schnur |
| **strong** | fort | forte | stark |
| **stuck** | coincé | incastrato | festsitzen |
| **student** | étudiant | studente | Student |
| **stupid** | stupide | stupido | dumm |
| **sturdy** | robuste | resistente | haltbar |
| **style** | mode | stile | Stil |

| English | French | Italian | German |
|---------|--------|---------|--------|
| **suddenly** | soudain | improvvisamente | plötzlich |
| **suitcase** | valise | valigia | Koffer |
| **summer** | été | estate | Sommer |
| **sun** | soleil | sole | Sonne |
| **sunbathe** | se faire bronzer | abbronzarsi | sich sonnen |
| **sunburn** | coup de soleil | bruciatura del sole | Sonnenbrand |
| **Sunday** | dimanche | domenica | Sonntag |
| **sunglasses** | lunettes de soleil | occhiali da sole | Sonnenbrille |
| **sunny** | ensoleillé | assolato | sonnig |
| **sunset** | coucher de soleil | tramonto | Sonnenuntergang |
| **sunscreen** | huile solaire | protezione solare | Sonnencreme |
| **sunshine** | soleil | sole | Sonnenschein |
| **sunstroke** | insolation | insolazione | Sonnenstich |
| **suntan (n)** | bronzage | abbronzatura | Sonnenbräune |
| **suntan lotion** | lotion solaire | crema per il sole | Sonnenöl |
| **supermarket** | supermarché | supermercato | Supermarkt |
| **supplement** | supplément | supplemento | Zuschlag |
| **surprise (n)** | surprise | sorpresa | Überraschung |
| **swallow (v)** | avaler | ingoiare | schlucken |
| **sweat (v)** | transpirer | sudare | schwitzen |
| **sweater** | pull | maglione | Pullover |
| **sweet** | doux | dolce | süß |
| **swim** | nager | nuotare | schwimmen |
| **swimming pool** | piscine | piscina | Schwimmbad |
| **swim suit** | costume de bain | costume da bagno | Badeanzug |
| **swim trunks** | maillot de bain | costume de bagno | Badehose |
| **Switzerland** | Suisse | Svizzera | Schweiz |

| English | French | Italian | German |
|---|---|---|---|
| **synthetic** | synthétique | sintetico | synthetisch |

## T                              T

| **table** | table | tavolo | Tisch |
|---|---|---|---|
| **tail** | queue | coda | Schwanz |
| **take out (food)** | pour emporter | da portar via | mitnehmen |
| **take** | prendre | prendere | nehmen |
| **talcum powder** | talc | borotalco | Babypuder |
| **talk** | parler | parlare | reden |
| **tall** | grand | alto | hoch |
| **tampons** | tampons | tamponi | Tampons |
| **tape (cassette)** | cassette | cassetta | Kassette |
| **taste (n)** | goût | gusto | Gaschmack |
| **taste (v)** | goûter | assaggiare | probieren |
| **tax** | taxe | tasse | Steuer |
| **teacher** | professeur | insegnante | Lehrer |
| **team** | équipe | squadra | Team |
| **teenager** | adolescent | adolescente | Jugendlicher |
| **telephone** | téléphone | telefono | Telefon |
| **television** | télévision | televisione | Fernsehen |
| **temperature** | température | temperatura | Temperatur |
| **tender** | tendre | tenero | zart |
| **tennis** | tennis | tennis | Tennis |
| **tennis shoes** | chaussures de tennis | scarpe da tennis | Turnschuhe |
| **tent** | tente | tenda | Zelt |
| **tent pegs** | piquets de tente | picchetti della tenda | Zelthäringe |
| **terrible** | terrible | terribile | schrecklich |

| English | French | Italian | German |
|---|---|---|---|
| **thanks** | merci | grazie | danke |
| **theater** | théâtre | teatro | Theater |
| **thermometer** | thermomètre | termometro | Thermometer |
| **thick** | épais | spesso | dick |
| **thief** | voleur | ladro | Dieb |
| **thigh** | cuisse | coscia | Schenkel |
| **thin** | mince | sottile | dünn |
| **thing** | chose | cosa | Ding |
| **think** | penser | pensare | denken |
| **thirsty** | soif | assetato | durstig |
| **thongs** | pinces | sandali infradito | Badelatschen |
| **thread** | fil | filo | Faden |
| **throat** | gorge | gola | Hals |
| **through** | à travers | attraverso | durch |
| **throw** | jeter | tirare | werfen |
| **Thursday** | jeudi | giovedì | Donnerstag |
| **ticket** | billet | biglietto | Karte |
| **tight** | serré | stretto | eng |
| **timetable** | horaire | orario | Fahrplan |
| **tired** | fatigué | stanco | müde |
| **tissues** | mouchoirs en papier | fazzolettini | Taschentuch |
| **to** | à | a | nach |
| **today** | aujourd'hui | oggi | heute |
| **toe** | orteil | dito del piede | Zeh |
| **together** | ensemble | insieme | zusammen |
| **toilet** | toilette | toilette | Toilette |
| **toilet paper** | papier hygiénique | carta igienica | Klopapier |
| **tomorrow** | demain | domani | morgen |
| **tonight** | ce soir | stanotte | heute abend |

| English | French | Italian | German |
|---------|--------|---------|--------|
| too | trop | troppo | zu |
| tooth | dent | dente | Zahn |
| toothbrush | brosse à dents | spazzolino da denti | Zahnbürste |
| toothpaste | dentifrice | dentifricio | Zahnpasta |
| toothpick | cure-dent | stuzzicadenti | Zahnstocher |
| total | total | totale | Völlig |
| tour | tour | giro | Tour |
| tourist | touriste | turista | Tourist |
| towel | serviette de bain | asciugamano | Handtuch |
| tower | tour | torre | Turm |
| town | ville | città | Stadt |
| toy | jouet | giocattolo | Spielzeug |
| track (train) | voie | binario | Gleis |
| traditional | traditionnel | tradizionale | traditionell |
| traffic | circulation | traffico | Verkehr |
| train | train | treno | Zug |
| train station | gare | stazione | Bahnhof |
| translate | traduire | tradurre | übersetzen |
| travel | voyager | viaggiare | reisen |
| travel agency | agence de voyage | agenzia di viaggi | Reisebüro |
| traveler's check | chèque de voyage | traveler's check | Reisescheck |
| tree | arbre | albero | Baum |
| trip | voyage | viaggio | Fahrt |
| trouble | trouble | guaio | Schwierigkeiten |
| T-shirt | T-shirt | maglietta | T-Shirt |
| Tuesday | mardi | martedì | Dienstag |
| tunnel | tunnel | tunnel | Tunnel |
| tweezers | pince à épiler | pinzette | Pinzette |
| twins | jumeaux | gemelli | Zwillinge |

| English | French | Italian | German |
|---------|--------|---------|--------|

## U

## U

| | | | |
|---------|--------|---------|--------|
| ugly | laid | brutto | häßlich |
| umbrella | parapluie | ombrello | Regenschirm |
| uncle | oncle | zio | Onkel |
| under | sous | sotto | unter |
| underpants | slip | mutandine | Unterhose |
| understand | comprendre | capire | verstehen |
| underwear | sous vêtements | mutande | Unterwäsche |
| unemployed | au chômage | disoccupato | arbeitslos |
| unfortunately | malheureusement | sfortunatamente | unglücklicherweise |
| United States | Etats-Unis | Stati Uniti | Vereinigte Staaten |
| university | univerisité | università | Universität |
| up | en haut | su | hoch |
| upstairs | en haut | di sopra | oben |
| urgent | urgent | urgente | dringend |
| us | nous | noi | uns |
| use | utiliser | usare | nutzen |

## V

## V

| | | | |
|---------|--------|---------|--------|
| vacancy (hotel) | chambre libre | camare libere | Zimmer frei |
| vacant | libre | libero | frei |
| valley | vallée | valle | Tal |
| vegetarian (n) | végétarien | vegetariano | Vegetarier |
| very | très | molto | sehr |
| vest | gilet | panciotto | Weste |
| video | vidéo | video | Video |
| video recorder | magnétoscope | video registratore | Videogerät |
| view | vue | vista | Blick |

| English | French | Italian | German |
|---------|--------|---------|--------|
| **village** | village | villaggio | Dorf |
| **vineyard** | vignoble | vigneto | Weinberg |
| **virus** | virus | virus | Virus |
| **visit (n)** | visite | visita | Besuch |
| **visit (v)** | visiter | visitare | besuchen |
| **vitamins** | vitamines | vitamine | Vitamine |
| **voice** | voix | voce | Stimme |
| **vomit (v)** | vomir | vomitare | sich übergeben |

## W

**W**

| English | French | Italian | German |
|---------|--------|---------|--------|
| **waist** | taille | vita | Taille |
| **wait** | attendre | aspettare | warten |
| **waiter** | garçon | cameriere | Kellner |
| **waitress** | madame, mademoiselle | cameriera | Kellnerin |
| **wake up** | se réveiller | svegliarsi | aufwachen |
| **walk (v)** | marcher | camminare | gehen |
| **wallet** | portefeuille | portafoglio | Brieftasche |
| **want** | vouloir | volere | möchte |
| **warm (adj)** | chaud | caldo | warm |
| **wash** | laver | lavare | waschen |
| **watch (n)** | montre | orologio | Uhr |
| **watch (v)** | regarder | guardare | beobachten |
| **water** | l'eau | acqua | Wasser |
| **water, tap** | l'eau du robinet | acqua del rubinetto | Leitungswasser |
| **waterfall** | cascade | cascata | Wasserfall |
| **we** | nous | noi | wir |
| **weather** | temps | tempo | Wetter |

| English | French | Italian | German |
|---------|--------|---------|--------|
| **weather forecast** | météo | previsioni del tempo | Wettervorhersage |
| **wedding** | mariage | matrimonio | Hochzeit |
| **Wednesday** | mercredi | mercoledì | Mittwoch |
| **week** | semaine | settimana | Woche |
| **weight** | poids | peso | Gewicht |
| **welcome** | bienvenue | benvenuto | willkommen |
| **west** | ouest | ovest | Westen |
| **wet** | mouillé | bagnato | naß |
| **what** | que | che cosa | was |
| **wheel** | roue | ruota | Rad |
| **when** | quand | quando | wann |
| **where** | où | dove | wo |
| **whipped cream** | crème chantilly | panna | Schlagsahne |
| **white** | blanc | bianco | weiß |
| **who** | qui | chi | wer |
| **why** | pourquoi | perchè | warum |
| **widow** | veuve | vedova | Witwe |
| **widower** | veuf | vedovo | Witwer |
| **wife** | femme | moglie | Ehefrau |
| **wild** | sauvage | selvaggio | wild |
| **wind** | vent | vento | Wind |
| **window** | fenêtre | finestra | Fenster |
| **wine** | vin | vino | Wein |
| **wing** | aile | ala | Flügel |
| **winter** | hiver | inverno | Winter |
| **wish (v)** | souhaiter | desiderare | wünschen |
| **with** | avec | con | mit |
| **without** | sans | senza | ohne |
| **women** | dames | donne | Damen |

| English | French | Italian | German |
|---------|--------|---------|--------|
| **wood** | bois | legno | Holz |
| **wool** | laine | lana | Wolle |
| **word** | mot | parola | Wort |
| **work (n)** | travail | lavoro | Arbeit |
| **work (v)** | travailler | lavorare | arbeiten |
| **world** | monde | mondo | Welt |
| **worse** | pire | peggio | schlechter |
| **worst** | le pire | peggiore | schlechteste |
| **wrap** | emballer | incartare | umwickeln |
| **wrist** | poignet | polso | Handgelenk |
| **write** | écrire | scrivere | schreiben |

## Y / Z                   Y / Z

| English | French | Italian | German |
|---------|--------|---------|--------|
| **year** | année | anno | Jahr |
| **yellow** | jaune | giallo | gelb |
| **yes** | oui | si | ja |
| **yesterday** | hier | ieri | gestern |
| **you (formal)** | vous | Lei | Sie |
| **you (informal)** | tu | tu | du |
| **young** | jeune | giovane | jung |
| **youth hostel** | auberge de jeunesse | ostello della gioventù | Jugendherberge |
| **zero** | zéro | zero | null |
| **zip-lock bag** | sac en plastique à fermeture | busta de plastica sigillablile | Gefrierbeutel |
| **zipper** | fermeture éclair | chiusura lampo | Reißverschluß |
| **zoo** | zoo | zoo | Zoo |

# APPENDIX

# Tongue twisters

Tongue twisters are a great way to practice a language—and break the ice with local Europeans. Here are a few that are sure to challenge you, and amuse your hosts.

### French tongue twisters (Tire-langues):

**Bonjour madame la saucissonière! Combien sont ces six saucissons-ci? Ces six saucissons-ci sont six sous. Si ces saucissons-ci sont six sous, ces six saucissons-ci sont trop chers.**

Hello madame sausage-seller! How much are these six sausages? These six sausages are six cents. If these are six cents, these six sausages are too expensive.

**Je veux et j'exige qu'un chasseur sachant chasser sans ses èchasses sache chasser sans son chien de chasse.**

I want and demand that a hunter who knows how to hunt without his stilts knows how to hunt without his hunting dog.

**Ce sont seize cent jacynthes sèches dans seize cent sachets secs.**

There are 600 dry hyacinths in 600 dry sachets.

**Ce sont trois très gros rats dans trois très gros trous roulant trois gros rats gris morts.**

There are three fat rats in three fat rat-holes rolling three fat grey dead rats.

## Italian tongue twisters (Scioglilingua):

Trentatrè trentini arrivarono
a Trento tutti e trentatrè
trottorellando.

Thirty-three people from Trent arrived
in Trent, all thirty-three trotting.

Chi fù quel barbaro barbiere che
barberò così barbaramente a
Piazza Barberini quel povero
barbaro di Barbarossa?

Who was that barbarian barber in
Barberini Square who shaved that poor
barbarian Barbarossa?

Sopra la panca la capra canta,
sotto la panca la capra crepa.

On the bench the goat sings, under
the bench the goat dies.

Tigre contro tigre.

Tiger against tiger.

## German tongue twisters (Zungenbrecher):

Zehn zahme Ziegen zogen Zucker
zum Zoo.

Ten domesticated goats pulled sugar
to the zoo.

Blaukraut bleibt Blaukraut und
Brautkleid bleibt Brautkleid.

Bluegrass remains bluegrass and a
wedding dress remains a wedding
dress.

| | |
|---|---|
| **Fischer's Fritze fischt frische Fische, frische Fische fischt Fischer's Fritze.** | Fritz Fischer catches fresh fish, fresh fish Fritz Fisher catches. |
| **Die Katze trapst die Treppe rauf.** | The cat is walking up the stairs. |
| **Ich komme über Oberammergau, oder komme ich über Unterammergau?** | I am coming via Oberammergau, or am I coming via Unterammergau? |

## English tongue twisters:

After your European friends have laughed at you, let them try these tongue twisters in English:

**If neither he sells seashells, nor she sells seashells, who shall sell seashells? Shall seashells be sold?**

**Peter Piper picked a peck of pickled peppers.**

**Rugged rubber baby buggy bumpers.**

**The sixth sick sheik's sixth sheep's sick.**

**Red bug's blood and black bug's blood.**

**Soldiers' shoulders.**

**Thieves seize skis.**

**I'm a pleasant mother pheasant plucker. I pluck mother pheasants. I'm the most pleasant mother pheasant plucker that ever plucked a mother pheasant.**

# Let's Talk Telephones

Smart travelers use the telephone every day. It's a snap to make a hotel reservation by phone the morning of the day you plan to arrive. If there's a language problem, ask someone at your hotel to talk to your next hotel for you.

In every western European country, card-operated public phones are speedily taking the place of coin-operated phones. Each country sells telephone cards good for use in its country. Get a phone card at any post office at the beginning of your trip to force yourself to find good reasons to use the local phones—for making hotel reservations, calling tourist information offices, and phoning home. Telephone cards work for local, long distance, and international calls made from card-operated public phones throughout that country. When using a card-operated phone, pick up the receiver, insert your card in the slot in the phone, dial your number, make your call, then retrieve your card. The price of your call is automatically deducted from your card as you use it. If you have a phone card phobia, you'll usually find easy-to-use "talk now-pay later" metered phones in post offices.

To make calls to other European countries, dial the international access code of the country you're calling from (00 in France, Germany, Austria, Italy, and Switzerland), then the country code of the country you're calling, followed by the area code without its initial zero, and finally the local number. The main exception is France, which has no area codes, but you still drop the zero—the initial digit of all of France's ten-digit numbers. To make an international call to

APPENDIX

France, dial the international access code of the country you're calling from, France's country code (33), then the ten-digit number (without the initial zero).

When dialing long distance within a country, start with the area code (including its zero), then dial the local number. To call anywhere within France, just dial the ten-digit number directly.

Calling the USA from any kind of phone is easy if you have an ATT, MCI or SPRINT calling card. Or call home using coins (costs $1 for 20 seconds), and ask the other person to call you back at your hotel at a specified time. Europe-to-USA calls are twice as expensive as direct calls from the States. Midnight in California is breakfast in Paris.

Hotel room phones are reasonable for local calls, but a terrible rip-off for long-distance calls. Never call home from your hotel room unless you are using a calling card service such as ATT, MCI, or SPRINT.

## Advantages of calling cards:

If you plan to call home often, get a ATT, MCI, or SPRINT calling card. Each card company has a toll-free number in each European country which puts you in touch with an American operator who takes your card number and the number you want to call, puts you through and bills your home phone number for the call (at the cheaper USA rate of about $1.25 a minute plus a $3.50 service charge). If you talk for at least 3 minutes, you'll save enough to make up for the service charge.

## ATT, MCI, & SPRINT calling card operators:

| Country | ATT | MCI | SPRINT |
|---|---|---|---|
| Austria | 022-903-011 | 022-903-012 | 022-903-014 |
| France | 0800-990-011 | 0800-990-019 | 0800-990-087 |
| Germany | 0130-0010 | 0130-0012 | 0130-0013 |
| Italy | 172-1011 | 172-1022 | 172-1877 |
| Switzerland | 0800-89-0011 | 0800-89-0222 | 0800-89-9777 |

## International access codes:
If you're dialing direct, these are the numbers you dial first when calling out of a country.

| | | | |
|---|---|---|---|
| Austria: | 00 | Italy: | 00 |
| France: | 00 | Switzerland: | 00 |
| Germany: | 00 | USA/Canada: | 011 |

## Country codes:
After you've dialed the international access code, then dial the code of the country you're calling.

| | | | | | |
|---|---|---|---|---|---|
| Austria: | 43 | Germany: | 49 | Portugal: | 351 |
| Belgium: | 32 | Greece: | 30 | Spain: | 34 |
| Britain: | 44 | Hungary: | 36 | Sweden: | 46 |
| Czech Rep.: | 42 | Italy: | 39 | Switzerland: | 41 |
| Denmark: | 45 | Netherlands: | 31 | Turkey: | 90 |
| France: | 33 | Norway: | 47 | USA/Canada: | 1 |

APPENDIX

## Weather
First line is average daily low (°F.); second  line average
daily high (°F.); third line, days of no rain.

|  | J | F | M | A | M | J | J | A | S | O | N | D |
|---|---|---|---|---|---|---|---|---|---|---|---|---|
| **FRANCE** | 32 | 34 | 36 | 41 | 47 | 52 | 55 | 55 | 50 | 44 | 38 | 33 |
| Paris | 42 | 45 | 52 | 60 | 67 | 73 | 76 | 75 | 69 | 59 | 49 | 43 |
|  | 16 | 15 | 16 | 16 | 18 | 19 | 19 | 19 | 19 | 17 | 15 | 14 |
| **ITALY** | 39 | 39 | 42 | 46 | 55 | 60 | 64 | 64 | 61 | 53 | 46 | 41 |
| Rome | 54 | 56 | 62 | 68 | 74 | 82 | 88 | 88 | 83 | 73 | 63 | 56 |
|  | 23 | 17 | 26 | 24 | 25 | 28 | 29 | 28 | 24 | 22 | 22 | 22 |
| **GERMANY** | 23 | 23 | 30 | 38 | 45 | 51 | 55 | 54 | 48 | 40 | 33 | 26 |
| Munich | 35 | 38 | 48 | 56 | 64 | 70 | 74 | 73 | 67 | 56 | 44 | 36 |
|  | 15 | 15 | 18 | 15 | 16 | 13 | 15 | 15 | 17 | 18 | 15 | 16 |

## Metric conversions (approximate)

1 inch = 25 millimeters          1 foot = .3 meter
1 yard = .9 meter               1 mile = 1.6 kilometers
1 sq. yard = .8 sq. meter       1 acre = 0.4 hectare
1 quart = .95 liter             1 ounce = 28 grams
1 pound = .45 kilo              1 kilo = 2.2 pounds
1 centimeter = 0.4 inch         1 meter = 39.4 inches

1 kilometer = .62 mile
Miles = kilometers divided by 2 plus 10%
(120 km ÷ 2 = 60, 60 + 12 = 72 miles)
Fahrenheit degrees = double Celsius + 30
32° F = 0° C, 82° F = about 28° C

# Your tear-out French cheat sheet

| Good day. | **Bonjour.** | bohn-zhoor |
| Do you speak English? | **Parlez-vous anglais?** | par-lay-voo ahn-glay |
| Yes. / No. | **Oui. / Non.** | wee / nohn |
| I don't speak French. | **Je ne parle pas français.** | zhuh nuh parl pah frahn-say |
| I'm sorry. | **Désolé.** | day-zoh-lay |
| Please. | **S'il vous plaît.** | see voo play |
| Thank you. | **Merci.** | mehr-see |
| No problem. | **Pas de problème.** | pah duh proh-blehm |
| It's good. | **C'est bon.** | say bohn |
| You are very kind. | **Vous êtes très gentil.** | vooz eht treh zhahn-tee |
| Goodbye. | **Au revoir.** | oh vwahr |
| Where is...? | **Où est...?** | oo ay |
| ...a hotel | **...un hôtel** | uhn oh-tehl |
| ...a youth hostel | **...une auberge de jeunesse** | ewn oh-behrzh duh zhuh-nehs |
| ...a restaurant | **...un restaurant** | uhn rehs-toh-rahn |
| ...a supermarket | **...un supermarché** | uhn soo-pehr-mar-shay |
| ...a pharmacy | **...une pharmacie** | ewn far-mah-see |
| ...a bank | **...une banque** | ewn bahnk |
| ...the train station | **...la gare** | lah gar |
| ...the tourist info office | **...l'office du tourisme** | loh-fees dew too-reez-muh |
| Where are the toilets? | **Où sont les toilettes?** | oo sohn lay twah-leht |
| men / women | **hommes / dames** | ohm / dahm |
| How much is it? | **Combien?** | kohn-bee-an |

| | | |
|---|---|---|
| Write it? | **Ecrivez?** | ay-kree-vay |
| Cheap. | **Bon marché.** | bohn mar-shay |
| Cheaper. | **Moins cher.** | mwan shehr |
| Cheapest. | **Le moins cher.** | luh mwan shehr |
| Is it free? | **C'est gratuit?** | say grah-twee |
| Included? | **Inclus?** | an-klew |
| Do you have...? | **Avez-vous...?** | ah-vay-voo |
| I would like... | **Je voudrais...** | zhuh voo-dray |
| We would like... | **Nous voudrions...** | noo voo-dree-ohn |
| ...this. | **...ceci.** | suh-see |
| ...just a little. | **...un petit peu.** | uhn puh-tee puh |
| ...more. | **...encore.** | ahn-kor |
| ...a ticket. | **...un billet.** | uhn bee-yay |
| ...a room. | **...une chambre.** | ewn shahn-bruh |
| ...the bill. | **...l'addition.** | lah-dee-see-ohn |
| one | **un** | uhn |
| two | **deux** | duh |
| three | **trois** | twah |
| four | **quatre** | kah-truh |
| five | **cinq** | sank |
| six | **six** | sees |
| seven | **sept** | seht |
| eight | **huit** | weet |
| nine | **neuf** | nuhf |
| ten | **dix** | dees |
| At what time? | **À quelle heure?** | ah kehl ur |
| Just a moment. | **Un moment.** | uhn moh-mahn |
| Now. | **Maintenant.** | man-tuh-nahn |
| soon / later | **bientôt / plus tard** | bee-an-toh / plew tar |
| today / tomorrow | **aujourd'hui / demain** | oh-zhoor-dwee / duh-man |

# Your tear-out Italian cheat sheet

| | | |
|---|---|---|
| Good day. | Buon giorno. | bwohn jor-noh |
| Do you speak English? | Parla inglese? | par-lah een-glay-zay |
| Yes. / No. | Si. / No. | see / noh |
| I don't speak Italian. | Non parlo l'italiano. | nohn par-loh lee-tah-leeah-noh |
| I'm sorry. | Mi dispiace. | mee dee-speeah-chay |
| Please. | Per favore. | pehr fah-voh-ray |
| Thank you. | Grazie. | graht-seeay |
| It's (not) a problem. | (Non) c'è problema. | (nohn) cheh proh-blay-mah |
| It's good. | Va bene. | vah behn-ay |
| You are very kind. | Lei è molto gentile. | lehee eh mohl-toh jayn-tee-lay |
| Goodbye! | Arrivederci! | ah-ree-vay-dehr-chee |
| Where is...? | Dov'è...? | doh-veh |
| ...a hotel | ...un hotel | oon oh-tehl |
| ...a youth hostel | ...un ostello della gioventù | oon oh-stehl-loh day-lah joh-vehn-too |
| ...a restaurant | ...un ristorante | oon ree-stoh-rahn-tay |
| ...a supermarket | ...un supermercado | oon soo-pehr-mehr-kah-doh |
| ...a pharmacy | ...una farmacia | oo-nah far-mah-chee-ah |
| ...a bank | ...una banca | oo-nah bahn-kah |
| ...the train station | ...la stazione | lah staht-seeoh-nay |
| ...tourist information | ...informazioni per turisti | een-for-maht-seeoh-nee pehr too-ree-stee |
| ...the toilet | ...la toilette | lah twah-leht-tay |
| men | uomini, signori | woh-mee-nee, seen-yoh-ree |
| women | donne, signore | don-nay, seen-yoh-ray |
| How much is it? | Quanto costa? | kwahn-toh kos-tah |

CHEAT SHEET

| Write it? | **Lo scrive?** | loh **skree**-vay |
| Cheap(er). | **(Più) economico.** | (pew) ay-koh-**noh**-mee-koh |
| Cheapest. | **Il più economico.** | eel pew ay-koh-**noh**-mee-koh |
| Is it free? | **È gratis?** | eh **grah**-tees |
| Is it included? | **È incluso?** | eh een-**kloo**-zoh |
| Do you have...? | **Ha...?** | ah |
| I would like... | **Vorrei....** | vor-**rehee** |
| We would like... | **Vorremo...** | vor-**ray**-moh |
| ...this. | **...questo.** | **kway**-stoh |
| ...just a little. | **...un pochino.** | oon poh-**kee**-noh |
| ...more. | **...di più.** | dee pew |
| ...a ticket. | **...un biglietto.** | oon beel-**yay**-toh |
| ...a room. | **...una camera.** | **oo**-nah kah-may-rah |
| ...the bill. | **...il conto.** | eel **kohn**-toh |
| one | **uno** | **oo**-noh |
| two | **due** | **doo**-ay |
| three | **tre** | tray |
| four | **quattro** | **kwah**-troh |
| five | **cinque** | **cheeng**-kway |
| six | **sei** | **sehee** |
| seven | **sette** | **seht**-tay |
| eight | **otto** | **ot**-toh |
| nine | **nove** | **nov**-ay |
| ten | **dieci** | **deeay**-chee |
| hundred / thousand | **cento / mille** | **chehn**-toh / **mee**-lay |
| At what time? | **A che ora?** | ah kay **oh**-rah |
| Just a moment. | **Un momento.** | oon moh-**mayn**-toh |
| Now. | **Adesso.** | ah-**dehs**-soh |
| soon / later | **presto / tardi** | **prehs**-toh / **tar**-dee |
| today / tomorrow | **oggi / domani** | **oh**-jee / doh-**mah**-nee |

# Your tear-out German cheat sheet

| | | |
|---|---|---|
| Good day. | **Guten Tag.** | **goo**-ten tahg |
| Do you speak English? | **Sprechen Sie Englisch?** | **shprekh**-en zee **eng**-lish |
| Yes. / No. | **Ja. / Nein.** | yah / nīn |
| I don't speak German. | **Ich spreche kein Deutsch.** | ikh **shprekh**-eh kīn doych |
| I'm sorry. | **Entschuldigung.** | ent-**shool**-dee-goong |
| Please. / Thank you. | **Bitte. / Danke.** | **bit**-teh / **dahng**-keh |
| No problem. | **Kein Problem.** | kīn proh-**blaym** |
| Very good. | **Sehr gut.** | zehr goot |
| You are very kind. | **Sie sind sehr freundlich.** | zee zint zehr **froynd**-likh |
| Goodbye. | **Auf Wiedersehen.** | owf **vee**-der-zayn |
| Where is...? | **Wo ist...?** | voh ist |
| ...a hotel | **...ein Hotel** | īn hoh-**tel** |
| ...a youth hostel | **...eine Jugendherberge** | ī-neh **yoo**-gend-hehr-behr-geh |
| ...a restaurant | **...ein Restaurant** | īn res-tow-**rahnt** |
| ...a supermarket | **...ein Supermarkt** | īn **zoo**-per-markt |
| ...a pharmacy | **...eine Apotheke** | ī-neh ah-poh-**tay**-keh |
| ...a bank | **...eine Bank** | ī-neh bahnk |
| ...the train station | **...der Bahnhof** | dehr **bahn**-hohf |
| ...the tourist information office | **...das Touristeninformationsbüro** | dahs **too**-ris-ten-in-for-maht-see-**ohns**-bew-roh |
| ...the toilet | **...die Toilette** | dee toh-**leh**-teh |

**CHEAT SHEET**

| | | |
|---|---|---|
| men / women | **Herren / Damen** | **hehr**-ren / **dah**-men |
| How much is it? | **Wieviel kostet das?** | vee-**feel kos**-tet dahs |
| Write it? | **Schreiben?** | **shrī**-ben |
| Cheap / Cheaper / Cheapest. | **Billig / Billiger / Am Billigsten.** | **bil**-lig / **bil**-lig-er / ahm **bil**-lig-sten |
| Is it free? | **Ist es umsonst?** | ist es oom-**zohnst** |
| Included? | **Eingeschlossen?** | **īn**-geh-shlos-sen |
| Do you have...? | **Haben Sie...?** | **hah**-ben zee |
| I would like... | **Ich hätte gern...** | ikh **het**-teh gehrn |
| We would like... | **Wir hätten gern...** | veer **het**-ten gehrn |
| ...this. | **...dies.** | deez |
| ...just a little. | **...nur ein bißchen.** | noor īn **bis**-yen |
| ...more. | **...mehr.** | mehr |
| ...a ticket. | **...ein Karte.** | īn **kar**-teh |
| ...a room. | **...ein Zimmer.** | īn **tsim**-mer |
| ...the bill. | **...die Rechnung.** | dee **rekh**-noong |
| one | **eins** | īns |
| two | **zwei** | tsvī |
| three | **drei** | drī |
| four | **vier** | feer |
| five | **fünf** | fewnf |
| six | **sechs** | zex |
| seven | **sieben** | **zee**-ben |
| eight | **acht** | ahkht |
| nine | **neun** | noyn |
| ten | **zehn** | tsayn |
| At what time? | **Um wieviel Uhr?** | oom vee-**feel** oor |
| Just a moment. | **Moment.** | moh-**ment** |
| now / soon / later | **jetzt / bald / später** | yetzt / bahld / **shpay**-ter |
| today / tomorrow | **heute / morgen** | **hoy**-teh / **mor**-gen |

## Faxing reservations

Most hotel managers know basic "hotel English." Use this handy form for your fax.

. . . . . . . . . . . . . . . . . . . . . . . . . . . . . . . . .

One page fax            My fax #:_____

To:                           Today's date: ____ / ____ / ____

From:                                day   month   year

Dear Hotel _____,

     Please make this reservation for me:

Name: _____

Total # of people: ____      # of rooms: ____      # of nights: ____

Arriving: ____ / ____ / ____    Time of arrival (24-hour clock): _____
        day   month   year        (I will telephone if later)

Departing: ____ / ____ / ____
           day   month   year

Room(s):   Single   Double   Twin    Triple    Quad    Quint

With:    Toilet    Shower    Bath     Sink only

Special needs:    View    Quiet    Cheapest room    Ground floor

Credit card:   Visa    Mastercard     American Express

Card #: _____     Exp. date: _____

Name on card: _____

If a deposit is necessary, you may charge me for the first night. Please fax or mail me confirmation of my reservation, the type of room reserved, the price, and if the price includes breakfast. Thank you.

Signed: _____     Phone: _____

Address: _____

# Rick Steves' Europe Through the Back Door Catalog

*All of these items have been especially designed for independent budget travelers. They have been thoroughly field tested by Rick Steves and his globe-trotting ETBD staff, and are completely guaranteed. Prices include a free subscription to Rick's quarterly newsletter/catalog.*

## Back Door Bag convertible suitcase/backpack   $75

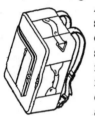

At 9"x21"x13" this specially-designed, sturdy, functional bag is maximum carry-on-the-plane size (fits under the seat), and your key to foot-loose and fancy-free travel. Made in the USA from rugged, water-resistant 1000 denier Cordura nylon, it converts from a smart-looking suitcase to a handy backpack. It has hide-away padded shoulder straps, top and side handles, and a detachable shoulder strap (for toting as a suitcase). Beefy, lockable perimeter zippers allow easy access to the roomy (2500 cubic inches) main compartment. Two large outside pockets are perfect for frequently used items. A nylon stuff bag is also included. Over 50,000 Back Door travelers have used these bags around the world. Rick Steves helped design this bag, and lives out of it for 3 months at a time. Comparable bags cost much more. Available in black, grey, navy blue and très chic forest green.

## European railpasses

...cost the same everywhere, but only ETBD gives you a free hour-long "How to get the most out of your railpass" video, free advice on your itinerary, and your choice of one of Rick Steves' 13 country guidebooks or phrase books. For starters, call 425/771-8303, and we'll send you a free copy of Rick Steves' Annual Guide to European Railpasses.

## Moneybelt                                                    $8

Absolutely required no matter where you're traveling! An ultra-light, sturdy, under-the-pants, one-size-fits-all nylon pouch, our svelte moneybelt is just the right size to carry your passport, airline tickets and traveler's checks comfortably. Made to ETBD's exacting specifications, this moneybelt is your best defense against theft—when you wear it, feeling a street urchin's hand in your pocket becomes just another interesting cultural experience.

*Prices are good through 1998—maybe longer. Orders will be processed within 2 weeks. Please add $3 per order (not per item) for shipping within the USA/Canada. Washington residents please add 8.6% sales tax. Send your check to:*

## Rick Steves' Europe Through the Back Door
120 Fourth Ave. N, PO Box 2009
Edmonds, WA 98020

## More books by Rick Steves...

*Now more than ever, travelers are determined to get the most out of every mile, minute and dollar. That's what Rick's books are all about. He'll help you have a better trip* **because** *you're on a budget, not in spite of it. Each of these books is published by John Muir Publications, and is available through your local bookstore, or through Rick's free Europe Through the Back Door newsletter/catalog.*

## Rick Steves' Europe Through The Back Door

Updated every year, *ETBD* has given thousands of people the skills and confidence they needed to travel through the less-touristed "back doors" of Europe. You'll find chapters on packing, itinerary-planning, transportation, finding rooms, travel photography, keeping safe and healthy, plus chapters on Rick's favorite back door discoveries.

## Mona Winks: Self-Guided Tours of Europe's Top Museums

Let's face it, museums can ruin a good vacation. But *Mona* takes you by the hand, giving you fun and easy-to-follow self-guided tours through Europe's 20 most frightening and exhausting museums and cultural obligations. Packed with more than 200 maps and illustrations.

## Europe 101: History and Art for the Traveler

A lively, entertaining crash course in European history and art, *Europe 101* is the perfect way to prepare yourself for the rich cultural smorgasbord that awaits you.

**Rick Steves' Best of Europe**
**Rick Steves' France, Belgium & the Netherlands**
**Rick Steves' Italy**
**Rick Steves' Germany, Austria & Switzerland**
**Rick Steves' Great Britain & Ireland**
**Rick Steves' Scandinavia**
**Rick Steves' Spain & Portugal**
**Rick Steves' Russia & the Baltics**

For a successful trip, raw information isn't enough. In his country guidebooks, Rick Steves weeds through each region's endless possibilities to give you candid, straightforward advice on what to see, where to sleep, how to manage your time, and how to get the most out of every dollar. Rick personally updates these guides every year.

**Rick Steves' European Phrase Books: French, Italian, German, Spanish/Portuguese, and French/Italian/German**

Finally, a series of phrase books written especially for the budget traveler! Each book gives you the words and phrases you need to communicate with the locals about room-finding, food, health and transportation—all spiced with Rick Steves' travel tips, and his unique blend of down-to-earth practicality and humor.

---

**www.ricksteves.com**

Rick Steves' popular Web site is packed full of travel tips, late-breaking book updates, and more. You can even sign up to get Rick's free monthly e-mail newsletter!

## What we do at Europe Through the Back Door

At ETBD we value travel as a powerful way to better understand and contribute to the world in which we live. Our mission at ETBD is to equip travelers with the confidence and skills necessary to travel through Europe independently, economically, and in a way that is culturally broadening. To accomplish this, we:

■ Teach budget European travel skills seminars;

■ Research and write guidebooks to Europe;

■ Write and host a Public Television series;

■ Sell European railpasses, our favorite guidebooks, maps, travel bags, and travel accessories;

■ Provide European travel consulting services;

■ Organize and lead free-spirited Back Door tours of Europe;

■ Run a Travel Resource Center in espresso-correct Edmonds, WA;

...and we travel a lot.

## Back Door 'Best of Europe' tours

If you like our independent travel philosophy but would like to benefit from the camaraderie and efficiency of group travel, our Back Door tours may be right up your alley. Every year we lead friendly, intimate 'Best of Europe' tours, free-spirited 'Bus, Bed & Breakfast' tours, and regional tours of France, Italy, Britain, Ireland, Germany-Austria-Switzerland, Spain-Portugal, Scandinavia, and Turkey. For details, call 425/771-8303 or go to www.ricksteves.com and ask for our free newsletter/catalog.